WALTER HILTON

COLLECTION

2 BOOKS

AETERNA PRESS

PUBLISHED BY AETERNA PRESS.
COVER DESIGN BY AETERNA PRESS.

ISBN-13: 978-1-78647-107-9

AVAILABLE AS AN E-BOOK:
WWW.AETERNAPRESS.COM

CONTENTS

WALTER HILTON COLLECTION

Walter Hilton was an English Augustinian mystic. The first book of The Scale of Perfection (it is worth noting that the title is editorial, appearing only on half the manuscripts of Book One of the Scale) is addressed to a woman recently enclosed as an anchoress, providing her with appropriate spiritual exercises; the bulk of its ninety-three chapters deal with the extirpation of the 'foul image of sin' in the soul – the perversion of the image of the Trinity in the three spiritual powers of Mind, Reason and Will (reflecting the Father, Son and Holy Spirit respectively, according to a tradition drawn from St Augustine) – through a series of meditations on the seven deadly sins. The second book, which opens by addressing itself to Hilton's former reader, who, he says, has further questions, seems from its style and content rather to be addressed to a larger, perhaps more sophisticated audience; its major themes are the reformation of the soul in faith alone and in both faith and feeling. This latter is described in an extended metaphor as a spiritual journey to Jerusalem, or 'peace' in meditation, a gift which is also its own giver, Christ. The first book of the Scale was apparently written some time before the second and was circulated independently.

THE SCALE OR LADDER OF PERFECTION

WALTER HILTON

AVAILABLE IN PAPERBACK.

WITH AN ESSAY ON THE SPIRITUAL LIFE OF MEDIAEVAL ENGLAND BY THE REV. J. B. DALGAIRNS, PRIEST OF THE ORATORY

MOSES PLUS PROFECIT IN MONTE ADORANDO QUAM MULTITUDE MAGNA BELLANTIUM

SCANNED AND EDITED BY HARRY PLANTINGA, 1995

THE SCALE OR LADDER OF PERFECTION

PUBLISHERS' NOTE

OF all the old English ascetical works which were extant before the Reformation none have maintained their reputation longer than Walter Hilton's "Scale of Perfection." Hilton was a canon of Thurgarton in Nottinghamshire, and died in 1395. His "Scale of Perfection" is found in no less than five MSS. in the British Museum alone. Wynkyn de Worde printed it at least three times—in the years 1494, 1519 and 1525. Many other editions were printed at the same period.

After the Reformation it was a favourite book of Father Augustine Baker's, the well-known author of "Sancta Sophia," and his comments on it are among his MSS. at Downside. In 1659 Father Baker's biographer and editor, Dom Serenus Cressy, O.S.B., published an edition of the "Scale," the title-page of which claims that "by the changing of some antiquated words [it is] rendered more intelligible." Another edition appeared in 1672, and yet another in 1679.

Within our own times two editions have been published—one by the late Father Ephrem Guy, O.S.B., in 1869, the other, a reprint of Cressy's, in 1870, with an introduction by Father Dalgairns on the "Spiritual Life of Mediaeval England." Cressy's text has again been used in the present edition, and Father Dalgairns's Essay is also reprinted in this volume.

AN ESSAY on the Spiritual Life of Mediaeval England

IT is only very gradually that we are obtaining a real knowledge of the Middle Ages. Hitherto it has been one of those subjects which no one could approach without getting into a passion. Just as no one can talk soberly of Mary, Queen of Scots, so it would appear as if few could keep their tempers in speaking or writing of the mediaeval time. The fact is that it is only by little that we can understand a period so very different from our own. A chaotic time is always a time of great contrasts, when profound ignorance exists side by side with considerable learning in individual instances, when heresies are wild and monstrous, while faith is touchingly simple and devoted. The real difficulty is to estimate the condition of the masses. It requires a patient spirit of research into minute details and dry statistics, united with a reverential admiration, a sifting criticism as well as a devout imagination, to avoid overweighing isolated instances and attaching undue importance to outstanding and striking features. I am not going to enter upon this dangerous ground. My only anxiety is to protest against what I cannot but consider a great error, both historically and ecclesiastically, the assumption that the Middle Ages are the model time of Christianity. It matters little what a man thinks about mediaeval architecture, vestments and embroidery, but it does matter a good deal what principles a man holds as to what may be called the philosophy of Church History. If he conceives the grand story of God's Church as though it were a pyramid, the apex of which is formed by the Middle Ages, while modern Christendom is on the downward side, then his whole view of Christianity is wrong. The Church never grows old, and it has advantages in the nineteenth century which it had not in the thirteenth. What, however, strikes a student of history most forcibly is that the more minutely we know the ages which are past, the more we learn the oneness of the spirit amidst all outward differences of form. We are every day obtaining more knowledge about the Middle Ages. Much has come to light since, thirty years ago, I wrote some "Lives of English Mediaeval Saints" at Littlemore, and, little as I have been able to follow the progress of history since then, I have seen enough to acknowledge that recent publications have brought with them the conviction that there was far more interior and mystical life amongst our ancestors than appeared at first sight.

Very much has been done for us by such learned bodies as the Early English Text Society, and by such men as Pfeiffer in Germany and Lecoy de la Marche in France. Now we not only possess sermons like those of St Bernard addressed to monks in the cloister, but we have the identical vernacular sermon which roused to passionate grief the mediaeval sinner, and drew tears of sweet devotion from the eyes of the citizens of Cologne, Paris and London, or the peasants of country parishes in the Black Forest or the Weald of Kent. We have the English prayers which were said before the Rosary was invented, and the devotions which touched the hearts of men and women living in the midst of that world which seems so strange and so far off to us. I must confess that without any depreciation of our grand old Cathedrals, "The Wooing of our Lord" and "The Ancren Riwle" have more charms for me than a thousand painted windows. I know the thoughts which flowed from hearts which have long since ceased to beat, and I can understand, as I never did before, the grim old warriors and their wives who look so unearthly side by side upon their tombs. One touch of grace makes me feel akin to them.

The perusal of this literature has, however, far more than a sentimental interest. It has now become simply ludicrous to look upon the devotional ideas of the Middle Ages as made up of indulgences and gifts to monasteries. These, of course, had their right place, as they have now; but, if ever it was doubtful, no one now can doubt that the mediaeval sinner knew quite as well as the gentleman of the nineteenth century that if he offended God and did not resolve never to offend Him again, he would infallibly be lost, though he left all his lands to the neighbouring convent. Priests might sing Requiems, and nuns might recite their Office, but nought could avail the impenitent before the judgement seat of Christ. If any man doubt it, let him read a sermon preached by Berthold of Regensburg, somewhere near Toggenburg or Sargans, not far from where the railway now skirts the lovely lake of Wallen. The barefooted Franciscan introduces, in his dramatic way, a man who had kept possession of ill-gotten gains rising up in the midst of the congregation, and saying: "Ho! Brother Berthold, I have done good to the brotherhood, and I make my confession every year; I have often entertained you at my house; I am in the confraternity, and have besought your prayers, that when I am dead you may watch over my body with song and lections." "Thou hast done well," is the Brother's answer, "and as soon as thou art dead we will sing for thee, and read long vigils, and chant beautiful Masses for thy soul, and loud Requiems, and bring thee in procession from thy parish church into our minster, and lay thee before the altar. But, I tell thee, if thou hast not restored what thou hast robbed, then, if all the tears and the raindrops which were ever shed or rained since the world began were turned into monks and brothers, grey monks and black, Preachers and Minorites—yea, into patriarchs and prophets, martyrs and confessors, widows and virgins, and if they were to read and to sing and weep tears of blood before God for thee to the day of judgement, they would do thee no more good than if they did all this for the foul fiend." Such was mediaeval doctrine in the year 1256. Moreover, it results from many hitherto unknown documents, that there was much more of what we should now call spirituality everywhere in the Middle Ages than even Catholics were disposed to think. It is even plain that nations were not reduced to one uniform standard. There was, for instance, a type of devotion which was peculiarly English, and the object of the present essay is to point this out. Of course, I can only treat the subject cursorily, for want of space, and I will confine myself to one portion of mediaeval life intimately connected with the book which is here presented to the reader.

Very little is known of Walter Hilton, the author of the "Scale or Ladder of Perfection." It is very likely that more might be known if any one took the trouble to search the manuscripts of the British Museum. Something perhaps also might be done towards amending the text of this book if the edition of 1659, of which this is a reprint, were compared with the old black letter of

Wynkyn de Worde. The present edition, however, has solely a spiritual, not a critical object, and, therefore, I confine myself to the little which lies on the surface of history about this mystical writer, without inquiring further. Fortunately, Father Guy has lately, in his excellent edition of "The Scale of Perfection," thrown light on the life of Walter Hilton, by proving that he did not belong to the Carthusian Order, but was a Canon of Thurgarton, in Nottinghamshire. Tanner had already published an extract from a manuscript, which gave 1395 as the year of his death. No one, however, had as yet perceived that this fact disproves the ordinary account of his having been a member of Henry VI's Carthusian monastery at Sheen, since that house was not founded till several years later. It might still be argued that he belonged to some other house of the Order. As, however, there is no authority for his having been a Carthusian except the erroneous account of his having belonged to Sheen, and as the passage quoted by Tanner distinctly affirms him to have died at Thurgarton, Father Guy seems to me to have sufficiently proved his point. It is not hard to see how the mistake arose. Walter Hilton had evidently a great devotion to the Carthusian Order, and there is still extant in manuscript a panegyric of it, addressed to Adam Horsley, an officer of the King's Exchequer, who by his advice became a disciple of St Bruno. On the other hand, we shall presently see abundant proof that the devotion of the Carthusians to Walter Hilton was no less great. There was something in the "Scale of Perfection" which attracted the monks whom the Christian instincts of Henry VI planted in the neighbourhood of his palace of Richmond, as well as their brethren of the Charterhouse, who kept up a witness for God in the heart of London.

There is, however, an especial reason why the book should have found its way to Sheen. We know from Dugdale that a benefactor of the monastery had assigned out of the manors of Lewisham and Greenwich twenty marks a year for the maintenance of an anchoret, whose cell was in its precincts. Thus there dwelt in the midst of the Carthusians one of those recluses to whose instruction the book is dedicated, and a description of whom will form a considerable part of this essay.

Now it is not a little strange that a large portion of English vernacular literature has direct reference to this form of the solitary life. We possess, besides Hilton's "Scale of Perfection," two other most remarkable books, addressed to or written by anchoresses. They will serve as specimens of the spiritual life of our ancestors at several very striking periods.

It is very remarkable that the most startling form of the life of the desert saints should have continued in England up to the very moment of the Reformation. The Anchorets or Anchoresses (for there were solitaries of both sexes) were more lonely than hermits in the sense that they were far more of recluses. The hermit lived, it is true, in an out of the way place, in a forest, or in one of those many uncultivated spots of which an English common or down are the sole relics, but which were easily to be found in a country not yet entirely cultivated; while the anchorets were commonly attached to a church, and were thus not far from their fellowmen. They were, however, immured within the four walls of their habitation, while the hermit was a free denizen of the woods. As we know from St Godric, he might have his garden and his cow. The anchorets, on the contrary, were strictly confined to their cells. They were the descendants of solitaries like St Thais and those other recluses of whom we read in the annals of the Nile desert, who were strictly shut up in their hut and only held conversation with others through a window, which also served as a passage for their food. This sort of life, then, was by no means peculiar to the Oriental contemplative who fled from the old worn-out world of a decrepit civilization. The same taste for solitude in its most extreme form was a part of the young and vigorous life of those Teutonic nations whom Christianity converted after the Roman and Hellenic culture had disappeared. While the blood of the old Vikings was still fresh in their veins, men and women left the brilliant and varied world of the Middle Ages, which was still full of life and movement, to shut themselves in a cell, with no prospect but the black yews and crosses of the church-yard. This was a solitude far deeper than that of the great monasteries, each of which was a little world. It is evident that these recluses were by no means rare. There is many a foundation on record for the perpetual entertainment of a recluse. Several Pontificals contain a regular office for these enclosures. Very often the anchoret was a chaplain attached to a church, who said Mass in his cell. The anchoress was more commonly near a church, into which she could look through a window, and thus take part in its holy ceremonies. Incidental mention is often made of such recluses in the troubled history of the times. Two anchorets were burned in the church at Mantes, when William the Conqueror set fire to the town. Richard II, before setting out on his dangerous encounter with Wat Tyler, went to confession to the anchoret in Westminster Abbey. It is probable that these holy men were often spiritual directors, while, as we shall presently see, many souls in sorrow and trouble, came to the window of the maiden anchoress for advice and consolation. It is true that from their very position the recluses were exposed to great temptations. Sometimes hypocrites were to be found among them, as is known from the life of St Stephen of Obazine, where we hear of a pretended anchoret who decamped with sums of money entrusted to him. The life is more intelligible in the case of a priest who had the adorable Sacrifice to offer up, confessions to hear, and Office to recite; but what would be the occupation of the hearts and brains of many an English maiden during the long days and nights which she thus spent in the narrow circle of the four walls which thus encaged her? What spells did she use to cool the restless fever in her veins? This is revealed to us by those treatises which we are now to consider.

The first is the "Ancren Riwle," a book for anchoresses, first published by the Camden Society. The authorship of this remarkable book is very uncertain, or rather it is unknown. There is not a vestige of evidence to connect it with St Richard of Chichester, to whom it has been ascribed. On the faith of a manuscript, it has been assigned to Simon of Ghent Bishop of Salisbury, and supposed to have been written by him for some sisters living at Tarant in Dorsetshire. It has also been contended that Richard Poore, Bishop of the same See, was its author. The only thing that is certain is that it was written by a Dominican, for the list of prayers which the writer enumerates as having been in use among the lay brothers of his Order, are nearly identical with those ordered in the Rule of St Dominic. As the Black Friars did not come to England till 1221, the book could not have been originally written for the sisters at Tarant, who before that date are known to have been Cistercian and not recluses; nor can one of the above-named prelates be its author, for they never belonged to the Order. Whoever was its author, it is evident that it must have been written before French had penetrated to any great extent into the English tongue. A few such expressions as Deulefet (Dieu le fait) and "sot" (foolish), show the presence of the Norman; and "annui" proves how early an importation from France was weariness of spirit in England. But the newness of words of French origin proves how little two centuries of Norman rule had succeeded in Romanizing the old language of the Saxon. Though the recluses to whom the book is addressed evidently could read French, yet the whole language and tone of thought is essentially English. The anchoresses, then, were English girls, in the thirteenth century. Their very names are unknown, though at that time, probably in the reign of our Henry III, their renunciation of the world was much spoken of among our ancestors. "Much word is of you, how gentle women ye be, for godliness and for nobleness yearned after by many, sisters of one father and one mother, in the blossom of your youth having forsaken all the world's blisses, and become anchoresses." A rich neighbour sent them all necessaries "from his hall." They had maidens to wait upon them, and to provide all that they wanted from without. They themselves, however, never stepped beyond the threshold of their hermitage. One window looked into the church, and from thence they assisted at the holy Sacrifice of the Mass. At another window, answering to the grill of an enclosed convent, they gave audience to visitors; but from the moment of their seclusion they never left their house, till they were carried out for burial.

What could be the meaning of this apparition in the bustling times of the thirteenth century. Though society was gradually settling down, yet it was a restless age. Men did not travel for pleasure, nor were there yearly migrations to the seaside; yet there was still a good deal of wandering. The great migrations of nations were over long before, and the majority of the agricultural population was still practically tied to the soil; yet crusades and pilgrimages often drew men to the far East and across the Alps. The scholar wandered from university to university for knowledge; the merchant was not tied to his desk, but travelled from fair to fair with all his precious wares; the minstrel disseminated news, and sung his ballads. There was a world then, with pomps and vanities, as there is now; a gay, parti-coloured, motley world, at which the Church frowned and preached. The eternal war between God and the world was going on. It is quite true there was less of the chronic excitement which is now wearing the strength of souls with its wasting fever. Pleasures were intermittent, and life more even. Balls were few, and generally took place in the daytime; public tournaments were few and far between. Yet society was still heaving with conflicting elements. Archbishops were often in exile, Emperors were under the ban of the Church; the Pope himself oftener in Viterbo than in Rome. English barons were harassing their king with Oxford Provisions; Simon de Montfort was devising a real English Parliament where the middle classes were represented. All the while these maidens of the period were praying to God day and night.

This is the secret of their life. Wherever men believe in prayer, you are sure to have the monastic life in some shape or other. If they have none, they will soon cease to believe in prayer, as is fast becoming the case in all Protestant countries. Wherever the Christian idea is strong, men who are by their position necessarily involved in the strife of the world will be glad to know that men and women who are separated from its turmoils and its sins are offering prayers to God for them.

It is plain that such was the occupation, and such the idea of the anchoress. It is also true that they did a great deal more than pray. The very dangers against which the author of her rule warns her are a proof that all had many visitors. He warns her against becoming a "babbling" or "gossiping anchoress," a variety of the species evidently drawn from the life; a recluse whose cell was the depository of all the news of the neighbourhood at a time when newspapers did not exist. Her habitation is not to be the storehouse where the neighbours placed objects of value, that they might be safe from the robber's hand.

All this proves that the good anchoress had means of exercising charity towards her fellow creatures. Many a sorrowing soul came to the window, and received balm for her wounded spirit from behind the black curtain and the white cross which hung there. Through her servants she might even practise hospitality to those who wanted it, and they might act as schoolmistresses to little girls who otherwise would frequent schools where boys were taught. All this is quite true, yet it is plain that the chief business of the anchoress was prayer.

It is very difficult for men living in the modern world to understand a life of prayer; yet they must accept it as a real fact. Thousands of Christians have lived such a life without becoming either praying machines like the Buddhists or fakirs like the Brahmins. The principle of Christian asceticism is as far apart from Manicheism as possible. It is simply the principle of expiatory suffering and prayer involved in the very idea of the sacrifice of Christ. The gulf which separates the anchoress from the fanatic is the love of Jesus. Of course this is nothing new to Catholics. Yet I think that even Catholics are not aware to what extent this is true of mediaeval devotion, and above all of England. Looking at the England of to-day it is very difficult to realize the fact that, whilst such a feeling towards our Lord is the very foundation of all Christian devotion, there is undoubtedly a kind of tender, pathetic love which is to be found in old English writers, and which is peculiarly their own. If I were asked to select the grace which is prominent in their writings, I should say that it was piety in the sense in which the word is applied to the gift of the Holy Ghost. The literature which is now before us is an excellent specimen of this spirit, because of the great interior freedom which was allowed to anchorets. They were less liturgical, and had fewer regulations than the religious Orders. "In this wise," says the Rule, "answer to him that asketh you of your Order, and whether it is white or black; say that ye are both, through the grace of God, of St James's order, about which he wrote, Immaculatum se custodire ab hoc saeculo, that is, as I said before, From the world to keep himself clean and unstained.' Herein is religion, and not in the white hood nor in the black, nor in the white nor in the grey cowl. Thus it is in a convent; but wherever woman liveth or man liveth by himself alone, eremite or anchoret, on outward things whereof no scandal cometh, he need lay little stress." The anchoress had no peculiar habit, and her office was, as has been said, not that of the choir, but that of the lay brothers. She is encouraged to say English prayers. At midday she made a meditation on the crucifix. Holy meditations are especially recommended to her. Though, according to the practice of the Church at the time, she made only fifteen Communions a year, yet there is a marked devotion to the Blessed Sacrament throughout the treatise. Its perpetual presence in the church is held out as a refuge against temptation, and it is plain that from the window which looked into the church, the anchoress often knelt in prayer, with her eyes fixed upon the altar where Jesus lay in the Sacrament of His love. Let me give a few specimens of these meditations of the thirteenth century. These then were the veritable thoughts which went through the hearts of English anchoresses as they knelt before the crucifix five hundred years ago:

"Jesus; true God! God's Son! Jesus, true God, true Man! Man, maiden-born! Jesus, my holy love, my own sweetness! Jesus, mine heart, my joy, my soul's health! Jesus, sweet! Jesus, my love, my light, my healing oil, my honey-drop! Thou all that I hope in! Jesus, my weal, my winsomeness, blithe bliss of my breast! Jesus, teach me that Thou art so soft, and so sweet, yet, too, so lovely and so lovesome that the Angels ever behold Thee, and yet are never full of looking on Thee! Jesus, all fair, before whom the sun is but a shadow, for she loseth her light and becometh ashamed of her darkness before Thy bright face. Thou that givest her light, and whose is all that brightness, enlighten my dark heart. Give brightness to Thy bower, even my soul that is sooty. Make her worthy to be Thy sweet abode. Kindle me with the blaze of Thy enlightening love. Let me be Thy bride, and learn me to love Thee, the loving Lord! Wo that I am so strange with Thee; but as Thou hast bodily separated me from the world, separate me eke in heart; turn me altogether to Thee, with true love and belief."

In another place, after a beautiful and minute description of the crucifixion, and how the "hellbairns" betrayed and crucified Him, she breaks out: "Ah! Jesus, my life's love, what heart is there that will not break when he thinketh hereof; how Thou, that art the Saviour of mankind, and the remedy for all bales, didst thole such shame for the honour of mankind. Men speak oft of wonders and of strange things divers and manifold that have befallen, but this was the greatest wonder that ever befell upon earth. Yea, wonder above wonders that that renowned Kaiser, crowned in Heaven, maker of all that is made, to honour His foes would hang between two thieves. Ah, how can I live for ruth that see my darling on the rood, and His limbs so drawn that I may tell each bone in His body! Ah, how do they now drive the iron nails through Thy fair hands into the hard rood and through Thy noble feet! Ah, now from those hands and feet so lovely streams the blood so ruefully! Ah, now they offer to my love, who says He thirsts, two evil drinks in His blood-letting, vinegar, sourest of all drinks, mingled with gall, that is the bitterest of all things! Ah, now, sweet Jesus, yet besides all Thy woe, to eke it out with shame and mockery, they laugh Thee to scorn when Thou hangest on the rood! Ah that lovely body that hangs so ruefully, so bloody, and so cold! Ah, how shall I live, for now dies my love for me on the dear rood, hangs down His head, and sends forth His soul? But it seems to them that He is not yet fully tormented, nor will they let the pitiful body rest in peace. They bring forth Longinus with the broad sharp spear. He pierces His side, cleaves the heart, and there come flowing out of that wide wound the Blood that bought us, the water that washes the world of guilt and sin. Ah, sweet Jesus, Thou openest for me Thy heart, that I may know Thee truly, for there I may openly see how much Thou lovedst me. With wrong should I refuse Thee my heart, since Thou hast bought heart for heart. Jesus, sweet Jesus, thus Thou foughtest for me against my soul's foes. Thou didst settle the contest for me with Thy body, and hast made of me, a wretch, Thy beloved and Thy spouse. Brought Thou hast me from the world to Thy bower. I may there so sweetly kiss Thee, and embrace Thee, and of Thy love have ghostly liking. What may I suffer for Thee for all that Thou didst thole (endure) for me? But it is well for me that Thou be easy to satisfy. A wretched body and a weak I bear upon earth, and that, such as it is, I have given Thee and will give Thee to Thy service. Let my body hang with Thy body nailed on the rood, and enclosed within four walls, and hang I Will with Thee, and never more leave my cross till that I die."

These extracts suffice to give us an insight into the inner life of the anchoresses of the thirteenth century. They were supported in their long imprisonment by the love of our Lord. Their thoughts were fed by the image of Jesus. This is expressed in characteristic words: "After the death of an earnest knight man hangeth high in church his shield to his memory. All so is this shield, that is, the crucifix, set in church in such place that it may soonest be seen, for to think thereby on the knightship of Jesus Christ which He did on the rood." Here is evidently a passionate, chivalrous love of our Lord. The Rule is very full of child-like piety, and at the same time of shrewd common sense. Its whole tone is as different as possible from that of the hermit of modern fancy. There are no images of Alexandrian orgies, no hobgoblins worse than the anchoress's cat, which is especially exempt from the ban which proscribes pet animals. She is nothing but a simple girl, who has given up the free life of English country maidens for the love of Christ.

Very different is the next anchoress who comes under our consideration. One of the most remarkable books of the Middle Ages is the hitherto almost unknown work called "Sixteen Revelations of Divine Love made to a devout servant of our Lord, called Mother Juliana, an Anchoress of Norwich." It contains visions and passages of such beauty as to rival the revelations of the Blessed Angela of Foligno. We shall find it well worth studying.

But little is known of Mother Juliana. Her very name has been hitherto unnoticed. It appears, however, most probable that she is the Juliana Lampit to whom a knight, Shakespeare's "good Sir Thomas Erpingham," who commanded the English archers at Agincourt, left a legacy in his will in 1424. Her cell was at the east end of the church-yard of St Julian's Church at Norwich. She was thirty years old and a half in May, 1373, and, as she appears to have died in 1443, she must have lived to be a hundred. She thus lived through some of the most stirring times of English history. She saw Poitiers and Agincourt, and the death of Joan of Arc.

Nothing can show more forcibly how profoundly the minds of men in the fourteenth century were stirred down to their lowest depths than the appearance in an obscure anchoress of those fundamental questions concerning good and evil, which, however laid to rest in times of peaceful faith, are sure to start up afresh whenever the minds of men are strongly moved. We know that the time was marked by an outburst of mystical life in Germany, and that Eckhart, Tauler and the Blessed Henry Suso are proofs of the existence of a deeply speculative as well as religious spirit; but we were not prepared to find it in England. This is the more remarkable because there is no trace of any connexion between the German and English movement. In one short passage alone, Juliana, in the crude English expression, "unmade kind is God," might seem to give utterance to the doctrine so prominent in Eckhart that creatures, considered as eternally present to God's mind, are identical with God. It was such expressions as these which drew upon the Dominican the censure of the Church, which, after his submission, he modified, and which reappear in writers of his school, such as the Blessed Henry Suso, but with explanations which render them harmless. Their occurrence in Mother Juliana is very remarkable. We might be tempted to suppose that they were an importation into Norwich through the immigration of Flemish weavers. We must, however, remember that this school of mysticism, represented by Ruysbrock, appeared later in Flanders than in the Rhineland. These views, then, are only another proof, among many, of the simultaneous appearance of ideas in places unconnected with each other. Like volcanoes, distant from each other, bursting out into flame at one and the same moment, they reveal the existence of some fiery depths at work in the very heart of Christendom. In Juliana's mind, however, this view of creation is only subordinate to that which absorbs and agonizes her whole being—the mystery of the existence of sin. Like the faces of fiends which grin in stone down upon us from the roof of a Gothic cathedral, the thought haunted her cell and mocked her at her prayers. In her mind it does not take the shape of the modern difficulty of the existence of suffering, eternal or temporal. It is true that even in this shape the difficulty was not entirely unknown to the Middle Ages. In Dante's great poem, for instance, the question of the eternal destiny of the heathen is treated with a freedom which we should not have expected. Even in the preceding century Brother Berthold is obliged to answer both popular and learned objections to the doctrine of everlasting punishment. This, however, is never doubted by Mother Juliana. With her the difficulty is the possibility of the existence of such a horror as sin in creatures, which, even in the natural order, are so connected with God that in Him they "move and have their being." Above all, in the supernatural order, how could there be sin in souls predestinated to heaven? "How may this be? For I know by the common teaching of holy Church, and by mine own feeling, that the blame of our sins continually hangeth upon us from the first man unto the time when we come up into Heaven. And between these two contraries my reason was greatly troubled by my blindness, and could have no rest, for dread that His blissful presence should pass from my sight, and I to be left in unknowing how He beheld us in our sin. My longing endured, Him continually beholding; and yet I could have no patience in great fear and perplexity." Her mind is torn because she must hate sin, "as holy Church teacheth," yet that hateful thing exists in the predestinate. In vain she takes refuge in the views of the schoolmen that sin has "no manner of substance, ne no part of being, ne it might not be known but by the pain thereof." It was but poor comfort that sin, being a defect and therefore a negation, can be no object of cognition. The fiend was too powerful to be laid by metaphysical distinctions. Conscience and "the doom of the Church" alike cried out that it was a horrid fact, an "ugly sight," and that many creatures "shall he damned to Hell without aid, as holy Church teacheth me to believe." The agony of soul still continued: "I cried inwardly with all my might, seeking unto God for help, moaning thus: Ah! Lord Jesus, King of bliss, how shall I be eased?'"

This is very different from the "Ancren Riwle." There we saw none but the ordinary temptations of the soul, "the world and the flesh." Here is a soul racked by the agony of perplexity, torn by the throes of doubt. It is not the fruit of modern scepticism, "the spirit which always contradicts." She takes for granted all the grand mysteries of Heaven and earth. It is this very certainty which causes intolerable pain. This soul has a tremendous grasp of the reality of God, which she expresses with terse energy. "The Trinitie is God," she exclaims, "God is the Trinitie, the Trinitie is our maker, the Trinitie is our keeper, the Trinitie is our everlasting lover, the Trinitie is our endless joy and our blisse, by our Lord Jesus Christ, and in our Lord Jesus Christ; and this was showed in the first sight (vision) and in all. For when Jesus appeareth, the

Blessed Trinity is understood as unto my sight." Yet with all this, there was that "ugly sight" of sin, obscuring the very face of God, shaking "the holy Church in sorrow and anguish and tribulation, as men shaketh a cloth in the wind," coming like a dark cloud between her and the crucifix. Truly here is an anchoress worth studying, if only because it gives us a new and unexpected insight into the mediaeval time.

The fact is hers was a dismal age. The more we study history, the more preposterous it seems to lump together into one the whole of those ages commonly called the Ages of Faith. There is as much difference between the twelfth and fourteenth centuries as between the fourteenth and the nineteenth. The power of the Church throughout the Middle Ages has certainly been much exaggerated. There were continual fluctuations of victory and defeat. Even in the thirteenth century she was by no means omnipotent; certainly at the beginning of the fourteenth her influence was sensibly growing less. I wish, however, just now especially to point out that, simultaneously with the fierce attack of Europe on the Papacy, of which the treatment of Boniface VIII by Philip the Fair was the beginning, there came an undoubted outburst of sin, a marked progress in vice. It is absurd to look for the cause of this enmity in the Papacy itself. Boniface laid claim to nothing whatsoever which was not successfully claimed by Innocent III. The causes were to be found in society itself, in profound social changes which were bringing on political revolutions. The unchristian principles which from the first were contained in chivalry, its courts of love, and its impure literature, were now getting entirely the upper hand over its high and virtuous ideal. The germ of all this wickedness had been at an early period brought over to England by the Queen of Henry II, the Eleanor of the South of France. Since John England had been ruled by men who, with all their faults, were good and religious—Henry, Dante's "king of simple life," and the noble Edward, his son; but the brilliancy of Cressy and Poitiers cannot blind us to the licentiousness of the court of Edward III, even though we disbelieve the common story of his affection for the Countess of Salisbury. Minute details on the subject of dress and manners, from contemporaries of Mother Juliana, come to us from too many sources to leave a doubt on the degeneracy of the times. The dress and demeanour of the ladies of the upper classes scandalized the people, and were a distinct change for the worse. "In these days," says Knighton, "arose a murmur and clamour among the people, that whenever there was a tournament, there came a great concourse of ladies of the court, costly and beautiful, but not of the best of the kingdom, in divers and wonderful rich apparel, in divided tunics, one part of one colour and one of another, with short caps and bands in the manner of cords wound round the head, and zones well bound round with gold or silver, and in pouches across their bodies knives called daggers, and thus they proceeded on chosen coursers or well-governed horses to the place of tournament; and so expended and devastated their goods, and vexed their bodies with scurrilous wantonness, that the murmurs of the people sounded everywhere; and thus they neither feared God nor blushed at the chaste voice of the people." Evidently these ladies of the period were worse than their grandmothers. Let any one call to mind the Parson's sermon in the "Canterbury Tales," and he will see that this immodesty continued in the reign of Richard II. This change of manners was, however, by no means confined to England. Loud complaints arose from every land in Europe. Dante's sad and beautiful description of the simplicity of the old Florentine life which he had known in his early years, and his indignant lines against the low dresses introduced among the Florentine ladies of the fourteenth century, are too precise to allow us to suppose them to be the product of a morbid mind. The sober prose of the chronicle bears out the language of the poet. "People at this time," says the Roman author of Rienzi's life, "began to change much in their habits, both in dress and conduct." Documents from Pavia, Piacenza and Milan bear witness to the same change for the worse, especially in the modesty of the young. As for France, the universal voice accuses it of being the centre of corruption and vice. Already, at the end of the preceding century, a preacher of the south of France attacks customs which only appeared later elsewhere. Villani traces Florentine degeneracy to the visit of the French in 1384. The same degeneracy appears in Germany. Landino, a commentator on Dante, mentions a circumstance of German life which resembles St Chrysostom's invectives against the public baths of the Eastern Empire. The whole subject is thus summed up by a competent writer : "Since the end of the thirteenth century the comfort and material prosperity of all classes in Italy, the Netherlands, France and Germany were much greater owing to the spread of commerce and intercourse. On all sides are seen a tendency to luxury and a rapid change of fashion which already, under Philip IV, called forth a formal sumptuary ordinance for the nobility, clergy and citizens." It was just one of those periods in which the heart of Christians like Mother Juliana are profoundly stirred by the sight of the increasing wickedness of mankind.

Nor need we wonder that the knowledge of the wickedness of the world should have reached the cell of the recluse. It so happens that the anchoress lived in the centre of these political revolutions, which were the result of this very degeneracy of chivalry. Norwich, with its 60,000 inhabitants, was the second city in the kingdom, and represented more interests than even London.

No one can fail to have been struck with the prominence of financial details in the annals of the reign of Edward III. The great conqueror is forced to leave his great crown and his little crown and his Queen's crown in pledge, and his nobles as hostages for his debts, before he can set sail from the continent and return to his own kingdom. A great part of his revenues came from taxes on wool, and as Norwich was the great seat of woollen manufactures, it acquired an immense preponderance in an age when almost daily alternations between protectionist and free-trade principles prove the attention paid to its peculiar branch of commerce. The city was therefore always profoundly stirred by England's revolutions, and wild storms surged up to the very doors of the cell of the Anchoress of Carrow. Every party in the realm was represented there. About seventy years before Juliana's birth there had been fighting in the streets between the partisans of the Abbey and the citizens. The old-world privileges of the Church, given in times when the monks were almost the only agriculturists, became galling to the rich wool-merchants of Norwich, and a bloody fight had been the result. The agitation had, however, worked deeper down; and a lower stratum of society was in process of upheaval. In the great insurrection of 1381 the French Revolution had been well-nigh anticipated. Two elements of strife were at work, and each affected Norwich. First there was the rebellion of labour against property. The awful visitation of the Black Death had carried off a vast proportion of the ill-fed, comfortless villains. The result was a great rise in wages, which Parliament attempted to keep down by legislation. This produced a long strike among the labourers, who fled from the uncultivated fields and flocked into the towns. From one single manor, that of Cossey, no fewer than eighteen villains in one year fled to Norwich; out of these eight received their freedom on the plea of their having had a domicile for a year and a day. This occurred earlier in the century, but by Juliana's time hundreds must thus have been turned into free manufacturers instead of serfs. In that one city there were congregated all the conflicting elements of society—the rich Abbey, the wealthy merchant, the Flemish manufacturer and the freed serf. This of itself, however, might have been insufficient to raise the storm if it had not been for a cause to which I have adverted. The increasing and ruinous luxury of the nobles produced a grinding oppression of the poor. This had always been contained in the bosom of feudalism. In that system those who were not possessors of land, the villains and the serfs, had but little to trust to but the conscience of their lord and the customs which regulated their services. As long as the lord had comparatively simple wants, the serf was less oppressed. But when a licentious court showed an example of prodigality, the infection spread through the whole of the feudal hierarchy. The knight still swore to defend the poor and the oppressed, but when he wanted money for his multiplied needs, the temptation to wring it out of the vassal was too strong to be resisted. Here again we have a cloud of witnesses from all sides. The evil had begun earlier in France. "The order of knighthood," says James of Vitry in a sermon, "is now-a-days in many cases corrupt; they use their strength like furious madmen. Many harry their vassals by corv?es, as they are called, and give them no bread to eat." "Let the serf be too happy that I have left him his calf and spared his life," said a nobleman, who had carried off a poor man's cow. Matters had become ten times worse at the period of which we are writing. The world had less conscience, and there are fewer stories on record of the signal punishment of the oppressor. "Jacques Bonhomme will not pull out his purse unless you beat him, but Jacques Bonhomme will pull out his purse because he will be beaten," was the common talk. Jacques Bonhomme took a fearful revenge. The horrible rebellion of the Jacquerie was the result. In England it took a longer time to stir up these elements of horror. There was a better feeling amongst us, and the Commons in the Good Parliament presented a petition for a law to forbid the lords of the demesnes to exercise sovereign authority by taxing the villain. The king answered that he would act as seemed good to him. The answer cost England a civil war. Six years later London was in the hands of Wat Tyler at the head of the Kentish serfs, and the blood of the Archbishop of Canterbury stained the streets of the city. Men perpetrated horrible crimes, but they were maddened by an unjust tax, levied by officials who insulted the honour of those who were nearest and dearest to them. Here again Norwich was in the midst of the fight. A dyer of Norwich was at the head of the peasants, and its Bishop, of the noble house of Spencer, in full armour, with a few lancers, rode and hewed down the insurgents, and arrested their leader. While all these horrors were enacted at the city gates, Juliana was leading her life of miraculous prayer. Amidst decaying chivalry and chaotic revolt the saints of God were suffering. It is remarkable that on the same blood-stained flats of Norfolk, over which formerly, in quieter times, St Walstan, of the royal house of Cedric, had driven the plough as a poor labourer, now in this most troubled century, an English peasant maiden, Jane the Meatless, was adoring and loving the Blessed Sacrament, which for many years was almost her only food.

Into this witch's cauldron was thrown another ingredient. Up to this time Europe can hardly be said to have given birth to an indigenous heresy. Such errors as those of Berengarius and Gilbert de la Por?e were chiefly confined to the schools, and only affected the laity in a comparatively small degree. Heresies of the Albigensian class were the descendants of Gnostics and Manichees.

Public opinion was against them, and the very jongleurs in their songs satirized the Vaudois. We find, however, in the fourteenth century the beginning of a distinct revolt of the cultivated class against Christianity. They are already numerous enough to fill the sixth circle of Dante's Hell. In the case of Fredrick II it was still possible to refer his scepticism to what has been well called Ghibelline culture. But now out of the dismal tombs arise at once spirits who belonged to both the great parties of the time. Farinata was a Ghibelline, Cavalcante was a Guelph. Hitherto England had been singularly free from intellectual revolts against the Church. The Dominican author of the "Ancren Riwle" thanks God that England is free from heresy. In Mother Juliana's time, however, the land was stained with native error. It is to the disgrace of Wycliffe that while he taught doctrines which, notwithstanding his disclaimers, struck at the root of all property, he played into the hands of the party of the rapacious nobles, headed by the Duke of Lancaster. The citizens of London rose in disgust against the priest who insulted their bishop and was protected by the man who was the defender of abuses, which the Black Prince rose from his bed of death to oppose in his place in Parliament. We have not, however, anything to do with Wycliffe's social views. I must advert to the speculative part of his system in order to contrast it with that of the recluse of Norwich, for there is sometimes a coincidence of language which might deceive the unwary. Little do they know of Wycliffe who look upon him as a sort of modern Evangelical because he translated the bible and abused the mendicant Orders. That he was a morning-star of the Reformation we have no difficulty in allowing, a fitting Lucifer for such a day. Some writers have connected him with Ockham, because Merton College had the honour of producing both. In point of fact, the two doctors were at the very opposite extremes of the poles of scholastic thought. Wycliffe identifies nominalism with heresy and held realism in its most intrepid form. "We meet in him," says a Protestant writer, "with elements which in their logical evolution would have led to Pantheism." What they did lead to, according to the same authority, was "a denial of free-will" in God and man. So thoroughly and absolutely did he identify in God the idea and the fact, the order of thought and the order of being, that he denies to God the conception of any possible things beyond what is or will be actual. Thus creation, present or future, is the measure of God's omnipotence. The old metaphysical bull-dog of the North country, the "quidam Borealis" of Walsingham, hung on with all his teeth to his premisses, in spite of the immorality of the conclusion. God, according to him, was neither more nor less free in the creation of the world than in the generation of the Son. I need not say that this is direct Pantheism, since it makes the universe a necessary part of

God. Wycliffe saw and was not scared by the fearful danger of throwing the causality of evil upon God. He tries to escape from it, indeed, by the scholastic view that sin is but a negation, and therefore cannot be the object of the Divine ideas. But he did not fear to say that all things happen by absolute necessity. "Accordingly all sin appears to him a necessary thing; all is required in order to the beauty of the universe." This might have appeared at first sight as unintelligible nonsense, but it has borne a most bitter fruit. Unfortunately a good deal of what some are inclined to dismiss as metaphysical subtlety leads to endless misery, and turns to very intelligible blasphemy. The slightest acquaintance with the schoolmen will enable us to see that Wycliffe's views are an audacious perversion of scholastic principles. His denial of possible things in God is a shameless use of St Thomas's "Actus Purus," and his theory of evil a still more shameless abuse of the view that sin is a defect not a substance.

We are now in a condition to show how groundless is the notion that Mother Juliana's expressions in the least imply a tendency to the errors of Wycliffe. Both fact and doctrine render such a notion preposterous. It so happens that we have Walsingham's testimony that "Faith and religion remained inviolate in the diocese of Norwich." The martial prelate whom we met just now threatened to burn any Lollard whom he caught, and would, without doubt, have kept his word. The recluse was under ecclesiastical jurisdiction, and was too marked a person to escape if her works had had a really Wycliffite tendency. Furthermore, her tender devotion to our Lady, her reverence for the saints, her very mode of life rendered it impossible. Wycliffe denied the necessity of confession, calls the canonization of saints blasphemous, and enclosure within stone walls a result of "the cursed spirit of falsehood." The only passages which would lend a colour to such an imputation on the recluse are those which we have already quoted, and others which imply strong views about predestination, the impossibility of the ultimate fall of the elect, and the loving care of God for the souls of the elect if they fall into sin. All these coincidences only show how deeply the minds of men were stirred, since we find views on these subjects in the very cell of the recluse. It would be simple ignorance to suppose that such thoughts were confined to Wycliffe, and could only be derived from him. Bradwardine had already made them familiar. How far even the popular mind was tossed about by questions of free-will and grace is plain from the fact that in Chaucer the Nun's Priest mentions Bradwardine's book; and the existence of these disputes is thus referred to as well-known to an assembly such as that which composed the Canterbury Pilgrims, to mine host of the Tabard, to the miller and the reeve.

What has already been proved contrary to fact can still be shown to be impossible by a comparison of doctrine. The few coincidences between Mother Juliana and Wycliffe are among the many proofs that the same speculative view often means different things in different systems. Both St Augustine, Calvin and Mahomet believe in Predestination, yet an Augustinian is something utterly different from a Scotch Cameronian or a Mahometan. The same words mean different things in the mouths of different people. The idea which runs through the whole of Mother Juliana is the very contradictory of Wycliffe's Pantheistic Necesitanarianism, The moment that a man believes in any real sense in a loving God he ceases to be a Pantheist. It is not enough to believe in a beneficent spirit, for universal benevolence may be a blind impulse, but since love is a free gift of self, a spirit who can love is free, and a being who is free is at once personal. The very basis, however, and the essence of Mother Juliana's views are her belief in the lovingness of God. Few since the beginning of Christianity have spoken of the love of God like this English recluse. After the agony of the black night of sin, her only consolation is to plunge into the great abyss of God's love. "Thus Jesus Christ, that does good again evil, is our very Mother. We have our being of Him, where the ground of Motherhood beginneth, with all the sweet keeping of love that endlessly followeth. As verily as God is our Father, as verily is God our Mother; and that showeth He in all; and namely in these sweet words there He saith, I it am,' that is to say, I it am, the might and the goodness of the Fatherhead; I it am, the wisdom and the kindness of the Motherhead; I it am, the light and the grace that is all blessed love; I it am, the Trinity; I it am, the Unity; I it am, the high sovereign goodness of all manner things; I it am that maketh thee to long; I it am, the endless fulfilling of all true desires.' Our high Father, Almighty God, which is being, He knoweth us and loved us from before any time. Of which knowing in His full deep marvellous charity, by the far-seeing endless counsel of all the blessed Trinity, He would that the Second Person should become our Mother, our Brother, and our Saviour. Whereof it followeth that as verily as God is our Father, verily God is our Mother." In a perfect rapture of love, she goes on, "Our kind Mother, our gracious Mother, for He would all whole become our Mother in all things; He took the ground of His work full low and full mildly in the maiden's womb. In this low place He arrayed Him, and dight Him all ready in our poor flesh, Himself to do the service and the office of Motherhead in all things. We wit that all our mothers bear us to pain and to dying, what is that but our very Mother Jesus? He alone beareth us to joy and to endless living, blessed mote He be. Thus He sustained us with Him, in pain and travail, unto the full time that He would suffer the sharpest thorns and grievous pains that ever were or shall be, and died at the last. And when He had done and so borne us to bliss, yet might not all this suffice to His marvellous love. And that He showed in these high ever-passing words of love, If I might suffer more, I would suffer more.' He might no more die, but He would not stint working. Wherefore Him behoveth to feed us, for the dear-worthy love of motherhood hath made Him debtor to us. The mother may give her child to suck her milk; but our precious Mother Jesus, He may feed us with Himself and doth full continuously and tenderly with the Blessed Sacrament. This is precious food of very life, and with all the sweet sacrament He sustaineth us full mercifully and graciously. And so He meant in these blessed words, when He said, I it am that Holy Church preacheth thee and teacheth thee.' That is to say, all the health and life of the sacraments, all the virtue and the grace of my word, all the goodness that is ordained in Holy Church to thee, I it am.' The mother may lay her child tenderly to her breast; but our tender Mother Jesus He may homely lead us into His blessed by His sweet open side, and show us there in party of the Godhead. And that showeth He in the ninth Revelation, giving the same understanding in His sweet word when He saith, Lo how I love thee.'" This is the key-note of her whole book, the solution of all her doubts. She attempts no reasoning, and has no logical answer to her difficulties. She simply plunges into the depths of God's love. "There I was learned that I should only enjoy in our blessed Saviour Jesus, and trust in Him for all things. And thus our good Lord answered to all questions and doubts that I might make, saying full comfortably: ' I may make all things well, and I can make all things well, and I shall make all things well, and I will make all things well, and thou shalt see thyself that all manner of things shall be well." This, after all, is the sole refuge of poor humanity. Yet it is not a mere sentiment. It is based on a deep view of God's great attributes. God is not merely a benevolent being. She distinguishes His pity from His love. Down in the depths of His eternity there has been a longing, which she calls "a ghostly thirst," a "love-longing." "For as truly as there is a property (attribute) in God of ruth and pity, as verily there is a property in God of thirst and longing. And this property of longing and thirst cometh of the endless goodness of God; right as the property of pity cometh of His endless goodness; and though He have longing and pity, they are sundry properties (different attributes) as to my sight."

Put this side by side with Wycliffe's deep growl at abuses rather than sin, his heaven of brass, and his iron destiny; it looks like and is a different religion. Not only the feeling which actuates, but the intellectual basis which animates it is the direct contradiction of his whole system. She belongs to the genuine school of English mystics which we have pointed out. Her love for Jesus is of the same kind as that found in the "Ancren Riwle." The supernatural events of her life remind us of what has been often thought to be peculiar to Continental devotion. Here is a poor English recluse, who has visions not unworthy of being read by the side of those of her great contemporary, St Catherine of Siena. This is a phase of English mediaeval life which we little suspected. Juliana is a recluse very different from the creatures of the imagination of writers on comparative morals. So far from being cut off from sympathy with her kind, her mind is tenderly and delicately alive to every change in the spiritual atmosphere of England. Every storm was felt with an electric shock through her inmost being. The earthquake council made the cell of the poor recluse rock to and fro as violently as the stones of old St Paul's. The four walls of her narrow home seem to be rent and torn asunder, and not only England, but Christendom appears before her view. It was not the crucifix which came before her in her visions, but the very form of the crucified Jesus, "with the plenteous bleeding of the head, the great drops of blood falling down from under the garland of thorns." And this was seen at Norwich, the English Manchester of the fourteenth century, when Cressy and Poitiers were still fresh in men's minds, and the Black Prince was lying sick at Berkhampstead. At that time England had not separated itself from the great stream of Christian life.

A further proof the intimate connection between the spiritual and social life of England is furnished us by the history of the remarkable treatise to which this Essay serves as an introduction. The precise time when it was actually written is unknown; all that is certain is that the "Scale of Perfection" must have been written before 1395, when its author died. As Juliana's book was written in 1370, it is plain that there cannot have been any great difference in date between the composition of the two works. It tells much for the spiritual life of England that in the fourteenth century such a treatise as the "Scale of Perfection" should have been written. It is, however, to the subsequent history of the book that I wish to point rather than to its origin; it so happens that the period assigned for the commencement of Walter Hilton's influence coincides with that of the close of Mother Juliana's life. Unlike Mother Juliana's book, which remained comparatively unknown, Walter Hilton's treatise evidently had a wide circulation. The number of existing manuscripts scattered through various cathedral and other libraries bear witness to its popularity. It was translated into Latin by a Carmelite early in the fifteenth century. It was high in repute with the Carthusians, and this in itself is a guarantee of its being extensively read. No order was so respected in England and other Teutonic countries as the Carthusian. Those who speak most mournfully of the bad state of Christendom just before the Reformation, always make an honourable exception of the sons of St Bruno. They were spiritual directors of Gerard Groot in the Low Countries, and of Colet, More and Fisher in England. One of their especial employments was the translation and propagation of good spiritual books, as we know from Surius, through whom Tauler and Henry Suso were made known to the Church in a Latin dress. Walter Hilton was the favourite author of Margaret, Countess of Richmond, the spiritual child of Fisher. The art of printing was as yet in its infancy when the "Scale of Perfection" was at once printed in black letter by Wynkyn de Worde, and other editions rapidly appeared. This, then, is the remarkable fate of this book. A treatise on the spiritual life, originally written by an obscure author in a small house of Augustinian Canons in Nottinghamshire and addressed to the most solitary of all the varieties of monastic life, is chosen to be the guide of good Christians in the courts of kings and in the world. Throughout the dismal wars of the Roses, and the more dismal reign of Henry VIII, many a heart was strengthened and consoled by Walter Hilton. The very copy still exists which must have been in the hands of the martyred Carthusians, the glow from whose pallid faces lit up the cell of Sir Thomas More as he gazed down at them as they were dragged on the hurdle to execution. The selfsame book was to be found in the palace of the mother of Henry VII. How she loved it, the rude lines in Wynkyn de Worde's edition will testify:

This heavenly book more precious than gold,
Was lately directed with great humility,
For godly pleasure therein to behold
Unto the right, noble Margaret, as ye see,
The King's Mother of excellent bounty,
Harry the Seventh, that Jesus him preserve,
This mighty Princess hath commanded me
T' imprint this book her grace for to deserve.

Now, all this is very worthy of remark. Here is a book written for a recluse, yet printed and recommended as a book of devotion, not for the cloister, but for good Christians in the world. This is quite a new feature, and points at once to fact that that the interior life was spreading in England. What is the significance of this fact? Enough has been already said to show that the religious life of the Middle Ages was not the formal ritualism which many have supposed. German scholars have done a vast deal to destroy this illusion by the publication of old religious books in the vernacular tongue. We have only got to look at Mone's collection of mediaeval hymns, and to observe the frequent notices of translations, not only into German, but into French and Italian, to be convinced that the songs of the Church were accessible to the poor, and even in common use amongst them in their own language. Jacopone de Todi's beautiful hymns are a proof of the popularity of spiritual songs other than the liturgical hymns of the Breviary. There are extant also hymns sung and prayers said in various languages—French, Provenc,al, German and English—to be used at the Elevation, the Holy Communion, and on various feasts. Didactic books of devotion in the vernacular tongue, such as Tauler's "Nachfolge," "L'Internelle Consolation," and in English the "Ayenbite of Inwit" or Remorse of Conscience prove that spiritual reading was practiced. It is plain then that our mediaeval ancestors were by no means so chained to the letter, so unspiritual as some have supposed. Nevertheless it is true that the "Scale of Perfection" is a step forward, indicating a greater spread of the spiritual life among Christians in the world.

The fact is that there was arising, at the close of the feudal period, a new class, which had to be legislated for. We often use the terms mediaeval and modern without much reflection on the real difference between society as it was constituted then and now. The feudal society was a great hierarchy of duties. Of course, wherever Christianity exists property must involve duties; in the mediaeval time property and duty were absolutely synonymous. Property was held on condition of certain services, and was forfeited when these were withheld. In theory the feudal sovereign was the owner of the soil, and the nobles held their lands of him on a definite tenure. Combined with this was the view that each noble was despotic on his own land, and administered justice to the serfs who lived upon it. Horridly oppressive and tyrannical as the system became in fact, it was founded on the notion of reciprocal obligations. The noble defended and fought for the serf, who in his turn laboured for the lord. The consequence of this state of things was that there did not exist a single man who had nothing to do. Independently of the absence of available wealth and of means of being comfortable, the very fact of possessing something implied that a man must work. Every little lord who possessed as much as a tower was fully occupied in the administration of justice, in the government of his vassals, and in actual war or the keeping himself ready for it. Robbery, injustice and crime were very possible; idleness could not exist. The result of this was that there was no such thing as a class of persons in society who had a great deal of time on their hands and were not compelled to do anything. In times when money was scarce life was a struggle. Ladies took a personal share in the work of the kitchen, and overlooked their servants from the gallery in the hall. Even hunting was an occupation as well as an amusement; men hunted stags for the sake of the venison, instead of foxes for the love of sport. The fish of the stream and the birds which were struck down by the hawk were an object to the lord. Gardens and parks were few, and forests many. The marks of the plough can still be traced close up to the ruined castle wall. Life was a more earnest, personal affair in the Middle Ages than now.

Gradually this state of things passed away. Warwick the King-maker has been rightly called the last of the Barons. In Henry VI we may consider that we have the last of mediaeval kings. The Middle Ages find their euthanasia in this pallid, saintly monarch, just as a former state of things was closed by St Edward the Confessor. Edward IV, the favourite of the citizens of London, brave, but unchivalrous, faithless, irreligious and unchaste, was a king of a far other type. The wars of the Roses utterly destroyed the old feudal baron. Men were hardly conscious of the change, and the Duke of Norfolk might still boast "that he was as good as a king when he was on his own estate at Norwich." The dream cost him his head. It was only gradually that men became aware of the vast, silent change which had been consummated. The feudal world had passed away, and modern society had taken its place. As far as concerns us, the result is the total disruption of all necessary connection between property and occupation, the creation of a very large class of men and women who can live, if they please, without doing anything at all. I do not mean to say that any man breathing is born without duties; but I mean that there is a very large class of beings who can eat, drink and perform all the functions of life whether they do their duties or not.

It is evident that this state of things requires something peculiar to meet it. What is to be done with all this superfluity of unemployed life? What is a man thus set free from obligation to do with his time? In the Middle Ages life itself imposed an unvarying rule of living. Is man now to live without a rule? A thousand moral and religious questions start up and cry out for an answer. Things have become possible now which were not possible before. Men and women can spend their lives in an unvarying round of amusements and excitements, even without supposing them to seek vicious pleasures. Theatres, operas, balls, novels—things unknown to their ancestors—may make up their life. Is this right? Is it safe? A most momentous question this, which requires an answer. Here is a new thing upon earth, or at least a state of things which has not existed since the Teutonic nations were converted—the upper classes of society able to live in a constant round of amusement, and thinking themselves satisfactorily sure of salvation, because of the hypothetical absence of great sin. Are unlimited balls and unlimited sacraments compatible? Or is a worldly life a perilous one for those who live it? Or rather ought not Christians to spend more time in prayer, in devotion, in voluntary almsgiving and works of charity, in proportion as they are set free from many duties? Is not life more dangerous and salvation more insecure because of this terrible invasion of the world, with audacious requirements and unblushing exigencies? Considering the cool impudence with which the world insists on his own innocence, nay, has even the impertinence to look upon its general mode of life as a duty to society, it does seem as if this new attitude of the world called for new rules and a greater strictness to counteract its dangers.

Now, the "Scale of Perfection" is valuable because it is an English book containing an answer to this question. If not written for, it was at least adopted by an English princess, a king's mother, living at court in the reign of Henry VII. In fact, it contains the old English Catholic view before Protestantism existed. The answer to the above question is unequivocal, and is contained in the following words: "When men and women who are free from worldly businesses if they will, and may have their needful sustenance without much solicitude about it, especially religious men and women—and other men also in secular estate, that have good abilities and understanding, and may, if they will dispose themselves, come to much grace; these men are more to blame than those who are so busied with worldly things which are so needful to be done. Verily it is perilous for a soul not to seek to make any further progress." The only safe thing is to "set his heart fully to come to more grace and give himself heartily to prayer, meditating and other good wishes."

Such was the old Catholic life, before we were corrupted by the society of Protestants. The moral of the book is that a supernatural life is common to all Christians, and that there is no such infinite distinction between Christians in the world and religious. Both, in different degrees and modes, are not safe unless they aim at "profiting in grace." Of course, much in Walter Hilton's book is inapplicable to us, yet all who are not repelled by the unusual English will find it a very beautiful spiritual treatise. It is not a regimental book, and contains few rules. No one will find in it "a rule of life." It is simply occupied in laying down principles. A book written in the fourteenth century cannot be expected to establish minute practical rules for the nineteenth. It will, however, be very valuable as a specimen of the old traditional Catholic spiritual life in England. The basis of all spiritual life in all ages must after all be the same; and this book, written so long ago in the forgotten house of Canons at Thurgarton, may help us now in fighting our battle of life in this very different time. In this respect it will be a lesson to us. Rather mystical than ascetical, it contains an antidote to the prevailing tendency to restless activity, even in devotion. Above all, it is remarkable for containing the old English tradition of a most tender, personal love for our blessed Lord.

Now that we are threatened by a great influx of Protestant morals, through the increasing intercourse of Catholics with the world, it will be well if this book reminds us of our past history. The great apostasy of the Reformation could never have been successful if a terrible outbreak of worldliness had not sapped the first principles of Christian life among the nobility and gentry of England. Nothing will save us now in dangerous times but the supernatural principles of our Faith carried out in our lives.

BOOK I

PART I

CHAPTER I: THAT THE INWARD STATE OF THE SOUL SHOULD BE LIKE THE OUTWARD

GHOSTLY Sister in Christ Jesus, I pray thee that in the calling to which our Lord hath called thee for His service, thou rest contented, and abide constantly therein, travailing busily with all the powers of thy soul to fulfil in truth of good life (by the grace of Jesus Christ) the state which thou hast taken in exterior likeness and seeming; and as thou hast forsaken the world, as it were a dead man, and turned to our Lord bodily in sight of men, so thou be in thy heart as it were dead to all earthly loves and fears, and turned wholly to our Lord Jesus Christ; for be thou well assured that a bodily turning to God without the heart following is but a figure and likeness of virtues, and not the truth in itself. Wherefore wretched men and women are they who, neglecting the care of their interior, show only exteriorly a form and likeness of holiness, in habit or clothing, in speech and outward carriage and works, casting their eyes upon other men's deeds, and judging their defects, esteeming themselves to be something, when indeed they are just nothing, and so deceive themselves. Do not thou so; but together with thy body turn principally thy heart to God, and frame thy interior to His likeness, by humility and charity and other spiritual virtues, and then art thou truly turned to Him. I say not that thou mayest early on the first day be turned to Him in thy soul in perfection of virtues as thou mayest with thy body be enclosed in a house; but my meaning is, that thou shouldst know that the end of thy bodily enclosure is that thou mightest thereby the better come to a spiritual enclosure; and even as thy body is enclosed from bodily converse with men, even so thine heart might be enclosed from the inordinate loves and fears of all earthly things. And that thou mayest the better come thereto, I shall in this little treatise yield thee the best instructions and helps that I know or can.

CHAPTER II: OF THE ACTIVE LIFE, AND THE EXERCISES AND THE WORKS THEREOF

THOU must understand that there are in the holy Church two manner of lives (as saith St Gregory) in which a Christian is to be saved. The one is called Active, the other Contemplative; without living one of these two lives no man may be saved. The Active consisteth in love and charity exercised exteriorly by good corporal works, in fulfilling of God's commandments and of the seven works of mercy, corporal and spiritual, towards our Christian brethren. This life pertains to all worldly men that have riches and plenty of worldly goods to dispose of, and to all those (be they learned or unlearned, lay men or spiritual persons) that are in office or state to govern, or have care of others; and generally all worldly men are bound to the practice of this kind of life according to their best knowledge and ability, and as reason and discretion shall require. If he much good have, then much good for to do; if he little have, less may he do; and if he naught have, then must he have a good will. Such works as these (be they corporal or spiritual) are works of the Active life. Also a great part of it consists in great bodily deeds which a man exerciseth upon himself, as great fasting, much watching, and other sharp penance, to chastise the flesh with discretion for sins formerly committed. As also to mortify thereby the lusts and likings of the flesh, and to make it pliable and obedient to the will of the spirit. These works though they be but Active, yet they help very much, and dispose a man in the beginning to attain afterwards to contemplation, if they be used with discretion.

CHAPTER III: OF THE CONTEMPLATIVE LIFE, AND THE EXERCISES AND WORKS THEREOF

CONTEMPLATIVE life consisteth in perfect love and charity, felt inwardly by spiritual virtues; and in a true and certain sight and knowledge of God and spiritual matters. This life belongs to them especially who for the love of God forsake all worldly riches, honours, worships and outward businesses, and wholly give themselves soul and body (according to all the knowledge and ability that is in them) to the service of God, by exercises of the soul.

Now then, since it is so (dear sister) that the quality of thy state requireth of thee to be contemplative (for that is the intent of thy enclosing, that thou mightest more freely and entirely apply thyself to spiritual exercises), it behoveth thee to be right busy both night and day in labour of body and spirit, to attain as nigh as thou canst to that life by such means as thou mayest find to be best for the said end. But before I tell thee of the means, I shall tell thee a little more of this contemplative life, that thou mayest somewhat see what it is, and so set it as a mark in the sight of thy soul, whereto thou shalt tend, and direct all thy exercises and doings.

CHAPTER IV: OF THREE SORTS THAT BE OF CONTEMPLATION AND OF THE FIRST OF THEM

CONTEMPLATIVE life hath three parts. The first consisteth in knowing God, and of spiritual things gotten by reason and discourse, by teaching of men, and by study in holy Scripture, without spiritual gust, or affection, or inward relish felt by them; for they have it not by the special gift of the Holy Ghost, as persons truly spiritual have their knowledge, which, therefore, is very tasteful to them in their interior.

This part have especially in them learned men and great scholars, who, through long study and travail in holy Writ, attain to this knowledge more or less by the abilities of their natural wit, which God giveth to every one, more or less, that hath use of reason.

This knowledge is good, and may be called a kind or part of Contemplation, inasmuch as it is a sight of verity and a knowledge of spiritual things. Nevertheless it is but a figure and shadow of true Contemplation, since it hath no spiritual gust or taste in God, nor inward sweetness, which none feels but he that is in great love of charity; for it is the proper Well or Spring of our Lord, to which no alien is admitted. But the aforesaid manner of knowing is common both to good and bad, seeing it may be had without charity, and therefore it is not very contemplation. Of this kind of knowledge St Paul speaketh thus: If I knew all mysteries and all knowledge, and have not charity, I am nothing.

Nevertheless, if they that have it keep themselves in humility and charity, and according to their might fly worldly and fleshly sins, it is to them a good way, and a great disposing to true Contemplation if they desire and pray devoutly after the grace of the Holy Ghost. Other men have this knowledge, and turn it to pride and vain-glory, or unto covetousness and desire of worldly dignities, worships and riches, not humbly using it to the glory of God, nor charitably to the soul's good of their brethren. Some of them fall either into heresies and errors, or into other open sins, by which they discredit themselves and the holy Church. Of this knowledge St Paul speaks in these words: knowledge puffeth up, but charity edifies. This I knowledge alone lifteth up the heart to pride; but mix it with charity, and then it turns to edification.

This knowledge alone is but water, unsavoury and cold. And, therefore, if they that have it would humbly offer it up to our Lord, and pray for His grace, He would by His blessing turn their water into wine, as He did at the prayer of His Mother at the marriage feast; that is to say, He would turn their unsavoury knowledge into true wisdom, and their cold naked reason into spiritual light and burning love, by the gift of the Holy Ghost.

CHAPTER V: OF THE SECOND SORT OF CONTEMPLATION

THE second part of Contemplation lieth principally in affection, without spiritual light in the understanding or sight of spiritual things; and this is commonly of simple and unlearned men who give themselves wholly to devotion, and is had and felt in this manner: When man or woman being in meditation of God, through the grace of the Holy Ghost, feeleth fervour of love and spiritual sweetness, by occasion of thinking of Christ's passion, or of some of the works done by Him in His humanity; or he feeleth cause of great trust in the goodness and mercy of God for the forgiveness of his sins, or admires the liberality of His gifts of grace, or else feeleth in his affection a certain reverential fear towards God, and His secret judgements and justice, which yet he seeth not; or being in prayer, he findeth all the powers of his soul to be gathered together, and the thought and love of his heart to be drawn up from all transitory things, aspiring and tending upwards towards God by a fervent desire, and spiritual delight, and yet, nevertheless, during that time he hath no plain sight in the understanding of spiritual things, nor in particular of any of the mysteries or senses of the holy Scriptures; but only that for that time nothing seemeth so pleasing and delightful to him as to pray, or think as he then doth for the savoury delight and comfort that he findeth therein, and yet cannot he tell what it is, but he feeleth it well, for it is a gift of God, for out of it spring many sweet tears, burning desires, and still mournings, or contrition for sin, which scour and cleanse the heart from all filth of sin, and causeth it to melt into a wonderful sweetness in Jesus Christ, and to become obedient and ready to fulfil all God's will, insomuch that it seems to him he makes no reckoning what becomes of himself, so that God's will were fulfilled in him, and by him, with many other such good inspirations and desires which cannot be reckoned. Such feelings as these cannot be had without great grace, and whoso hath any of them or other such like, he is at that time in charity and the grace of God; which charity let him know to his comfort, will not be lost or lessened in him (though the fervour thereof may abate) but by a deadly sin.

And this may be called the second part of Contemplation, nevertheless, this part hath two degrees.

CHAPTER VI: OF THE LOWER DEGREE OF THE SECOND SORT OF CONTEMPLATION

THE lower degree of this feeling, men which are active may have by grace, when they are visited by our Lord, as mightily and as fervently as they that give themselves wholly to Contemplation and have this gift. But this feeling in his fervour cometh not alway when a man would, nor lasteth it full long. It cometh and goeth as He will that giveth it; and therefore whoso hath it, let him be humble, and thank God and keep it secret, unless it be to his confessor, and let him hold it as long as he may with discretion; and when it is withdrawn, let him not be daunted or troubled, but abide constant in the light of faith, an humble hope, with patient expecting till it come again. This is a little tasting of the sweetness of the love of God, whereof David saith thus in the Psalms: Gustate et videte quoniam suavis est Dominus—Taste and see how sweet our Lord is.

CHAPTER VII: OF THE HIGHER DEGREE OF THE SECOND SORT OF CONTEMPLATION

THE higher degree of this part may not be had nor held but of them which be in great rest and quiet both of body and mind, who by the grace of Jesus, and long travail corporal and spiritual, are arrived to a rest and quietness of heart and clearness of conscience. So that nothing is so pleasing to them as to sit still in quiet of body and to pray always to God, and to think on our Lord, and sometimes on the blessed name of Jesus, which is comfortable and delightful to them, by the remembering whereof they feel themselves moved and fed in their affection towards God. And not only the said name, but also all other kind of prayers (as the Pater Noster, the Ave, the Hymns and Psalms, and other devout prayers and sayings of holy Church) are turned, as it were, into a spiritual mirth and sweet songs, by which they are comforted and strengthened against all sins, and much relieved in their bodily pains or diseases. Of this degree speaketh St Paul thus: Be not drunk with wine, but be filled with the Holy Ghost, speaking to yourselves in psalms and hymns and spiritual songs, making melody an your hearts to our Lord. Whoso hath this grace, let him keep himself in humility and be ever desiring to come to more knowledge and feeling of God, which is to be had in the third sort of Contemplation.

CHAPTER VIII: OF THE THIRD SORT OF CONTEMPLATION

THE third sort, which is as perfect Contemplation as can be had in this life, consisteth both in knowing and affecting; that is, in knowing and perfect loving of God, which is when a man's soul is first reformed by perfection of virtues to the image of Jesus, and afterwards, when it pleaseth God to visit him, he is taken in from all earthly and fleshly affections, from vain thoughts and imaginings of all bodily creatures, and, as it were, much ravished and taken up from his bodily senses, and then by the grace of the Holy Ghost is enlightened, to see by his understanding Truth itself (which is God) and spiritual things, with a soft, sweet, burning love in God, so perfectly that he becometh ravished with His love, and so the soul for the time is become one with God, and conformed to the image of the Trinity.

The beginning of this Contemplation may be felt in this life, but the full perfection of it is reserved unto the bliss in heaven. Of this union and conforming to our Lord speaks St Paul thus: Qui adhaeret Deo unus spiritus est cum eo; that is to say, he who by ravishing of love is become united to God, God and that soul are not now two, but both one. And surely in this oneing consisteth the marriage which passeth betwixt God and the soul, that shall never be dissolved or broken.

CHAPTER IX: OF THE DIFFERENCE THAT IS BETWIXT THE SECOND AND THIRD SORT OF CONTEMPLATION

THE foresaid second sort of Contemplation may be termed a burning love in Devotion, and is the lower; this third a burning love in Contemplation, and is the higher. That is sweeter to the bodily feeling, this to the spiritual feeling inwardly, and is more worthy, more spiritual, more wonderful. For, indeed, it is a foretaste (so little as it is) and an earnest or handsell of the sight or Contemplation of heavenly joy, not clearly, but half in darkness, which shall be perfected and made a clear light and sight in the bliss of heaven; as St Paul saith: Now we see as through a glass darkly, but then we shall see face to face. This is the enlightening of the understanding in delights of loving, whereof David saith in the Psalter: Et nox illuminatio mea in deliciis meis—My night is my light in my delight. The other is milk for children, but this solid meat for perfect men, that have their senses exercised (as St Paul saith) for the discerning of good from evil.

To the perfection of this high Contemplation may no man come till he be first reformed in soul to the likeness of Jesus in the perfection of virtues: nor can any man living in mortal body have it continually and habitually in the height of it, but by times when he is visited. And as I conceive by the writing of holy men, it is a full short time, for soon after he returneth to a sobriety of bodily feeling; and of all this work charity is the cause. Thus, as I understand St Paul speaks of himself: For whether we be beside ourselves, it is to God, or whether we be sober, it is for your cause; it is the love of Christ that constraineth us; that is, whether we overpass our bodily senses in Contemplation, or we are more sober to you in our bodily feeling, the love of Christ straineth us. Of this part of Contemplation and of reforming to God speaketh St Paul openly, thus: But we all with open face, beholding as in a glass the glory of our Lord, are changed into the same image from glory to glory, even as by the spirit of the Lord. Which is as much as if in the person of himself and all perfect men he had said thus: We, first being reformed in virtues, and having the face of our soul uncovered by opening of our spiritual eye, behold as in a mirror the heavenly joy, being withal fulshaped and oned to the image of our Lord, from clearness of faith into clearness of understanding, or else from clearness of desire into that of blessed love; and all this is wrought in a man's soul by the spirit of our Lord, as saith St Paul.

This part of Contemplation God giveth where He will, to learned and unlearned, to men and to women, to them that are in government, and to solitary also. But it is special, and not common. And although a man who all his lifetime is active happen to have the gift of it through special grace or favour, yet the fulness of it may no man have, but he that is solitary and in life contemplative.

CHAPTER X: HOW THAT APPEARINGS OR SHEWINGS TO THE CORPORAL SENSES OR FEELINGS MAY BE BOTH GOOD AND EVIL

BY this that I have said may you somewhat understand that visions, or revelations, or any manner of spirit in bodily appearing, or in imagining, sleeping or waking, or also any other feeling in the bodily sense, made as it were spiritually, either by sounding in the ear, or savouring in the mouth, or smelling at the nose, or else any sensible heat, as it were fire glowing and warming the breast, or any other part of the body, or any other thing that may be felt by bodily sense, though it be never so comfortable and liking, yet be they not very Contemplation, but simple and secondary (though they be good) in respect of spiritual virtues, and of this spiritual knowing and loving of God accompanying true Contemplation. But all such manner of feeling may be good, wrought by a good angel, and they may be deceivable, wrought by a wicked angel, when he transfigureth himself into an angel of light. Wherefore sith they may be both good and evil, it appeareth they are not the best. For, mark ye well, that the devil may, when he hath leave, counterfeit in bodily feeling the likeness of the same things the which a good angel may work; for just as a good angel cometh with light, so can the devil. And as he can do this in matters of seeing, so can he do it in matters of the other senses. Whoso hath felt both, he can well tell which were good and which were evil. But he that never felt either, or else but one of them, may easily be deceived.

These two be alike in the manner of feeling outwardly, but they are full different within, and therefore they are not to be desired greatly, nor to be entertained lightly, unless a soul can by the spirit of discretion know the good from the evil, that he be not beguiled, as St John saith: Trust not every spirit, but essay first whether it be of God or no. Wherefore by one trial that I shall tell thee, methinketh thou shalt know the good from the evil.

CHAPTER XI: HOW THOU SHALT KNOW WHETHER THE SHOWING OR APPARITION TO THE BODILY SENSES AND FEELINGS BE GOOD OR EVIL

IF it be so that thou see any manner of light or brightness with thy bodily eye or in imagination, other than every man seeth; or if thou hear any pleasant, wonderful sounding with thy ear, or in thy mouth any sweet sudden savour, other than what thou knowest to be natural, or any heat in thy breast like fire, or any manner of delight in any part of thy body, or if a spirit appear bodily to thee, as it were an angel to comfort thee or teach thee; or if any such feeling, which thou knowest well that it cometh not of thyself, nor from any bodily creature, beware in that time, or soon after, and wisely consider the stirrings of thy heart; for if by occasion of the pleasure and liking thou takest in the said feeling or vision, thou feelest thy heart drawn from the minding and beholding of Jesus Christ, and from spiritual exercises, as from prayer, and thinking of thyself and thy defects, or from the inward desire of virtues, and of spiritual knowing and feeling of God, for to set the sight of thy heart and thy affection, thy delight and thy rest, principally on the said feelings or visions, supposing that to be a part of heavenly joy or angels' bliss, and thereupon comest to think that thou shouldst neither pray nor think of anything else, but wholly attend thereto, for to keep it and delight thyself therein: then is this feeling very suspicious to come from the enemy; and therefore, though it be never so liking and wonderful, refuse it and assent not thereto, for this is a sleight of the enemy. When he seeth a soul that would entirely give itself to spiritual exercises, he is wonderfully wroth; for he hateth nothing more than to see a soul in this body of sin to feel verily the savour of spiritual knowledge and the love of

God, which he himself, without the body of sin, lost wilfully. And therefore, if he cannot hinder him by open sinning, he will let and beguile him by such vanity of bodily savours or sweetness in the senses, to bring a soul into spiritual pride and into a false security of himself, weening that he had thereby a feeling of heavenly joy, and that he is half in paradise, by reason of the delight he feeleth about him, when indeed he is near to hell gates; and so by pride and presumption he might fall into errors or heresies, or phantasies, or other bodily or spiritual mischiefs.

But if it be so that this manner of feeling let not thy heart from spiritual exercises, but maketh thee more devout, and more fervent to pray, more wise to think ghostly thoughts, and though it be so that it astonish thee in the beginning, nevertheless afterward it turneth and quickeneth thy heart to more desire of virtues, and increaseth thy love more to God and to thy neighbour, also it maketh thee more humble in thy own eyes—by these tokens mayest thou know that it is of God, wrought by the presence and working of a good angel, and cometh from the goodness of God, either for the comfort of simple devout souls, for to increase their trust and desire towards God, to seek thereby the knowing and loving of God more perfectly by means of such comforts. Or else if they be perfect that feel such delight, it seemeth to them to be an earnest and as it were a shadow of the glorifying of the body, which it shall have in the bliss of heaven; but I wot not whether there be any such man living on earth. This privilege had Mary Magdalen (as it seemeth to me) in the time when she was alone in the cave thirty years, and every day was borne up with angels, and was fed both body and soul by their presence, as we read in her story.

Of this way of discerning the working of spirits speaketh St John in his Epistle, thus: Omnis spiritus qui solvit Jesum, hic non est ex Deo—Every spirit that loosed or unknitteth Jesus, he is not of God. These words, I confess, may be understood in many manners, nevertheless, one way I may understand them to this purpose, as I have said. This knitting and fastening of Jesus to a man's soul is wrought by a good will and a great desire to Him, only to have Him and see Him in His bliss spiritually. The greater this desire is, the faster is Jesus knit to the soul; and the less this desire is, the looser is He knit; whatsoever spirit, therefore, or feeling it is which lesseneth this desire and would draw it down from the stedfast minding of Jesus Christ and from the kindly breathing or aspiring up to Him, this spirit will unknit Jesus from the soul, and therefore is not of God, but is the working of the enemy. But if a spirit, or a feeling, or a revelation make this desire more, knitting the knots of love and devotion faster to Jesus, opening the eye of the soul into spiritual knowing more clearly, and maketh it more humble in itself, this spirit is of God.

And hereby you may learn that you are not to suffer your heart willingly to rest nor to delight wholly in any such bodily feelings of such manner of comforts or sweetness, though they were good; but rather hold them in your sight naught, or little in comparison of spiritual desire and stedfast thinking on Jesus; nor shall you fasten the thought of your heart over much on them.

CHAPTER XII: HOW AND IN WHAT THINGS A CONTEMPLATIVE MAN SHOULD BE BUSIED

BUT thou shalt ever seek with great diligence in prayer that thou mayest come to a spiritual feeling or sight of God. And that is, that thou mayest know the wisdom of God, the endless might of Him, His great goodness in Himself and in His creatures; for this is Contemplation, and that other mentioned is none, thus saith St Paul: Being rooted and grounded in charity, we may be able to comprehend with all the saints what is the breadth and length and height and depth. That ye may know, he saith not, by sound of the ear nor sweet savour in the mouth, nor by any such bodily thing, but that ye may know and feel with all saints what is the length of the endless being of God, the breadth of the wonderful charity and the goodness of God, the height of His almighty Majesty and the bottomless depths of His wisdom. In knowing and spiritual feeling of these should be the exercise of a Contemplative man. For in these may be understood the full knowing of all ghostly things. This exercise is that one thing which St Paul coveted after, saying thus: This one thing I covet, which is that, forgetting those that are behind, and reaching forth to those things that are before, I press to the mark of the supernal vocation. Which is as much as if he had said, One thing is best for me to covet, and that is, that I might forget all things that be behind or backward, and I shall stretch out my heart ever forward for to feel and to grip the sovereign reward of endless bliss. Behind are all bodily things, forward or before are all spiritual things. And so St Paul would forget all bodily things, and even his own body also, that so he might see spiritual things.

CHAPTER XIII: HOW VIRTUE BEGINNETH IN REASON AND WILL AND IS PERFECTED IN LOVE AND LIKING, OR AFFECTION

THUS have I told thee a little of Contemplation what it is, to the intent that thou mightest know it and set it as a mark before the sight of thy soul, and to desire all thy lifetime to come to any part of it by the grace of our Lord Jesus Christ. This is the conforming of a soul to God, which cannot be had unless it first be reformed by some perfection of virtues turned into affection; which is when a man loveth virtues because they be good in themselves. Many a man hath the virtues of humility, patience and charity to his neighbour, and such other only in his reason and will, and hath no spiritual delight nor love in them, for ofttimes he feeleth grudging heaviness and bitterness for to do them, and yet nevertheless he doth them, but tis only by stirring of reason for dread of God. This man hath these virtues in reason and will, but not the love of them in affection. But when by the grace of Jesus and by ghostly and bodily exercise reason is turned into light and will into love, then hath he virtues in affection; for he hath so well gnawn on the bitter bark or shell of the nut that at length he hath broken it and now feeds on the kernel; that is to say, the virtues which were first heavy for to practise are now turned into a very delight and savour, so that he takes as much pleasure in humility, patience, cleanness, sobriety and charity as in any other delights. Verily till these virtues be turned thus into affection he may well have the second part of Contemplation, but the third, in sooth, shall he not have.

CHAPTER XIV: OF THE MEANS THAT BRING A SOUL TO CONTEMPLATION

Now seeing virtues dispose us to Contemplation, it behoveth us to use the means that may bring us to virtues. And they be three means which men most commonly use that give themselves to Contemplation: As reading of holy Scripture and good books, secondly, spiritual meditation; thirdly, diligent prayer with devotion. By meditation shalt thou come to see thy wretchedness, thy sins and thy wickedness; as pride, covetousness, gluttony, sloth and lechery, wicked stirrings of envy, anger, hatred, melancholy, wrath, bitterness and imprudent heaviness. Thou shalt also see thy heart to be full of vain flames and fears of the flesh and of the world. All these stirrings will always boil out of thy heart, as water runneth out of the spring of a stinking well, and do hinder the sight of thy soul, that thou mayest never see nor feel clearly the love of Jesus Christ, for know thou well that until the heart be much cleansed from such sins, through firm verity and diligent meditating on Christ's humanity, thou canst not have any perfect knowledge of God, Himself witnessing the same in His Gospel thus: Blessed are the clean in heart, for they shall see God. In meditation, likewise, shalt thou see those virtues which be needful for thee to have, as humility, mildness, patience, righteousness, spiritual strength, temperance, cleanness, peace and soberness, faith, hope and charity. These virtues thou shalt see in meditation, how good, how fair, how profitable they be; and by prayer thou shalt thereupon desire and get them. Without which third means of prayer thou canst not be contemplative, for Job saith thus: In abundantia ingredieris sepulchrum—In plenty shalt thou enter thy grave; that is in plenty of bodily works and spiritual virtues shalt thou enter thy grave, that is thy rect in Contemplation.

CHAPTER XV

SECTION I: WHAT A MAN SHOULD USE AND REFUSE BY THE VIRTUE OF HUMILITY

Now if thou desirest to prosecute spiritual works and exercises wisely, and to labour seriously in them, it behoveth thee to begin right low; three things needest thou first to have, upon which as on a firm ground thou shalt set all thy work, namely, humility, a firm faith, and resolute will and purpose to seek after God.

First, it behoveth thee to have humility on this manner: thou shalt in thy will and in thy feeling judge thyself unfitting to dwell among men and unworthy to serve God in conversation with His servants and as unprofitable to thy Christian brethren, wanting both skill and power to fulfil any good works of active life in help of thy neighbour, as other men and women do. And, therefore, as a wretch and an outcast and refuse of all men art shut up in a house alone, that thou shouldst not grieve nor offend man or woman by thy bad example, seeing thou canst not profit them by any well-doing. Beyond this it behoveth thee to look further, that since thou art so unable to serve our Lord by outward bodily works, how much more it behoveth thee to deem thyself unable and unworthy to serve him spiritually by inward exercises; for our Lord is a spirit, as the prophet saith: Our Lord is a Spirit before our face, and the most kindly service to Him is spiritual, as He saith Himself: True worshippers shall worship the Father in spirit and in truth. Thou then that art so gross, so lewd, so fleshly, so blind in spiritual things and in the understanding of thy own soul (which it behoveth thee first to know before thou canst come to the knowing of God), how shouldst thou feel or think thyself to be able or worthy to enjoy the estate or likeness of a contemplative life, which consisteth principally, as I have said, in spiritual knowing. This I speak to thee, not that thou shouldst repent thee of thy clothing, enclosing and state of life, but that thou shouldst feel this humility really in thy heart (if thou canst), for this is the very truth and no lie. And, thereupon, thou shalt night and day desire and endeavour to come in truth as near as thou canst to that state which thou hast taken upon thee, firmly believing it to be the best kind of state for thee (by the mercy of God) to exercise thyself in. And though it be so that thou canst not in this life attain to the perfection of that state, yet, at least, seek to make an entry into it, and trust assuredly to have the perfection thereof by the mercy of God in heaven. And truly this is my own case, who feel myself so wretched, frail and fleshly, and so far from the true feeling of that which I speak of, that in a manner I do nothing but cry, God mercy, and desire after it (as well as I can) with a hope that our Lord will bring me thereto in heaven. Do thou likewise; and better also, if God give thee grace.

The feeling of this lowness and humility will put out of thy heart all imprudent looking into other men's actions, and drive thee wholly to behold thyself, as if there were no other man living but God and thyself. And thou shalt deem and hold thyself more vile and more wretched than any one creature that liveth; insomuch that thou shalt hardly be able to brook and endure thyself, for the greatness and number of thy sins, and the filth which thou shalt feel in thyself.

Thus behoveth it thee sometimes to feel and judge of thyself, if thou mean to become truly humble. For I tell thee truly, if thou wilt be very humble, thou must think a venial sin in thyself more grievous and painful to thee and greater in thy sight sometimes than great deadly sins in other men. And this is most true in thy case who aimest at Contemplation, seeing whatsoever hindereth and letteth thy soul most from the feeling and knowing of God, oughteth to be most grievous and painful to thee. But a venial sin of thy own letteth thee more from the feeling and perfect love of Jesus Christ than any other man's sins can do, be they never so great.

It follows, therefore, that thou shouldst rise more in thy heart against thyself to hate and condemn in thyself all manner of sin which letteth thee from the sight of God, more than against the faults of other men; for if thy heart be clean from thy own sins, verily the sins of other men will not hurt thee. If, therefore, thou wilt find rest here and in heaven, do thou (according to the counsel of one of the holy Fathers) every day ask of thyself: What am I? and judge no man.

But thou wilt object, how may this be, seeing it is a deed of charity to tell men of their faults, and a deed of mercy to admonish them that they may mend?

To this I answer that in my mind, that to thee or any other that hath taken on them the state of a contemplative life, it belongeth not to leave the watching over thyself to behold and blame other men, unless there should be great need, so that a man were in danger to perish without it.

But those men that are active and have authority and charge of others, are bound by their office and by way of charity to look into, inquire and rightly to judge and correct other men's faults; not out of a desire and delight to punish them, but only for need, with the fear of God and in His name, and for the love of the salvation of their souls. Other men also who are active and have no care or charge of other men are bound to admonish other men of their faults out of charity only, and that when the sin is deadly and cannot well be corrected by another, and there is hope of amendment by being admonished else it is better to let it alone.

That this is good doctrine may be gathered by the practices of St John, who was a Contemplative, and St Peter, who was an Active man. For when our Lord at His last Supper with His disciples, at the motion of St Peter to St John, told St John how Judas should betray Him, St John told it not to St Peter, though he asked him, but turned him, and laid his head upon Christ's breast, and became ravished through love into the contemplation of the Divinity and divine secrets; and that so pleasingly and beneficially to himself that he forgot both Judas and St Peter, teaching thereby other Contemplatives how in the like occasion they should behave themselves.

By this that hath been said thou mayest learn neither to judge other men nor conceive willingly against them any evil suspicions, but love them, nor see any faults in them, but worship in thy heart such as lead Active lives in the world, and suffer many tribulations and temptations; which thou sitting in thy house feelest naught of; and they endure very much labour and care, and take much pains for their own and other men's sustenance, and many of them had rather (if they might) serve God (as thou dost) in bodily rest and quietness. Nevertheless, they in the midst of their worldly business, avoid many sins, which thou, if thou wert in their state, shouldst fall into, and they do many good deeds, which thou canst not do. There is no doubt but many do thus, but which they be, thou knowest not; and therefore it's good for thee to worship them all, and set them all in thy heart above thyself as thy betters, and cast thyself down at their feet, as being the vilest and lowest in thy own sight. For there is neither dread nor danger in making thyself never so low beneath others, though in the sight of God, at the same time, thou hast more grace than others; but danger there is in being too high, and lifting up thyself in thy thoughts willingly above any other man, though he were the most wretched and the most sinful caitiff that is in the earth; for our Lord saith: He that humbleth himself shall be exalted, and he that exalteth himself shall be brought low.

This part of humility doth it behove thee to have in thy beginning; and by it, and for the grace, shalt thou come to the perfection of it, and so of all other virtues. For whoso hath one virtue, hath all other virtues; as much as thou hast of humility, so much hast thou of charity, of patience, and of other virtues; though they be not shown or appear outwardly. Be, therefore, busy to get humility, and hold it fast, for it is the first and the last of all other virtues.

The first, as being the foundation, as saith St Augustine: If thou think to build a high house of virtues, lay first a deep foundation of humility. Also, it is the last; for it is the maintainer and conserver of all other virtues. St Gregory saith: He that gathereth (or striveth to keep) virtues without humility, is like him that maketh or carrieth the powder of spices in the wind. Do thou never so good deeds, fast, watch, or anything else, if thou hast not humility, it is naught which thou dost.

Nevertheless, if thou feelest not this humility in thy heart with affection, as thou wishest, do as thou mayest, humble thyself in will, by reasoning and arguing with thyself, judging that by right thou shouldst be so humble, and think of thyself as I have said, albeit thou do not so feel it within thee, and in that respect hold and esteem thyself the verier wretch, that thou canst not feel thyself to be that which in truth thou art. And if thou do so, though thy flesh rise against it, and will not assent to thy will, be not too much daunted, nor troubled, but bear with and suffer such false feelings of thy flesh, as a pain, and then despise and reprove that feeling, and break down that rising of thy heart, as if thou wouldst be well contented to be spurned and trodden under other men's feet. So by the grace of Jesus Christ, through stedfast thinking on the humility of His precious Manhood, shalt thou much abate the stirrings of pride; and the virtue of humility, that was first only in thy naked will, shall be turned into feeling of affection. Without which virtue, either in true will, or in feeling of affection, whoso disposeth himself to serve God in a contemplative life, like to a blind man, he will stumble, and never attain thereto. The higher he climbeth by bodily penance, and other virtues, and hath not this humility, the lower he falleth. For as St Gregory saith: He that cannot perfectly despise himself, he hath never yet found the humble wisdom of our Lord Jesus Christ.

SECTION II: HOW HYPOCRITES AND HERETICS, FOR WANT OF HUMILITY, EXALT THEMSELVES IN THEIR HEARTS ABOVE OTHERS

HYPOCRITES and heretics feel not this humility neither in good-will nor in affection, but full cold and dry are their hearts and reins from the soft feeling of this virtue, and by so much the further are they from it, as they esteem they have it. They gnaw on the dry bark without, but the sweet kernel and the inward taste of it they never come to. They make a show of outward humility in habit and holy speech, in a low carriages and (as they would make show) in many corporal and spiritual virtues. But in the will and affection of their heart, where humility should be, it is but feigned. For they judge, and despise, and set at naught other men that will not do as they do and teach; they esteem them either fools for want of knowledge, or to be blinded by fleshly living. And, therefore, lift they themselves up on high in their own sight above all others, weening that they live better than others, and that they only have the truth and verity of right living and of spiritual feeling, and of the singular grace of God both in knowledge and affection above all others. And out of this sight of themselves riseth a delight in their hearts, in which they worship and praise themselves, as if there were none but they. They praise and thank God with their lips, but in their hearts, like thieves, they steal His worship and praise, and place it in themselves, and so have neither humility in will nor affection.

A wretched caitiff or sinner which falleth all day, and is sorry that he doth so, though he hath not humility in affection, yet hath he it in good will; but an Heretic or an Hypocrite hath neither; for they have the condition of the Pharisee, who came, as our Lord saith in the Gospel, with the Publican into the Temple to pray. And when he came, he prayed not, nor asked aught of God, for he thought he had no need; but he began to thank God, and said thus: Lord, I thank Thee that Thou givest me more grace than others, that I am not like other men, robbers, luxurious, or other such sinners. He looked beside him, and saw the Publican, whom he knew for a wretch, knocking on his breast, only crying for mercy; then he thanked God he was not such a one as he, for Lord, said he, I fast twice a week, and I pay my tithes duly. When he had done, our Lord said: He went home without grace as he came, and got just nought.

But thou wilt say, wherein did this Pharisee amiss, since he thanked God and spoke the truth? I answer he did amiss, inasmuch as he judged and reproved the Publican in his heart, who was justified of God. And he also did amiss, for he thanked God only with his mouth, but secretly in his heart he willingly delighted in himself through pride and glorying in the gifts of God, stealing to himself the honour of them, and the praise and love due to God. This is the condition verily of Heretics and Hypocrites, they will not willingly pray, and if they pray, do not humble themselves, acknowledging their wretchedness, but feigningly thank and love God, and speak of Him with their mouth, but their delight is vain and false, and not in God, and yet they do not think so, for they cannot love God. And as the wise man saith: Praise is not comely in the mouth of a sinner. Wherefore it is profitable for me, and for thee, and for such other wretches, to leave the condition of this Pharisee, and feigned loving of God, and follow the Publican in lowliness, asking of mercy and forgiveness of sins, and grace of spiritual virtues, that we may afterward, with a clean heart, truly thank Him and love Him, and yield wholly all honour without feigning; for our Lord asketh thus by His Prophet: Upon whom shall My Spirit rest? He answereth Himself, and saith: Upon none but upon the humble, poor and contrite in heart, and him that trembleth at My words. If, therefore, thou wilt have the Spirit of God ruling in thy heart, have humility and dread Him.

CHAPTER XVI: OF A FIRM FAITH NECESSARY THERETO, AND WHAT THINGS WE OUGHT TO BELIEVE THEREBY

THE second thing which it behoveth thee to have is a firm faith in all the articles of thy belief, and in the Sacraments of the holy Church, believing them stedfastly with all thy will in thy heart. If thou feel any stirring in thy heart against any of them, by suggestion of the enemy to put thee in doubt of them, be thou stedfast, and dread not therefore, but forsake thine own wit, without disputing or ransacking of them, and set thy faith in general on the faith of the holy Church, and make no reckoning of the stirrings of thy heart which seem to be contrary thereto; for those stirrings are not thy faith, but the faith of the holy Church is thy faith, though thou never see it nor feel it. And bear those suggestions patiently as a scourge of our Lord, by which He will cleanse thy heart and make thy faith stedfast. Also it behoveth thee to embrace and honour in thy heart all the laws and ordinances made by the prelates and rulers of the Church, either in declaring of the Faith, or concerning the Sacraments, or in general concerning all Christian men, meekly and truly assenting to them though thou understandest not the cause of making such ordinances; and though thou shouldst think that some of them were unreasonable, yet shalt not thou judge them or find fault with them, but reverence and honour them although they little concern thy particular. Neither entertain thou any opinion or fancy or singular conceit under colour of more holiness (as some unwise people do) either out of thy own imagination, or by the teaching of any other man, which thwarteth the least ordinance or general teaching of the Church.

Moreover, together with such faith, thou shalt firmly hope that thou art ordained by our Lord to be saved as one of His chosen by His mercy, and stir not from this hope whatsoever thou hearest or seest, or what temptation befalls thee. Though thou think thyself so great a wretch that thou art worthy to sink into hell, for that thou doest no good nor servest God as thou shouldst, yet hold thee in this truth and in this hope, and ask mercy, and all shall be well with thee. And though all the devils in hell appeared in bodily shapes, saying to thee, sleeping or waking, that thou shouldst not be saved; or all men living on earth or all the angels in heaven (if possible) should say the same, yet believe them not, nor be stirred much from thy hope of salvation. This I speak to thee, because some are so weak and simple that when they have given up themselves wholly to serve God to their power, and feel any stirrings of this kind within them by the suggestion of the enemy, or any of his false prophets (which men call soothsayers) that they shall not be saved, or that their state or manner of living is not pleasing to God, they be astonished and moved with such words, and so through ignorance fall sometimes into great heaviness, and as it were into despair of salvation.

Wherefore it is (as it seems to me) necessary for every one (that by the grace of God is in a full and resolute will to forsake sin, and as clearly as his conscience telleth him, suffereth no deadly sin to rest in him, but he goes soon to confession for it, and humbly betakes himself to the sacraments of the Church) to have a good trust and hope of salvation. Much more then should they trust and hope, who give themselves wholly to God, and eschew venial sins the best they know and can.

But on the other hand, as perilous it is for him who lieth wittingly in deadly sin, to have trust in salvation, and in hope of this trust will not forsake his sin, nor humble himself truly to God and the holy Church.

CHAPTER XV: OF A FIRM AND RESOLUTE INTENT AND PURPOSE NECESSARY HERETO

THE third thing needful for thee to have in thy beginning was an entire and firm intention; that is to say an entire will and a desire only to please God, for this is charity, without which all is nought which thou doest, and thou shalt set thine intent always to search and travail how thou mayest please Him, resting no time willingly from some good exercises, either bodily or ghostly. Neither shalt thou set a time in thy heart that thus long thou wilt serve Him, and then suffer thy heart willingly to fall down to vain thoughts and idle exercises, imagining it needful to do so for preserving of thy health, leaving the keeping of thy heart and good exercises, and seeking rest and comfort for a time outwardly from thy bodily senses or inwardly from vain thoughts, as it were for recreation of thy spirit, that thereby it may be more quick and lively for spiritual employments. But I trow thou wilt not find it so. I say not that thou wilt be able fully and continually to perform this thy intent and purpose, for ofttimes thy bodily necessities, such as eating, drinking, sleeping and speaking and the frailty of thy flesh shall let and hinder thee, be thou never so careful.

But my meaning and desire is that thy will and intent be always wholly to be exercised bodily and spiritually, and to be no time idle, but always lifting up thy heart by desire to God and to heaven, whether thou be eating or drinking or doing any corporal work as much as thou canst, intermit it not willingly. For if thou have this intent it will make thee quick and ready to thy exercises; and if thou fall through frailty or negligence upon any idle occupation or vain speech, it will smite thy heart as sharply as a prick, and make thee account irksome, and be weary of all such vanities, and turn again speedily to inward thinking of Jesus Christ or to some good exercise.

As to thy body, it is good to use discretion in eating, drinking and sleeping, and in all manner of bodily penance, and in long vocal prayer, and in all bodily and sensible feelings and fervours, or earnestness of devotions, and tears and the like, and in discoursing with the imagination in times of aridities and want of the feeling of grace. In all these works it is good to use discretion, for the mean is the best. But in destroying of sin by keeping thy heart, and in the continual desire of virtues and the joys of heaven, and to have the spiritual knowledge and love of Jesus Christ, hold there no mean, for the greater it is the better it is, for thou must hate sin and all fleshly loves and fears in thy heart without ceasing, and love virtue and purity and desire them without stinting if thou canst. I say not that all this is needful to salvation, but I trow it is speedful and much helping. And if thou keep this full intent, thou shalt profit more in one year in virtues than thou shalt without it in seven.

CHAPTER XVIII: A BRIEF REHEARSAL OF WHAT HATH BEEN SAID, AND OF AN OFFERING MADE OF THEM ALTOGETHER TO JESUS

Now I have told thee of the end thou shouldst set in thy desire, and draw towards it as nigh as thou canst, as also what is needful for thee to have in thy beginning, namely, humility, firm faith and an entire and strong will and purpose, upon which ground thou shalt build thy spiritual house by prayer and meditation and other spiritual virtues.

Furthermore, pray thou or meditate thou, or any other good deed or exercises which thou dost, be it either good by grace or defective through thy own frailty, or whatsoever it be that thou seest, feelest or hearest, smellest or tastest, either outwardly or by thy bodily senses or inwardly by thy imagination, or knowest or perceivest by thy natural reason, bring it all within the truth and the rules of holy Church, and cast all into the mortar of humility and break it small with the pestle of the fear of God, and throw the powder of all this into the fire of desire, and so offer it up to God. And I tell thee for truth that well pleasing shall this offering be in the sight of our Lord Jesus, and sweet shall the smoke of that fire smell before His face.

The sum is this: draw all that thou seest and intendest within the truth of holy Church, and break thyself by humility, and offer up the desire of thy heart only to thy Lord Jesus, to have Him and nought else but Him. If thou do thus, I hope, by the grace of Christ, that thou shalt never be overcome by thine enemy. This St Paul teacheth us when he saith: Whether ye eat or drank, or whatsoever else ye do, do all in the name of our Lord Jesus Christ, forsaking yourselves and offering all up to Him; and the means which thou shalt use to this purpose are prayer and meditation.

PART II

CHAPTER I

SECTION I: OF PRAYERS AND THE SEVERAL SORTS THEREOF

PRAYER is profitable and speedful to be used for the getting of purity of heart by destroying of sin and bringing in virtues; not that thou shouldst thereby make our Lord know what thou desirest, for He knoweth well enough what thou needest, but to dispose thee and make thee ready and able thereby, as a clean vessel, to receive the grace which our Lord would freely give thee, which grace cannot be felt till thou be exercised and purified by the fire of desire in devout prayer. For though it be so that prayer is not the cause for which our Lord giveth grace, nevertheless it is a way or means by which grace freely given cometh into a soul.

But now thou wilt desire perhaps to know how thou shouldst pray and upon what thing thou shouldst set the point of thy thoughts in prayer, and also what prayer was best for thee to use. As to the first, I answer that when thou art wakened out of thy sleep, and art ready to pray, thou shalt feel thyself fleshly and heavy, tending ever downwards to vain thoughts, either of dreams or fancies, or of unnecessary things of the world or of the flesh, then behoveth it thee to quicken thy heart by prayer, and stir it up as much as thou canst to some devotion. In thy prayer set not thy heart on any bodily thing, but all thy care shall be to draw in thy thoughts from beholding any bodily thing, that thy desire may be as it were naked and bare from all earthly things, ever aspiring upward to Jesus Christ, whom yet thou canst never see bodily as He is in His Godhead, nor frame any image or likeness of Him in thy imagination; but thou mayest, through devout and continual beholding of the humility of His precious humanity, feel the goodness and the grace of His Godhead.

When thy desire and mind is gotten up, and as it were set free from all fleshly thoughts and affections, and is much lifted up by spiritual power unto spiritual favour and delight in Him and of His spiritual presence; hold thou therein much of thy time of prayer, so that thou have no great mind of earthly things, or if they come into thy mind that they do but trouble or affect thee little. If thou canst pray thus, thou prayest well, for prayer is nothing else but an ascending or getting up of the desire of the heart into God by withdrawing of it from all earthly thoughts. Therefore it is likened to a fire which, of its own nature, leaveth the lowness of the earth and always mounteth up into the air, even so desire in prayer, when it is touched and kindled of the spiritual fire, which is God, is ever aspiring up to Him that it came from.

They that speak of this fire of love know not well what it is; save this I can tell that it is neither any bodily thing nor felt by any sense of the body. A soul may feel it in prayer or in devotion, which soul is in the body, but it feeleth it not by any bodily sense; for though it is true that it works in and upon the soul, that the body itself is turned thereby into a heat and be as it were chafed through the labour and travail of the spirit, nevertheless the fire of love is not bodily, for it is only in the spiritual desire of the soul. And this is no riddle to any man or woman that have had the experience of devotion; but because some are so simple as to imagine that because it is called a fire that therefore it should be hot as bodily fire is, therefore have I set down thus much.

Now as to thy other question to know what prayer is best to be used, I shall give thee my opinion. Thou shalt understand that there be three kinds of vocal prayer.

The first is that which was made immediately by God Himself, as the Pater noster; the second those that are made more generally by the ordinance of holy Church, as Matins, Evensong and Hours; the third sort such as are made by pious men addressed to our Lord and to our Lady and to His saints.

As to these kinds of prayers that are called vocal, I judge that for thee that art religious and art bound by custom and thy rule to say thy Breviary it is most expedient to say it, and that as devoutly as thou canst, for in saying of them thou sayest also the Pater noster and other prayers likewise. And to stir thee up more to devotion there be ordained psalms and hymns, and such other which were made by the Holy Ghost, like as the Pater noster was. Therefore thou shalt not say them hastily nor carelessly, as if thou wert troubled or discontented for being bound to the recital of them; but thou shalt recollect thy thoughts to say them more seriously and more devoutly than any other prayers of voluntary devotion, deeming for truth that, seeing it is the prayer of holy Church, there is no vocal prayer so profitably to be used by thee as it is. Thus shalt thou put away all heaviness, and by God's grace turn thy necessity into good will and thy Obligation into a great freedom, so that it shall be no hindrance to thy other spiritual exercises. After this thou mayest, if thou wilt, use others, as the Pater noster or any other, and stick to those in which thou feelest most savour and spiritual comfort.

This kind of vocal prayer is commonly most profitable for every man in the beginning of his conversion, as being then but rude and gross and carnal (unless he have the more grace) nor cannot think of spiritual thoughts in his meditations, for his soul is not yet cleansed from his old sins. And therefore I hope it is most speedful to use this manner of prayer, as to say his Pater Noster and his Ave, and to read upon his psalter and such other. For he that cannot run easily and lightly by spiritual prayer, his feet of knowledge and love being feeble and sick by reason of sin, hath need of a firm staff to hold by, which staff is set forms of vocal prayer ordained by God and holy Church for the help of men's souls. By which the soul of a fleshly man that is alway falling downward into worldly thoughts and sensual affections shall be lifted up above them, and holden up as by a staff, and fed with the sweet words of those prayers as a child with milk, and guided and held up by them that he fall not into errors or fancies through his vain imaginations; for that in this manner of prayer is no deceit nor error to him that will diligently and humbly exercise himself therein.

And hereby thou mayest learn that those men (if any such there be) who in the beginning of their conversion, or soon after, having felt some spiritual comfort, either in devotion or knowledge, and are not yet stablished therein, leave such vocal prayer and other outward exercises too soon, and give themselves wholly to meditation, are not wise; for ofttimes in that time of rest which they take to themselves for meditation, imagining and thinking on spiritual things after their own fancies, and following their bodily feeling, having not yet received sufficient grace thereto, by indiscretion overtravel their wits and break their bodily strengths and so fall into fancies and singular conceits, or into open errors, and hinder that grace which God hath already given them, by such vanities. The cause of all this is secret pride and overweening of themselves; for when they have felt a little grace and some sensible devotion, they esteem it so much to surpass the graces and favours He doth to others that they fall into vain-glory. Whereas if they knew but how little it were in comparison of that which God giveth, or may give, they would be ashamed to speak anything of it, unless it were in a case of great necessity. Of this kind of vocal prayer speaketh David in the Psalms, thus: With my voice have I cried unto the Lord, with my voice have I prayed to our Lord. Behold how the prophet, for to stir other men to pray both with mouth and with voice, saith: With my voice I cried to God, and with my speech I besought our Lord.

There is another sort of vocal prayer which is not by any set common form of prayer; but is, when a man or woman, by the gift of God, feeling the grace of devotion, speaketh to God as it were bodily in His presence, with such words as suit most to his inward stirrings for the time, or as cometh to his mind, answerable to the feelings or motions of his heart, either by way of rehearsal of his sins and wretchedness, or of the malice and sleights of his enemy, or of the mercies and goodness of God. And hereby he crieth with desire of heart and speech of mouth to our Lord for succour and for help, as a man that were in peril among his enemies; or in sickness, showing his sores to God as to a physician, saying with David: Deliver me from my enemies, O Lord. Or else this: Heal my Soul, for I have sinned against Thee; or other suchlike words as they come to his mind.

And at other times there appears to him to be so much goodness and grace and mercy in God that it delighteth him with great affection of heart to love Him, and thank Him in such words and psalms as do most suit to that occasion, as David saith: Confess ye to the Lord because He is good, because His mercy endureth for ever.

This kind of prayer pleaseth God much, for it proceedeth wholly from the affection of the heart, and therefore never goeth away unsped or empty without some grace, and this prayer belongeth to the second part of contemplation, as I have said before. Whoso hath this gift of God fervently ought for a time to eschew the presence and company of all men, to be alone that he be not letted; whoso hath it let him hold it as long as he can, for it will not last long in its fervour. If the grace of it come plenteously, it is wondrous painful to the spirit, though it be much pleasant also to it; for it is much wasting to the body whoso useth it much, for it maketh the body (if the grace of it come in abundance) for to stir and move here and there as if the man were mad or drunk and could have no rest. This is a point of the passion of love, the which by great violence and mastery breaketh down and mortifieth all lusts and likings of any earthly thing, and woundeth the soul with the blessed sword of love, that it makes the body sink, not able to bear it. The touch of love is of so great power that the most vicious or fleshly man living on earth, if he were once strongly touched with this sharp sword, he would be right sober and grave a great while after, and abhor all the lusts and likings of the flesh and all earthly things which before he took most delight in.

Of this manner of feeling speaketh the prophet Jeremy thus: And there was made in my heart as a fire boiling, and shut up in my bones, and I fainted, not able to bear it; which words may be understood thus: The love and feeling of God was made in my heart, not fire, but as boiling or burning fire; for as material fire burneth and wasteth all bodily things where it cometh, right so doth spiritual fire (as is the love of God) burneth and wasteth all fleshly loves and likings in a man's soul. And this fire is shut up in my bones, as the prophet saith of himself, that is to say: This love filleth the powers of the soul, as the mind, reason and will, with grace and spiritual sweetness, as marrow filleth the bones, and that inwardly, and not outwardly in the senses. Nevertheless it is so mighty within that it worketh out into the body, and maketh it quake and tremble. And yet it hath so little to do with the bodily senses, and so unacquainted is the body with it that it cannot skill of it and cannot bear it, but faileth and falleth down as the prophet saith. Therefore our Lord tempereth it and withdraweth this fervour, and suffereth the heart to fall into more sobriety and softness. He that can pray thus often, he speedeth soon in his travail, and shall get more of virtues in a little time than another without this, or exercised in any other way of prayer, shall get in a long time for all the bodily penance he can do. Whoso hath this need not afflict his body with more penance than this brings along with it, which will be enough if it come often.

The third sort of prayer is only in the heart without speech, with great rest and quietness both of soul and body. A pure heart it behoveth him to have that shall pray after this manner; for such only attain to it who by long travail both of body and soul, or else by such sharp touches or motions of love, as I have before mentioned, have arrived to rest of spirit, so that his affections are turned into spiritual savour and relish, that he is able to pray continually in his heart, and love and praise God without great letting of temptations or of vanities, as is said before in the chapter of the second sort of Contemplation. Of this kind of prayer St Paul saith thus: If I pray with the tongue, my spirit prayed, but my mind is without fruit. What then? I will pray also in the spirit, I will pray also in the mind; I will sing in the spirit, I will sing also in the mind. That is to say: If I pray with my tongue only, by the consent of my spirit, and with painstaking and diligence, it is meritorious, but my soul is not fed by it, for it feeleth not the fruit of spiritual sweetness by understanding. What then shall I do, saith St Paul? And he answers, I will pray with the exercise and desire of the spirit, and I will also pray more inwardly in my spirit without labour, in spiritual savour and sweetness of the love and the sight of God, by the which sight and feeling of love my soul is fed. Thus (as I understand him) could St Paul pray.

Of this manner of prayer speaketh our Lord in holy Writ in a figure thus: Fire shall always burn upon the altar, which the priest shall nourish, putting wood underneath in the morning every day, that so the fire may not go out. That is, the fire of love shall ever be lighted in the soul of a devout and clean man or woman, the which is God's altar. And the priest shall every morning lay to it sticks and nourish the fire, that is this man shall, by holy psalms, clean thoughts and fervent desires, nourish the fire of love in his heart, that it go not out at any time. This prayer of rest or quiet our Lord giveth to some of His servants, as it were a reward of their travail, and an earnest of that love and sweetness which they shall have in the bliss of heaven.

SECTION II: HOW THEY SHOULD DO THAT ARE TROUBLED WITH VAIN THOUGHTS IN THEIR PRAYERS

BUT thou wilt say that I speak too high in this matter of prayer, which indeed is no mastery nor difficulty for me to write it, but it were a great piece of mastery for a man to practise it.

Thou sayest that thou canst not pray thus devoutly, nor so perfectly in heart as I speak of; for when thou wouldst have thy mind upward to God in thy prayer, thou feelest so many vain thoughts, either concerning thy own business or other men's, with many other lets and hindrances, that thou canst neither feel savour nor rest nor devotion in thy prayers, and ofttimes the more thou strivest to keep thy heart the further it is from thee and the harder, and sometimes continues so from the beginning to the end, that thou thinkest all lost that thou dost.

In answer to that which thou saidst, that I spake too high of prayer, I grant well that I spake more than I myself can or may do. Nevertheless I spake it for this intent that thou shouldst know how we ought to pray; and when we cannot do so, that we should acknowledge our weakness with all humility and God's mercy. Our Lord Himself hath commanded us thus: Thou shalt love the Lord thy God with all thy heart, with all thy soul and with all thy might. It is impossible for any man living to fulfil this bidding so fully as it is said. Yet our Lord hath bidden us so, to the intent, as St Bernard saith, that thereby we should know our feebleness, and then humbly cry for mercy, and we shall have it. Nevertheless I shall instruct thee in this point what to do as well as I can.

When thou goest about to pray, first make and frame betwixt thee and God in thy mind a full purpose and intention in the beginning to serve Him, then with all the powers of thy soul by thy present prayer, and then begin and do as well as thou canst. Though thou be never so much letted contrary to thy former purpose, be not afraid, neither be angry at thyself, nor impatient against God, because He giveth thee not the savour and spiritual sweetness in devotion as thou thinkest He giveth to others. But see therein thy own feebleness and bear it patiently, deeming it to be (as it is) feeble and of no worth in thy own sight, with humility of spirit; trusting also firmly in the mercy of our Lord, that he will make it good and profitable to thee, more than thou imaginest or feelest. For know thou well that thou art excused of thy duty, and thou shalt be rewarded for this (as well as for any other good work done in charity), though thy mind and intention may be not so fully set upon it as thou wishest. Therefore do what belongs to thee, and suffer our Lord to give what He will, and teach Him not. Think thyself wretched and negligent, and as it were in great fault for such things, yet for this fault and all other venials which cannot be eschewed in this wretched life lift up thy heart to God, acknowledging thy wretchedness, and cry God mercy, with a good trust of forgiveness, and strive no more therewith, nor stay any longer upon it, as if thou wouldst by main strength not feel such wretchedness, but leave off and go to some other good exercise, either corporal or spiritual, and resolve to do better the next time. Though thou shouldst fall another time into the same defect, yea, an hundred times, yea, a thousand, yet still do as I have said, and all will be well. Moreover a soul that never finds rest of heart in prayer, but all her life is striving with her thoughts, and is troubled and letted with them, if she keep her in humility and charity in other things, she shall have great reward in heaven for her good will and endeavours.

CHAPTER II

SECTION I: OF MEDITATION

THOU must understand that in meditation no certain rule can be set for every one to observe, for they are in the free gift of our Lord, according to divers dispositions of chosen souls, and according as we thrive in that state and in virtues, so God increaseth our meditations, both in spiritual knowing and loving of Him. For whoso is always alike, and at a stand in knowing of God and spiritual things, it seemeth that he profiteth and groweth but little in the love of God, which may be proved by the example of the apostles, who, when at Pentecost they were filled with burning love of the Holy Ghost, became thereby neither fools nor dolts, but became wonderful wise, both in knowing and speaking of God and spiritual things, as much as men could in mortal bodies. For thus saith the Scripture: They were all filled with the Holy Ghost, and began to speak the wonders of God; all which knowledge they got by ravishing in love, through the working of the Holy Ghost within them. Divers sorts of meditations there be which our Lord putteth in a man's heart. Some of them shall I tell thee of that thou mayest exercise thyself in them. In the beginning of the conversion of such a man as hath been much defiled with worldly or fleshly sins, commonly his thoughts are much upon his sins with great compunction and sorrow of heart, with great weeping and many tears humbly and busily asking mercy and forgiveness of God for them. And if he be deeply touched in conscience for them (for then our Lord will soon cleanse him from them), his sins will seem ever to be in his sight, and that so foul and so horrible, that hardly can he be able to brook or endure himself for them; and though he confess himself never so clearly of them, yet will he find difficulty and a fretting and biting in his conscience about them, thinking that he hath not confessed right. And scarce can he take any rest, or be quiet, insomuch that his body were not able to undergo such vexation and pain, were it not that our Lord of His mercy sometimes comforteth him by the consideration of His Passion, and devotion wrought in him thereto; or by some other means as He seeth good. After this manner worketh He in some men's hearts more or less, as He will, and this is through His great mercy, that not only will He forgive the sin or the trespass, but will both forgive the trespass and the pain due for it in Purgatory, for such a little pain here felt in the remorse and biting of conscience. Also, to make a man rightly to receive any special gift or degree of the love of God, it behoveth that he first be scoured and cleansed by such a fire of compunction for all his great sins before done. Of this kind of exercise of compunction often David speaks in the Psalter, but especially in the psalm, Miserere mei, Deus—Have mercy on me, O God.

And then sometime after this travail and exercise, and sometimes together with it, such a man that hath been so defiled with sins, or else another who, by the grace of God, hath been kept in innocence, our Lord bestoweth on him the meditation of His humanity, or of His birth, or of His Passion, and of the compassion of our Lady, St Mary. When this meditation is made by the help of the Holy Ghost, then it is right profitable and gracious, and thou shalt know it by this token: when thou art stirred to a meditation in God, and thy thoughts are suddenly drawn out from all worldly and fleshly things, and thou thinkest that thou seest in thy soul the Lord Jesus in a bodily likeness as He was on earth, and how He was taken by the Jews and bound as a thief, beaten and despised, scourged and judged to death, how lowly He bore the cross upon His back, and how cruelly He was nailed thereon; also of the crown of thorns upon His head, and of the sharp spear that sticked Him to the heart; and thou in this spiritual sight feelest thy heart stirred to so great compassion and pity of thy Lord Jesus, that thou mournest and weepest, and criest with all thy might of body and soul, wondering at the goodness, the love, the patience, the meekness of thy Lord Jesus, that He would, for so sinful a caitiff as thou art, suffer so much pain; and, nevertheless, thou seest so much goodness and mercy to be in Him that thy heart riseth up into a love and a joy and a gladness in Him, with many sweet tears, having great trust of the forgiveness of thy sins and the salvation of thy soul by the virtue of this precious Passion; so that when the meditation of Christ's Passion, or any part of His humanity is thus wrought in thy heart by such a spiritual sight, with devout affection answerable thereunto, know well that it is not of thy own working, nor the feigning or working of any evil spirit, but by the grace of the Holy Ghost. For it is an opening of the spiritual eye into the humanity of Christ, and may be called the fleshly love of God, as St Bernard saith, inasmuch as it is set upon the fleshly nature of Christ, and it is right good, and a great help for the destroying of great sins, and a good way to come to virtues, and so after to the Contemplation of the Godhead. For a man shall not come to the spiritual light in Contemplation of Christ's Godhead, unless first he be exercised in imagination with bitterness and compassion, and in stedfast thinking of His humanity. Thus St Paul did, and therefore first he saith: I desired to know nothing among you but Jesus Christ and Him crucified. As if he had said: My knowing and my faith is only in the Passion of Christ; and therefore he saith thus also: God forbid I should rejoice in anything, save in the cross of Christ. Nevertheless afterward he saith: We preach unto you Christ, the power of God and the wisdom of God. As who should say: First I preached of the humanity and Passion of Christ; now I preach to you of the Godhead, that Christ is the power of God, and the endless wisdom of God.

But this manner of meditation a man hath not always when he would, but only when our Lord will give it. Unto some He giveth it all their lifetime by fits, when He visiteth them; some men being so tender in their affections that, when they hear men speak or think themselves of this precious Passion, their hearts melt into devotion, and are fed and comforted thereby against all manner of temptations of the enemy, and this is a great gift of God. To some men He giveth it plentifully at the first, and afterwards withdraws it for divers causes, either if a man grow proud of it in his own eyes, or for some other sin by which he disableth himself to receive the grace; or else our Lord withdraweth it, and all other devotions sometimes, because He will suffer him to be tried with temptations of the enemy, and thereby will dispose a man to understand and feel our Lord more spiritually, for so He saith to His disciples: It is expedient for you that I go away from you [in my body], for except I go the Holy Ghost will not come. As long as He was with them they loved Him much, but it was fleshly according to His humanity, and therefore it was necessary that He should withdraw His bodily presence, that the Holy Ghost might come to them and teach them how to love Him and know Him more spiritually, as He did at Pentecost. Right so, it is expedient for some that our Lord withdraw a little the fleshly and bodily image from the eye of their soul, that their heart may be set and fixed more busily in spiritual desire and seeking of His divinity.

SECTION II: OF DIVERS TEMPTATIONS OF THE ENEMY, AND THE REMEDIES AGAINST THEM

NEVERTHELESS it behoveth a man to suffer many temptations first, which shall befall some men often after that their comfort is withdrawn, and that sundry ways by the malice of the enemy. As thus: when the devil perceiveth devotion much withdrawn, that the soul is left, as it were, naked for a time, then sendeth he to some temptations of lust, of gluttony, and these so hot and burning that they shall think they never felt so grievous ones in all their life before, even when they gave themselves most to such sins. Insomuch as they think it impossible to stand out long from falling without help. And, therefore, have they then much sorrow for lack of comfort and devotion which formerly they have had, and much dread also of falling from God by such open sins. All this the devil worketh (by God's permission) to make them repent of their good purposes, and turn back to their former courses of sinning. But whoso will abide, and suffer a little pain, and not turn again to sin for anything, the hand of our Lord is full near, and will help them right soon, for He hath much care of that man that is in such a case, though he knoweth it not; for so saith David in the person of our Lord: I am with him in trouble, I will deliver him, and he shall glorify Me. The devil tempteth others maliciously to spiritual sins, as to doubt of the articles of faith, or of the Sacrament of our Lord's blessed Body. Also to despair, or blaspheme of God or any of His saints, or to a wearisomeness of their own life, or to bitterness against others, or foolish melancholy and sadness, or too much fear of themselves, of doing hurt to their healths by giving themselves so much to serving of God. Some others, and namely solitary folks, he frighteth with dreads and ugly shapes appearing to their eyes or to their imaginations, causing often thereby great shakings and quakings in their bodies, either sleeping or waking, and so troubleth them that they can hardly take any rest. And also many other ways he tempteth, more than I can or may say.

The remedies for such may be these. First: that they put all their trust in our Lord Jesus Christ, and often call to mind His Passion and the pains that He suffered for us, and that they then believe stedfastly that all sorrows and travail which they suffer in such temptations, which to unskilful men may seem a forsaking by God, are indeed no such leavings or forsakings, but trials for their good, either for cleansing of their former sins or for the great increasing of their reward and the disposing of them for more grace, if they will but suffer awhile and stand fast, that they turn not again willingly to sin.

Another remedy is that they fear not, nor esteem these malicious stirrings for sins, nor lay to heart that despair or blasphemy, or doubtings of sacrament, or any such other, though never so ugly to hear; for the feeling of these temptations defile the soul no more than if they heard a hound bark or felt the biting of a flea. They vex the soul indeed, but do not harm it, if so be a man despise them and set them at nought, for it is not good to strive with them, as if thou wouldst cast them out by mastery and violence, for the more they strive with them the more they cleave to them. And therefore they shall do well to divert their thoughts from them as much as they can, and set them upon some business. And if they will still hang upon them, then it is good for them that they be not angry nor heavy through feeling of them; but with a good trust in God bear them (like a bodily sickness and scourge of our Lord for the cleansing of their sins as long as He pleaseth) out of love to Him, even as He was willing to be scourged and bear His cross for the love of them. Moreover, it is good for them to open their minds to some wise man in the beginning, before these temptations get rooting in their heart, and that they forsake their own wit and judgement and follow the counsel of another. But that they show them not unadvisedly or lightly to any unskilful or worldly man, who never felt such temptations, for such may happily by their unskilfulness bring a simple soul into despair.

Of this manner of temptations by which a man seemeth forsaken of God, and is not, the help and comfort is this: The Lord saith by His prophet, For a little space have I left thee, but in great mercy will I gather thee. For a moment of indignation have I hid my face a little while from thee, and in mercy everlasting will I have mercy on thee. As if He had said, I suffered thee to be troubled a little while, and in a point of My wrath I smote thee; that is to say, the penance and the pain that thou sufferest here is but a point or little prick of My wrath, in regard of the pain of hell or of purgatory. Yet in My manifold mercies I shall gather thee; when thou thinkest thyself forsaken, then will I of My great mercy gather thee again to Me; for when thou esteemest thyself, as it were, lost, then shall our Lord help thee, as Job saith: When thou shalt think thyself consumed, thou shalt arise as the daystar, and thou shalt have confidence. That is to say, when thou art brought so low by travail into temptation that thou despairest of help or comfort, like a forlorn man, yet stand stiffly in hope and pray to God, and verily thou shalt suddenly spring up as the day-star, in gladness of heart, and have a sure trust in God.

Moreover, for the comfort of such men, that they may not despair in temptation, the wise man saith thus of our Lord: In temptation He walketh with him, and bringeth fear and dread upon him, and torments him with His discipline, till He try him in his cogitations, and may trust His soul: And He will establish him, and make a direct way unto him, and make him glad, and will disclose His secrets to him, and will heap upon him as treasures knowledge of understanding and justice. The wise man, because he would have not despair in temptation, to comfort them saith thus: In temptation our Lord forsaketh not a man, but goeth with him from the beginning to the end. For he saith first, He chooseth him, and that is, when He draweth a man to Him by comfort of devotion, and afterward bringeth upon him sorrow and dread and trials, and that is when He withdraweth devotion and suffereth him to be tempted. And he saith that He tormenteth him in tribulation until He hath well tried him in his thoughts, and until a man will put all his trust in Him fully, and then He bringeth him out into the right way, and fasteneth him to Him, and gladdeneth him, and sheweth him His secrets, and giveth him His treasure of knowing and understanding of righteousness.

By these words may you see that these temptations or any other, be they never so ugly, are expedient and profitable to a man that by grace is in full will to forsake sin, if he will be willing to suffer and abide God's will, and not turn again to sin which he hath forsaken, for any sorrow, or pain, or dread of such temptations; but ever stand still in travail and in prayer with good hope. Our Lord of His endless goodness having pity and mercy of all His creatures, when He seeth time, will put to His hand and smite down the devil and all his power, and ease him of his travail, and put away all dreads and sorrows and darkness out of his heart, and brings into his soul the light of grace, opening the eye thereof to see, that all the travail that he hath had was expedient for him, giving him also fresh spiritual might to withstand all the suggestions of the fiend and all deadly sins without great difficulty, and leadeth him into a stability and settledness of virtue and good living; in which, if he keepeth himself humble to the end, then will He take him wholly to himself. Thus much have I said, that thou mightest not be troubled or letted with any such temptation, or too much afraid; but do as I have said, and better if thou canst, and I hope through the grace of Jesus Christ thou shalt never be overcome by thine enemy.

But after thou hast escaped these temptations, or else if our Lord hath so kept thee (as He doth many by His mercy) that thou hast not been troubled much with any such, then it is good for thee that thou beware of turning thy rest into idleness; for there is many a man that taketh rest upon him too soon, as if he were ripe for rest in Contemplation. But if thou wilt do well, begin a new game and a new travail, and that is, by meditation, to enter within into thy own soul, for to know what it is, and by the knowing thereof to come to the spiritual knowledge of God. For St Austin saith, By the knowing of myself I shall get the knowledge of God. I say not that such exercise is absolutely necessary, and thy bounden duty, unless thou feel thyself stirred up by grace, and as it were called thereto. For our Lord giveth divers gifts where He pleaseth, not all to one man, nor one to every man, save the gift of charity, which is common to all.

Therefore, if a man have received a gift from God, as devotion in prayer, or in the Passion of Christ, or any other, be it never so little, let him not leave it quickly for any other, unless he assuredly find and feel a better, but hold that which he hath, and exercise himself therein seriously, ever desiring a better when God will give it. Nevertheless, if that be withdrawn somewhat, and he seeth a better, and feeleth his heart stirred thereto, then seemeth it to be a calling of our Lord to the better, and then is it time that he follow after it, to get it, and fall to practise it as speedily as he may.

CHAPTER III: THAT A MAN SHOULD KNOW THE MEASURE OF HIS GIFT, THAT HE MAY DESIRE AND TAKE A BETTER WHEN GOD GIVETH IT

OUR holy Fathers heretofore taught us that we should know the measure of our gift, and therefore to work upon it, and according to it, and not take upon us, out of our head or imagination, to have more in our feeling or ability than indeed we have. We may ever desire the best, but we may not ever work the best or our utmost, because we have not yet received that grace and ability. A hound that runneth after the hare only because he seeth other hounds run, when he is weary, he stayeth and resteth, or turneth home again; but if he run because he seeth or is in view of the hare, he will not spare for weariness till he have caught her. Right so it is in the spiritual course, whoso hath grace, be it never so little, and wittingly leaveth it, and the working upon it, and putteth himself to the exercise or practice of another kind, for which he hath not as yet received a gift or grace, but doth it only because he seeth, readeth, or heareth that some others do so, he may perhaps run awhile till he be weary and then will he turn home again, and if he be not the more wary, may hurt his feet with such fancies before he get home. But he that continueth working upon such grace as he hath, and humbly beggeth by prayer perseverantly for more, and after feeleth his heart stirred to follow after the grace which he desired, he may securely run, if he keep himself humble. Therefore, desire of God as much as thou wilt or canst, without measure or moderation at all concerning any thing that belongs to His love or Heaven's bliss, for he that can desire most of God shall feel and receive most; but work as thou mayest and cry God mercy, for that thou canst not do. Thus St Paul seems to mean, when he said: Every one hath a proper gift of God, one so, and another so. Also, when he said: There are varieties of gifts, to one is given the word of wisdom, to another the word of knowledge, etc. And also when he said: To every one of us is given grace, according to the measure of the donation of Christ. And further, where he said: That we may know the things that are given us by God. He saith that every one hath his gift of God: For to every man that shall be saved is given a grace according to the measure of Christ's gift. Therefore it is speedful that we know the gifts that are given us by God, that we may work in them, for by those we shall be saved, as some by bodily works, and by deeds of mercy, some by great bodily penance, some by sorrow and weeping for their sins all their lifetime, some by preaching and teaching, some by divers graces and gifts of devotion shall be saved and come to bliss.

PART III

CHAPTER I: OF THE KNOWLEDGE OF A MAN'S SOUL AND THE POWERS THEREOF NECESSARY TO CONTEMPLATION

THERE is one work more very needful and expedient to travail, in which I esteem also to be the plain highway in our working (as much as may be) to Contemplation: and that is, for a man to enter into himself, to know his own soul and the powers thereof.

By this inward sight thou shalt come to see the nobility and dignity that naturally it had in its first creation; and thou shalt also see the wretchedness and the mischief which thou art fallen into by sin. From this sight will arise a desire with great longing in thine heart to recover again that dignity and nobleness which thou hast lost. Also thou shalt feel a loathing and detestation of thyself, with a great will and desire to destroy and beat down thyself and all things that let thee from that dignity and that joy. This is a spiritual work, hard and sharp in the beginning, for those that will go speedily and seriously about it. For it is an exercise in the soul against the ground of all sins, little and great, which ground is nought else but a false mistrusted love of man to himself. Out of this love, as St Austin saith, springeth all manner of sin, deadly and venial.

Verily until this ground be well ransacked and deep digged, and as it were dried up by casting out of all fleshly and worldly loves and fears, a soul can never spiritually feel the burning love of Jesus Christ nor have the homeliness of His gracious presence, nor have a clear sight of spiritual things by light in the understanding. This then must be the travail and labour of a man, to draw his heart and mind from the fleshly love and liking of all earthly creatures, from vain thoughts and from fleshly imaginations and from the love and vicious feeling of himself, so that the soul shall or may find or take no rest in any fleshly thoughts or worldly affections. Then inasmuch as the soul cannot as yet find her spiritual rest and satisfaction in the sight and love of Jesus, therefore it must needs be that in the meanwhile she must find and feel some pain and wearisomeness.

This pain and travail is somewhat straight and narrow, nevertheless I hope it is the way which Christ teacheth to them that would be His perfect lovers in the Gospel, saying: Strive to enter in at the strait gate, for strait is the gate, and narrow is the way that leadeth to life, and few men find it. How strait this way is, He telleth us in another place: Whoso will come after me, let him forsake himself and hate his own soul. That is to say, forsake all fleshly love and hate his own carnal life and vain liking of all his bodily senses for love of Me; and take the cross, that is suffer the pain of this awhile and then follow Me; that is to say, in Contemplation of My Humanity and of My Divinity. This is a strait and narrow way that no bodily thing can pass through it, for it is a slaying of all sin, as St Paul saith: Mortify your members that are upon earth, not the members of our body but of our soul, as uncleanness, lust, evil concupiscence, avarice, fond love to ourselves and earthly things. Therefore as thy endeavour has been heretofore to resist bodily sins and open temptations of the enemy, and that in matters as it were from without; right so it behoveth thee now, in this spiritual work within thyself, to batter down and destroy the ground of sin in thyself as much as thou canst. Which that thou mayest be better able to perform, I shall give thee the best counsel I can.

CHAPTER II: OF THE WORTHINESS AND EXCELLENCY OF THE SOUL AND HOW IT WAS LOST

THE soul of a man is a life consisting of three powers, Memory, Understanding and Will, after the image and likeness of the Blessed Trinity; inasmuch as the Memory was made strong and stedfast by the power of the Father to hold and retain God in perpetual remembrance, without forgetting, distracting or letting of any creature, and so it hath the likeness of the Father. The Understanding was made bright and clear, without error or darkness, as perfectly as a soul in a body unglorified could have, and so it hath the likeness and image of the Son, who is infinite wisdom. The Will and affections were made pure and clean, burning in love towards God, without sensual love of the flesh or of any creature by the sovereign goodness of God the Holy Ghost, and so it hath the likeness of the Holy Ghost, which is blessed love. Whereby you may see that man's soul (which may be called a created Trinity) was in its natural estate replenished in its three powers with the remembrance, sight and love of the most blessed uncreated Trinity, which is God.

This was the dignity and worth of man's soul by nature at his first creation, which thou hadst in Adam before the first sin. But when Adam sinned, choosing love and delight in himself and in the creatures, he lost all his excellency and dignity, and thou, also, in him, and fell from that Blessed Trinity into a foul, dark, wretched trinity; that is to say, into forgetting of God and ignorance of himself, and into a beastly love and liking of himself, and all this he did wittingly and willingly. For, as David saith in the Psalter: Man being in honour understood it not, and, therefore, he lost it, and became like a beast.

See then the wretchedness of thy soul, for as the Memory was something established and fixed upon God, so now it hath forgotten Him and seeketh its rest in the creatures, now in one creature and then in another, and never can find full rest, having lost Him in whom is full rest. So it is with the Understanding and the Will and affections, both which were pure in spiritual favour and sweetness but now is turned into a foul, beastly lust and liking in itself and in the creatures and in fleshly favours, both in the senses as in gluttony and lechery; and in the imagination, as in pride, vain-glory and covetousness, insomuch that thou canst do no good deed but it is defiled with vain-glory; nor canst thou easily make use of any of thy five senses cleanly upon anything that is pleasant, but thy heart will be taken and enflamed with a vain lust and liking of it, which putteth out the love of God from thy heart, so that no feeling of love or spiritual favour may come into it.

Every man that liveth in spirit understandeth well all this. This is the soul's wretchedness and our mischief for the first man's sin besides all other wretchedness and sins which thou hast wilfully added thereto. And know thou well that hadst thou never committed any sin with is thy body, either mortal or venial, but only this which is called original (for that is the first sin, and is nothing else but the losing of our righteousness which we were created in), thou shouldst never have been saved, had not our Lord Jesus Christ by His precious Passion delivered thee, and restored thee again.

And, therefore, if thou think I have herein spoken too high, because thou canst neither understand it well, nor practise it according as I have delivered, I will now descend to thee, and fall as low as thou canst desire, both for thy profit and my own. Then say thus: though thou be never so much a wretch, and hast committed never so great sins, do but forsake thyself and all thy works done, both good and bad, and cry God mercy, and ask salvation only by virtue of this precious Passion, and that with a good trust, and without doubt thou shalt have it. And as for original sin, and all other thou shalt be safe, yea, as safe as an anchoret that is enclosed. And not only thou, but all Christian souls that trust upon His Passion and humble themselves, acknowledging their wretchedness, asking mercy and forgiveness, and the fruit of this precious Passion only, and submitting themselves to the Sacraments of holy Church, though it be so that they have been encumbered with sin all their lifetime, and never had feeling of spiritual favour or sweetness, or ghostly knowledge of God, yet shall they in this faith, and in their good will, by virtue of this precious Passion of our Lord Jesus Christ be safe, and come to the bliss of Heaven.

All this thou knowest well, but yet it delights me to recite and speak of it, that thou mayest see the endless mercy of our Lord, how low He falleth to thee and to me and to all sinful caitiffs; ask mercy therefore, and have it. Thus saith the Prophet in the person of our Lord: Every one that calleth upon the Name of our Lord shall be saved; that is to say, asketh salvation by Jesus and His Passion.

This courtesy of our Lord some men understand aright, and are saved thereby, and others in trust of this mercy and this courtesy lie still in their sins, and think to have the benefit of it when they list, but they are mistaken, for they are taken ere they are aware, and so damn themselves.

But thou wilt object: If this be true that thou sayest, I wonder greatly at that which I find in some holy men's books, for some say (as I understand them) that he that cannot love this blessed Name Jesus nor find and feel in it spiritual joy and delight with sweetness, shall be a stranger to the bliss of Heaven, and never come there. Verily when I read these words, they astonished me, making me afraid. For I hope (as you have said) that through the mercy of our Lord they shall be safe, by keeping of the commandments and by true repentance for their former evil life, who never felt any such spiritual sweetness, in the Name of Jesus, and therefore I marvel the more, to find them say (as me thinketh) the contrary hereto.

To this I answer that (in my opinion) their saying (if it be well understood) is true, and no whit contrary to what I have said, for this Name Jesus is nothing else in English but healer or health. Now every man that liveth in this wretched life is spiritually sick, for there is no man that liveth without sin, which is a spiritual sickness, as St John saith of himself, and of other perfect men thus: If we say we have no sin, we beguile ourselves, and there is as no truth in us. Therefore he can never come to the joy of Heaven, till he be first healed of this ghostly sickness. But this spiritual healing may no man have (that hath the use of reason) except he desire it, and love it, and have delight therein, inasmuch as he hopeth to get it. Now the Name of Jesus is nothing else but this spiritual health; wherefore it is true that they say, that no man can be safe, unless he love and like the Name of Jesus; for no man can be spiritually healed, until he love and desire spiritual health; just as if a man were bodily sick, there could no earthly thing be so dear, nor so needful to him, nor so much would he desire it, as bodily health; for though thou shouldst give him all the dignities and riches of this world, and not make him whole (if thou couldst), thou pleaseth him not. Right so it is to a man that is sick spiritually, and feeleth the pain thereof; nothing is so dear, nor so needful, nor so much coveted by him, as is ghostly health, and that is Jesus, without whom all the joys of Heaven cannot please him. And this is the reason (as I take it) why our Lord when He took man's nature upon Him for our salvation, would not be called by a name betokening His infinite essence, or His wisdom, or His justice, but only by that which betokened the cause of His coming, namely, the salvation of man's soul, which salvation this name Jesus betokened. Hereby, then, it appeareth that none can be saved unless he love salvation, to have it through the mercy of our Lord Jesus only, by the merits of His passion; which love he may have that liveth and dieth in the very lowest degree of charity.

Also I may affirm on the other side, that he that cannot love this blessed name Jesus with a spiritual joy, nor increase in it with heavenly melody here, shall never have nor feel in Heaven the fulness of sovereign joy, which he that could so love it in this life by abundance of perfect charity in Jesus shall then have and feel in Heaven, and so may their saying be understood.

Nevertheless he shall be saved, and have great reward in Heaven from God, whosoever in this life is in the lowest degree of charity by keeping God's commandments. For our Lord saith: In My Father's house are sundry mansions. Some are perfect souls, who in this life are filled with charity and graces of the Holy Spirit, and sing most sweetly and lovingly to God in Contemplation of Him, with wonderful sweetness and heavenly savour. These because they have most charity and grace of the Holy Ghost shall have the highest reward in the bliss of heaven, for these are called God's darlings. Others there be, not disposed or enabled to Contemplation, nor having the perfection of charity (as the apostles and martyrs had in the beginning of the holy Church), these shall have a lower reward in the bliss of Heaven, for these are called God's friends, for thus doth our Lord call them: Eat, O My friends, and be inebriated, O My darlings. As if He had said: Ye that are My friends, because ye have kept My commandments, and preferred My love before the love of the world, and loved me more than any earthly thing, ye shall be fed with the spiritual food of the Bread of life. But ye that are more than My friends, that not only kept My commandments, but also of your own free will fulfilled My counsels, and loved Me entirely with all the powers of your souls, and burned in My love with spiritual delight (as especially did the apostles and martyrs and all other souls that through grace came to the gift of perfection) ye shall be made drunken with the noblest and freshest wine in My cellar, which is the supreme joy of love in heaven.

CHAPTER III

SECTION I: THAT A MAN SHOULD BE INDUSTRIOUS TO RECOVER AGAIN HIS ANCIENT DIGNITY AND REFORM WITHIN HIM THE IMAGE OF THE TRINITY, AND HOW IT MAY BE DONE

NEVERTHELESS, though this that I have said be true, through the endless mercy of God to thee and to me and to all mankind we are not, therefore, in confidence hereof to be more careless, or wilfully negligent in our living; but the more busy to please Him, and the rather, because now we are restored again in hope by the passion of our Lord, to the dignity and bliss which we had lost by Adam's sin. Though we should prove not to be able to recover it fully here in this life, yet should we desire and endeavour to recover the image and likeness of the dignity we had, so that our soul might be reformed, as it were in a shadow, by grace to the image of the Trinity which we had by nature, and hereafter shall have fully in bliss. For that is the life which is truly contemplative to begin here, in that feeling of love and spiritual knowing of God, by opening of the spiritual eye, which shall never be lost nor taken away, but shall be perfected in a far higher manner in heaven. Thus did our Lord promise to St Mary Magdalen (that was a true Contemplative) when He told her that she had chosen the better part (which was the love of God in Contemplation) that should never be taken from her.

I do not say that in this life thou canst recover so whole and so perfect a cleanness and innocency, knowing and loving of God, as thou hadst at first, and shalt have hereafter, neither mayest escape all the wretchedness and pains of sin; nor that thou living in mortal flesh canst wholly destroy and kill within thee all false vain loves, nor eschew all venial sins, but that they will (unless they be stopped by great fervour of charity) spring out of thy heart, as water doth out of a stinking well. But I wish that if thou canst not fully quench it, yet thou mayest somewhat slack it, and come as near as thou canst to cleanness of soul. For our Lord promised to the children of Israel, when He led them into the land of Promise, and in them by a figure to all Christians, saying: All the land which thy foot shall tread upon shall be thine. That is to say, so much land as thou canst tread upon with thy foot of true desire, so much shalt thou have in the land of Promise, namely, in the bliss of Heaven, when thou comest thither.

SECTION II: THAT THIS DIGNITY AND IMAGE IS RESTORED BY JESUS, AND HOW HE IS TO BE DESIRED, SOUGHT AND FOUND

SEEK, then, that which thou hast lost, that thou mayest find it; for well I wot, whosoever once hath an inward sight, but a little of that dignity and that spiritual fairness which a soul hath by creation, and shall have again by grace, he will loathe in his heart all the bliss, the liking and the fairness of this world, as the stink of carrion; and he will never have any will or mind to do other deed, night or day (save what mere need of nature requireth) but desire, mourn, seek, and pray how he may come again thereto.

Nevertheless inasmuch as thou hast not as yet seen what it is fully, for thy spiritual eye is not yet opened, I shall tell thee one word for all, in the which thou shalt seek, desire and find it; for in that one word is all that thou hast lost. This word is Jesus: I mean not this word Jesus painted upon the wall, as written in letters on the book, or formed by lips in sound of the mouth, or framed in thy mind by imagination, for in this wise may a man that is void of charity find Him; but I mean Jesus Christ, that blessed Person, God and Man, Son of the Virgin Mary, whom this name betokeneth; that is all goodness, endless wisdom, love and sweetness, thy joy, thy glory, and thy everlasting bliss, thy God, thy Lord, and thy salvation.

If, then, thou feelest a great desire in thy heart to Jesus, either by calling to mind this name Jesus, or by minding, or thinking, or saying of any other word; or in Prayer, or Meditation, or any other deed which thou dost; which desire is so much, that it putteth out, as it were, by force all other thoughts and desires of the world, and of the flesh, that they rest not in thy heart; then seekest thou well thy Lord Jesus. And when thou feelest this desire to God, or to Jesus (for it is all one), holpen and comforted by a ghostly might, insomuch that it is turned into love, affection, and spiritual savour and sweetness, into light and knowing of truth, so that for the time, the point of thy thought is set upon no other created thing, nor feeleth any stirring of vainglory, nor of self-love, nor any other evil affection (for they cannot appear at that time), but this thy desire is only enclosed, rested, softened, suppled, and anointed in Jesus, then hast thou found somewhat of Jesus; I mean not Him as He is, but a shadow of Him; for the better that thou findest Him, the more shalt thou desire Him. Then observe by what manner of prayer, or meditation, or exercise of devotion thou findest greatest and purest desire stirred up in thee to Him, and most feeling of Him, by that kind of prayer, exercise or work seekest thou Him best, and shalt best find Him. Therefore if it come into thy mind, asking as it were of thyself: What has thou lost, and what seekest thou? lift up thy mind and the desire of thy heart to Jesus Christ, though thou be blind, and canst see nought of His Godhead, and say that: Him hast thou lost, and Him wouldst thou have, and nothing but Him, to be with Him where His is. No other joy, no other bliss in Heaven or in earth, but Him.

And though it be so, that thou feelest Him in devotion, or in knowing, or by any other gift or grace, rest not there, as though thou hadst fully found Jesus; but forget that which thou hast found, and always be desiring after Jesus more and more, to find Him better, as though thou hadst right nought found in Him. For wot thou well, that what thou feelest of Him, be it never so much, yea, though thou wert ravished with St Paul into the third heaven, yet hast thou not found Jesus as He is in His joy, know thou, or feel thou never so much of Him, He is still above it. And therefore, if thou wilt fully find Him, as He is in His joy, do thou never cease from spiritual desiring and loving of Him, whilst thou livest.

Verily I had rather feel and have a true an; clean desire in my heart to my Lord Jesus Christ, though I see little of Him With my spiritual eye, than to have without this desire all the bodily penance of all men living, all visions, all revelations of Angels appearing, all songs and sounding to the ear, all tastes and smellings, fervours or any delights, or bodily feelings, and (to be brief) all the joys of heaven and earth which are possible to be had, without this desire to my Lord Jesus. David the Prophet felt (as I conceive) this desire in himself, when he said thus: What have I in Heaven but Thee, and what can I desire on earth besides Thee? As if he had said, Lord Jesus, what heavenly joy is liking to me without desire of Thee, whilst I am on earth, or without love of Thee when I come to Heaven? As who should say, right none. If, then, thou wilt feel anything of Him, bodily or spiritually, covet nothing but only to feel in truth within thee a desire of His grace and of His merciful presence, so that thou mayest think that it is not possible for thy heart to find any rest in anything but in Him. Thus coveted David, when he said thus: My soul hath coveted, or longed after, the desire of thy righteousness at all times. Seek, then, as David did, desire by desire. And if thou feelest, by thy desire in prayers and in meditations, the familiar presence of Jesus Christ in thy soul, bind thy heart fast thereto, that it fall not from it; and if thou shouldst stumble, that thou mayest soon find Him again.

Seek, then, Jesus, whom thou hast lost, for He would be sought, and is desirous to be found, for He Himself saith: Every one that seeketh findeth. The seeking is painful, but the finding is joyful; do, therefore, after the counsel of the wise man, if thou wilt find Him: If thou shalt seek wisdom (that is Jesus) like silver, and as treasures shalt dig her up, then shalt thou understand the fear of our Lord, and shalt find the knowledge of God. It behoveth thee to delve deep in thy heart, for therein Jesus is hid, and cast out perfectly all loves and likings, sorrows and fears of all earthly things, and so shalt thou find wisdom, that is Jesus.

Be thou, then, like the woman in the Gospel, of whom our Lord saith: What woman is there, that hath lost her groat and doth not light a candle, and turn her house upside down, and seek till she finds it? As who should say, there is none but would do so. And when she hath found it, she calleth to her friends, and saith to them thus: Make mirth with me and melody, for I have found my groat which I had lost. This groat is Jesus which thou hast lost, and if thou wilt find Him, light up a lanthorn, that is God's Word, as David saith: Thy Word is a lanthorn to my feet. By this lanthorn shalt thou see where He is, and how to find Him. And if thou wilt, thou mayest together with this, light up another lanthorn, that is the reason of thy soul. For as our Lord saith:

The lanthorn (or light) of thy body is thy bodily eye. Right so may it be said, that the lanthorn of thy soul is reason, by the which thy soul may see all spiritual things. By this lanthorn mayest thou find Jesus, that is if thou hold up this lanthorn from underneath the bushel, as our Lord saith: No man lighteth a (candle or) lanthorn to set it under a bushel, but upon a candlestick. That is to say, thy reason must not be overlaid with earthly business, or vain thoughts, and earthly affections, but always upwards, above all vain thoughts and earthly things as much as thou canst. If thou do so, thou shalt see all the dust, all the filth and small motes in thy house (for He is light itself), that is to say, all fleshly loves and fears in thy soul. I mean not perfectly all; for as David saith: Who knoweth all his trespasses? As who should say, no man. And thou shalt cast out of thy heart all such sins, and sweep thy soul clean with the besom of the fear of God, and wash it with thy tears, and so shalt thou find thy groat, Jesus; He is thy groat, thy penny, thy heritage.

This groat will not be found so easily as tis thought, for this work is not of one hour nor of one day, but many days and years, with much sweat and labour of body and travail of soul. And if thou cease not, but seek busily, sigh and sorrow deeply, mourn stilly, and stoop low, till thine eyes water for anguish and for pain, for that thou hast lost thy treasure Jesus, at the last (when His will is) well shalt thou find thy groat Jesus. When thou hast found Him, as I have said, that is when in purity of conscience feelest the familiar and peaceful presence of that blessed man Jesus Christ, at least a shadow or glimmering of Him; thou mayest, if thou wilt, call all thy friends to thee to make mirth with thee and melody, for that thou hast found thy groat Jesus.

See then the mercy and courtesy of Jesus. Thou hast lost Him, but where? Soothly in thy house, that is to say, in thy soul, that if thou hadst lost all thy reason of thy soul by its first sin, thou shouldst never have found Him again; but He left thee thy reason, and so He is still in thy soul, and never is quite lost out of it.

Nevertheless thou art never the nearer Him till thou hast found Him. He is in thee, though He be lost from thee; but thou art not in Him till thou hast found Him. This is His mercy also, that He would suffer Himself to be lost only there, where He may be found, so that thou needest not run to Rome, nor to Jerusalem to seek Him there, but turn thy thoughts into thy own soul where He is hid, as the Prophet saith: Truly thou art the hidden God, hid in thy soul, and seek Him there. Thus saith He Himself in the Gospel: The Kingdom of Heaven is likened to a treasure hid in the field, the which when a man findeth, for joy thereof, he goeth and selleth all that he hath, and buyeth that field. Jesus is a treasure hid in the soul. Then if thou couldst find Him in thy soul, and thy soul in Him, I am sure for joy thereof thou wouldst part with the liking of all earthly things to have Him. Jesus sleepeth in thy heart spiritually, as He did sometime bodily when He was in the ship with His disciples; but they, for fear of perishing, wakened Him, and soon after He saved them from a tempest. Do thou so, stir Him up by prayer, and waken Him with great crying of desire, and He will soon rise and help thee.

Nevertheless I believe thou sleepest oftener to Him than He doth to thee; for He calleth thee full oft with His sweet, secret voice, and stirreth thy heart full stilly, that thou shouldst leave all other jangling of other vanities in thy soul, and hearken only to Him. Thus saith David in the person of our Lord: Hear, O daughter, and consider; incline thine ear, and forget thy own people and thy father's house. That is, forget the people of thy worldly thoughts, and the house of thy fleshly and natural affections. Here thou seest how our Lord calleth thee, and all others that will hearken to Him. And what hindereth thee that thou canst neither see nor hear Him? Soothly there is so much din and noise in thy heart of vain thoughts and fleshly desires, that thou canst neither hear Him nor see Him? Therefore put away those unquiet noises, and destroy the love of sin and vanity, and bring into thy heart the love of virtues and full charity, and then shalt thou hear thy Lord speak to thee.

As long as Jesus findeth not His image reformed in thee, He is strange, and the farther from thee; therefore frame and shape thyself to be arrayed in His likeness, that is in humility and charity, which are His liveries, and then will He know thee, and familiarly come to thee, and acquaint thee with His secrets. Thus saith He to His disciples: Whoso loveth Me, he shall be loved of My Father, and I will manifest Myself unto him. There is not any virtue nor any good work that can make thee like to our Lord without humility and charity, for these two above all others are most acceptable to Him, which appeareth plainly in the gospel, where our Lord speaketh of humility thus: Learn of Me, for I am meek and humble in heart. He saith not, Learn of me to go barefoot, or to go into the desert, and there to fast forty days, nor yet to choose to yourselves disciples (as I did), but learn of Me meekness, for I am meek and lowly in heart. Also of charity He saith thus: This is My commandment, that ye love one another as I loved you, for by that men shall know you for My disciples. Not that you work miracles, or cast out devils, or preach, or teach, but that each one of you love one another in charity. If therefore thou wilt be like Him, have humility and charity, Now thou knowest what charity is, namely, To love thy neighbour as thyself.

CHAPTER IV

SECTION I: OF THE GROUND AND IMAGE OF SIN IN US, WHICH IS FIRST TO BE FOUND OUT AND LABOURED AGAINST, AND HOW IT IS TO BE DONE

THOU hast heard already what thy soul is, and what dignity and beauty it had, and how it lost it, and also how it may by grace and busy travail be somewhat recovered again, in feeling, in part in this life. Now I shall tell thee (according to my feeble ability) how thou mayest enter into thyself to see the ground of sin, and destroy it as much as thou canst, and so recover a part of thy soul's dignity.

To do this thou shalt cease for a time from all bodily works, and from all outward business as much as thou canst, then shalt thou draw thy whole thought into thyself from all thy bodily senses, which thou must hold in and restrain from wandering forth, so that thou take no heed of anything thou seest or hearest or feelest, and after this draw in thy thoughts nearer from all imaginations of any bodily deeds done before by thee, or of any other men's deeds; and this is not difficult to be done at that time when thou hast devotion, but thou must do it also when thou hast no such devotion, and then it will be somewhat difficult. And set thy intent and full purpose, as if thou wouldst not seek nor find anything but only the grace and spiritual presence of Jesus.

This will be painful; for vain thoughts will press into thy heart very thick, to draw thy mind down to them. And in doing thus thou shalt find somewhat, but not Jesus whom thou seekest, but only a naked remembrance of His name. But what then shalt thou find. Surely this: a dark and ill-favoured image of thy own soul, which hath neither light of knowledge nor feeling of love of God. This image, if thou behold it heedfully, is all inwrapped and clothed with black stinking rags of sin, as pride, envy, anger, covetousness, gluttony, sloth and luxury. This is not the image of Jesus, but the image of sin, which St Paul calleth a body of sin and of death. This image and this black shadow thou bearest about with thee wheresoever thou goest; out of this spring many great streams of sin, and small ones also. Just as out of the image of Jesus, if it be reformed in the beams of spiritual light will spring and ascend up towards heaven burning desires, pure affections, wise thoughts and all comeliness of virtues. Even so out of this image spring stirrings of pride, of envy and such other, which cast thee down from the comeliness of a man into a beast's likeness.

Peradventure now thou beginnest to think with thyself what this image is like, and that thou shouldst not study much upon it, I will tell thee. It is like no bodily thing. What is it then, sayest thou? Verily it is nought, or no real thing, as thou shalt find, if thou try by doing as I have spoken; that is, draw in thy thoughts into thyself from all bodily things, and then shalt thou find right nought wherein thy soul may rest.

This nothing is nought else but darkness of conscience, and a lacking of the love of God and of light; as sin is nought but a want of good, if it were so that the ground of sin was much abated and dried up in thee, and thy soul was reformed right to the image of Jesus; then if thou didst draw into thyself thy heart, thou shouldst not find this nought, but thou shouldst find Jesus; not only the naked remembrance of this name, but Jesus Christ in thy soul readily teaching thee; thou shouldst there find light of understanding and no darkness of ignorance, a love and liking of Him, and no pain of bitterness, heaviness or tediousness of Him. But because thou art not reformed, therefore when thy soul draweth into herself from all bodily things and delights, thou findest nothing but emptiness, darkness and heaviness; so that thou thinkest it an hundred years till thou be out again to some bodily delight or vain thoughts, and it is no wonder; for he that cometh home to his house, and findeth nothing but stink and smoke, and a chiding wife, he will quickly run out of it. Even so thy soul, finding no comfort in itself, but black smoke of spiritual blindness, or great chiding of guilty or fleshly thoughts, crying upon thee that thou canst not be in peace, verily it will quickly be weary of being alone and recollected, until it be out again. And this is the darkness of conscience.

Nevertheless, in this dark conscience it behoves him to labour and sweat; that is to say, it behoveth thee to draw thy thoughts into thyself from all bodily things as much as thou canst, and then when thou findest right nought but sorrow and pain, and blindness in this darkness, if thou wilt find Jesus, thou must suffer the pain of this dark conscience, and abide awhile therein. And here also thou must beware that thou take Jesus Christ into thy thoughts against this darkness in thy mind, by busy prayer and fervent desire to God, not setting the point of thy thoughts on that aforesaid nought, but on Jesus Christ whom thou desirest. Think stiffly on His Passion and on His humility, and through His might thou shalt arise. Do as if thou wouldst beat down this dark image, and go through-stitch with it. Thou shalt hate and loathe this darkness, and this nought, just as the devil, and thou shalt despise and all to break it. For within this nought is Jesus hid in His joy, whom thou shalt not find with all thy seeking, unless thou pass this darkness of conscience.

This is the ghostly travail I spake of, and the cause of all this writing is to stir thee thereto, if thou have grace. This darkness of conscience and this nought is the image of the first Adam. St Paul knew it well, for he said thus of it: As we have before borne the image of the earthly man, that is the first Adam, right so that we might now bear the image of the heavenly man, which is Jesus, the second Adam. St Paul bore this image oft full heavily, for it was so cumbersome to him that he cried out of it, saying thus: O who shall Deliver me from this body and this image of death? And then he comforted himself and others also thus: The grace of God through Jesus Christ.

SECTION II: WHAT THE SAID IMAGE OF SIN IS, PROPERLY, AND WHAT COMETH OUT OF IT

I HAVE already told thee of this image, that it is nought, Nevertheless, if thou canst not understand how this should be an image, seeing nought can be nothing else but nought, and so for all my telling thou canst make nothing of it, I shall therefore tell thee more plainly of this image as methinketh.

This image is a false inordinate love of thyself. Out of this there come all manner of sins by seven rivers, Which are these: pride, envy, anger, sloth, covetousness, gluttony and lechery. Lo, this is somewhat that thou mayest understand. By some one of these rivers runneth out all manner of sin, and putteth thee out of the state of charity, if it be a deadly sin; or letteth the fervour of thy charity if it be venial. Now mayest thou grope at least that this image is not altogether nought; but it is much of bad, for it is a great spring of love unto thyself, with such rivers as I have said.

But now, sayest thou, how can this be true? For I have forsaken the world, and am shut up in a monastery; I meddle with no man, I chide not, I strive not, I neither buy nor sell, I have no worldly business, but by the mercy of God keep myself chaste, and withhold me from delights. And, besides this, I pray, I watch, I labour bodily and ghostly, as well as I can; how should this image then be so much in me as thou speakest of?

To this I answer, granting thee that I hope thou dost all these works and more; and yet may it be true as I say. Thou art busy to thy power to stop these rivers without, but the spring within perhaps thou leavest whole. Thou art like to a man which had in his yard a stinking well, with many runnings from it, who went and stopped the runnings, and left the spring whole, and thought all was well; but the water sprang up at the ground of the well, and stood still insomuch that it corrupted all the fairness of his garden, and yet did no water run out. Right so may it be with thee, if it be so that thou hast by grace stopped the rivers of this image without, so far that all is done well, but beware of the spring within; surely unless thou stop and cleanse that as much as thou canst, it will corrupt all the flowers of the garden of thy soul, show they never so fair outwardly in sight of men.

But now, sayest thou, whereby shall I know that the ground is stopped, if I go about it? As to this I shall tell thee, how by trying and experience thou shalt know this image if it be in thee, and how much it is in thee, and thereby shalt thou know how much it is stopped in thee, and how little also. And inasmuch as pride is the principal river, I shall begin with it.

CHAPTER V

SECTION I: OF THE SEVEN DEADLY SINS, AND FIRST OF PRIDE, WHAT IT IS, AND WHEN IT IS A DEADLY SIN AND WHEN BUT VENIAL

PRIDE is nothing else (as the learned say) but love of thy own excellency, that is, of thy own worship. The more thou lovest and likest thine own honour, the more thou hast of this pride; the more thou hast of this image in thee. If thou feel in thy heart a stirring of pride, that thou art holier, wiser, better and more virtuous than others, that God hath given thee grace to serve Him better than others do, and thinkest all others beneath thee, and thyself above them, or any other thought of thyself, which showeth to the eye of thy soul an excellency and a surpassing of others, and thou feelest a love and delight in this stirring, and a vain pleasing in thyself, that indeed thou art so; this is a token that thou bearest this black image, which, though it be privy from the eyes of men, yet it appeareth openly in God's sight.

But thou sayest that thou canst not eschew such stirrings of pride, for oft thou feelest them against thy will, and therefore thou holdest them no sin; or, if they be sin, they be nought but venial.

As to this, I answer that the feeling of these stirrings of pride, or of any other sin, which spring either out of the corruption of this foul image or by incasting or suggestion of the enemy, is no sin so far as to the feeling of them. Nevertheless, when by negligence and thy own blindness this feeling is received unwarily in thy thoughts, and turned into love and liking, then is there sin in it more or less according to the measure of this love, sometime venial and sometime deadly.

This is a grace and privilege by virtue of Christ's passion granted to all Christians baptized in water and the Holy Ghost. For verily to Jews and Saracens, who believe not in Jesus Christ, all such stirrings are deadly sins. For St Paul saith: Whatsoever is done without faith in Christ is sin. But we Christians have this privilege through His mercy, that such feelings are no sins, but the pain of original sin.

But when it is venial and when it is deadly I cannot fully tell thee; nevertheless, a little I shall say, as methinketh. When the stirrings of pride are received and turned into liking, so far that the heart chooseth them for a full rest and a full delight, and seeketh no other end, but only the liking therein, then is this pride deadly sin; for he maketh and chooseth this delight as his god, without any opposing of his reason or will, and therefore it is deadly sin.

But now, sayest thou, who is such a fool as to choose pride for his God? No man living, sure, will do so. To this I answer that I cannot tell thee in special who sinneth deadly in pride. But in general I shall say that there be two sorts of pride, one bodily and the other spiritual. Bodily pride is of fleshly living men; spiritual is of hypocrites and heretics. These three sin deadly in pride; I mean such fleshly living men as St Paul speaks of: If ye live after the flesh, ye shall die. Then say I thus: That a worldly man who loveth and seeketh principally the worship of himself, and chooseth the liking of it as the rest of his heart, and the end of his bliss, he sinneth deadly.

But now thou wilt say: Who doth choose the love of his worship, credit or honour, instead of his God; I answer, that he that loveth his worship, as for to seem better and greater of estate than any other, and travaileth about it as much as he can; if he love it so much that for the getting, or keeping, or the saving of it, he breaketh the commandment of God, or breaketh love and charity to his neighbour, or is ready, or in full will to break it rather than he would forbear his worship, or lose anything of it, either in his name, or in his estate, or of fulfilling his will; soothly he sinneth deadly, for he loveth his worship, and chooseth it more than the love of God and of his neighbour. And nevertheless, the man that sinneth thus deadly will say with his mouth that he will not choose pride for his god, but he beguileth himself, for he chooseth it for his god in his deeds.

Nevertheless, another worldly man that loveth his own worship and pursueth after it, if he love it not so much, that he would not for the getting or the saving of it do a deadly sin, or break charity to his neighbour, he sinneth not deadly but venially, more or less according to the measure of his love and of his liking, with other circumstances.

But a man or woman that disposeth himself or herself, to live contemplatively, if it be so that he forsake himself as to his own will, and offer up himself wholly to God with a full general will, that he will not sin in pride wittingly, nor have any joy in himself wilfully, but only in God, as far as he can, and may; and notwithstanding after this full will offered up to God, feeleth many stirrings of vain-glory, and delighteth in them for the time (because at the first he did not so well perceive them), this liking is but venial sin, and, namely, if it be so, that when he cometh to himself he reproveth himself, and withstandeth this stirring with displeasure of his will, and asketh mercy and help of God; then the liking which before was some sin, our Lord of his mercy soon forgiveth it; and moreover he shall have reward for his good travail in withstanding it.

And this is a courtesy of our Lord, granted to all those who are specially His servants and domestics of His court, as are all those that for His love forsake, with a good true will, all worldly and all fleshly sin, and give themselves wholly both body and soul unto His service, with all their might and cunning, as do truly Anchorites enclosed, and all truly religious persons, who for the love of God and salvation of their own souls enter into any religious order approved by holy Church. Or else, if it be so, that they enter first for worldly respects, or for their bodily sustenance, or some other such; if they repent them and turn it into a spiritual respect, as for the service of God; these as long as they keep this will and pursue it as well as their frailty will permit, are true religious persons.

Also, what man or woman soever he be; in what degree soever he liveth in holy Church, priest, clerk or layman, widow, maid or wife that will for the love of God and salvation of his, or her, own soul forsake all the worships and likings of this world, in the world, in his or her heart truly and fully betwixt God and themselves, and all unnecessary business and earthly things, even to what they have bare need of, and offer up their will entirely to be His servants, in the constant exercise of devout prayers and holy thoughts, with other good deeds that they may do bodily and ghostly, and keep their will whole to God stedfastly, all such are God's special servants in holy Church. And for this good will and good purpose that they have by the gift of God, they shall increase in grace and in charity here all their life long; and they shall have for this special will a special reward in the bliss of heaven above other chosen souls, who offered not wholly their will and their body to God's service, neither openly nor privately as they did. All these, whom I call God's servants, and of His court more specially, if they, through frailty and ignorance, when they feel such stirrings of vainglory, for the time delight therein, and perceive not that they do so, for that their reason and senses are letted through that liking which they feel, so that they cannot so well see those stirrings, they sin not deadly in this liking of vainglory. For that will that they have in general set in their heart before, to please God, and to forsake all manner of sin, if they knew it, keepeth them here, that they sin not deadly in such stirrings, and in all other that come of frailty, and will keep them still as long as the ground of that will is kept whole.

I say moreover for thy comfort, and for the comfort of all others who live in the state of Anchorets enclosed, and also by God's grace, for the comfort of all them that enter into any religious order approved in holy Church, that all those who through the mercy of God among them shall be saved, shall have a special reward, and a singular worship in the bliss of heaven; for their state of living before other souls that had not that state in holy Church, though they were never so holy; which worship is better than all the worship of this world without comparison; for if thou couldst see what it is, thou wouldst not for the worship of this world, if thou mightest have it without sin, change thy state either of Anchoret or of religious, neither lose that singular reward in heaven, which reward is called the Accidental Reward.

Nevertheless, that other men may not mistake this that I say, therefore I shall say it more plainly. Thou shalt understand that there be two rewards in the bliss of heaven, which our Lord giveth to chosen souls. The one is Sovereign and Principal, and is called the Essential Reward, and that is the knowing and loving of God according to the measure of charity given by God to the soul while she lived here in mortal body. This reward is best and Sovereign, for it is God Himself, and is common to all the souls that shall be saved, in what state or degree soever they live in holy Church, more or less according to the quantity and the muchness of their charity in this life, what degree soever they live in. For he that loveth God by charity most shall have most reward in the bliss of heaven for he shall there love God and know Him most and that is the Sovereign, or Essential reward, and according to this reward it may and shall fall out, that some manner of man or woman, as a lord or a lady, knight or esquire, merchant or ploughman, or what degree he be, in man or Yeoman may and shall have more reward than some priest or friar, monk or canon, or Anchoret enclosed. And why so? Soothly, because he loved God more in charity.

Another reward there is that is Secondary, or Accidental, which our Lord giveth for special good deeds, which a man doth voluntarily, over that he is bound to do. Of these deeds three principal ones the Doctors of holy Church do make mention of, namely, Martyrdom, Preaching and Virginity. These works, inasmuch as they pass all others in excellency, shall have a special reward, which is called an Aureola, which is nought else but a singular worship and a special token ordained by God for reward of that special deed they did above others, over and above that Sovereign or Essential reward of the love of God which is common to him and to all others. Right so it is of all other special good deeds, which, if they be done sincerely, are specially acceptable in the sight of God, and in the judgement of holy Church are very excellent, as are the enclosing of Anchorets, done by the authority of holy Church, also entering into religion approved, and the stricter that the religion is, the more excellent is the deed in the judgement of holy Church.

Also after these, and beneath these, are the taking of the order of Priest, either for cure of men's souls, and to minister the Sacraments of holy Church, or else for singular Devotion to please God, and profit our neighbour, by the sacrifice of the precious body of our Lord Jesus Christ. Soothly these are special deeds, and declared to be excellent by the judgement of holy Church, and in the sight of our Lord. When they are done truly for God, they are excellent, and shall have special reward, each man in his degree, in the bliss of Heaven. The state of Bishop and Prelate is above all these deeds, as to the Accidental reward. That this is so, appeareth out of holy Writ, where it saith thus in the Prophet Daniel: But go thou until the time prefixed, and thou shalt rest and stand in thy lot until the end of the days; which is to say thus much: The Angel when he had showed Daniel the secrets of God, he said to him thus: Go thou to the rest of this bodily death, and thou shalt stand in thy lot as a prophet at the last day. And verily as Daniel shall stand as a prophet at the last day of doom, and have the worship and excellency of a prophet above the Sovereign blessed reward of the love and sight of God, right so shalt thou stand as an Anchoret in that lot, and a Religious in the lot of the Religious, and so shall it be with other excellent deeds, and have a singular worship, passing other men at the day of doom.

SECTION II: HOW PRIDE IN HERETICS AND IN HYPOCRITES IS DEADLY SIN

AN heretic sinneth deadly in pride, for he chooseth his rest and delight in his own opinion, and in his own sayings, for he imagineth them to be true; which opinion or sayings are against God and holy Church, and, therefore, he sinneth mortally in pride, for he loveth himself and his own will and wit so much, that though it be plainly against the ordinance of holy Church, he will not leave it, but resteth thereon, as upon the truth, and so maketh he it his god; but he beguileth himself, for God and holy Church are so united and accorded together that whoso doth against the one doth against both. And, therefore, he that saith he loveth God, and keepeth His biddings, and despiseth holy Church, and setteth at nought the laws and ordinances thereof, made by the head and supreme thereof appointed to govern all Christians, he lieth, for he chooseth not God, but chooseth the love of himself, contrary to the love of

God, and so sinneth mortally. And wherein he imagineth most to please God, he most displeaseth Him; for he is blind, and will not see.

Of this blindness and this false resting of an heretic in his own feeling, speaketh the wise man thus: There is a way that seemeth right to a man, and the last end of it bringeth him to endless death. This way specially is called heresy: for other fleshly sinners that sin mortally and lie therein, commonly condemn themselves, and feel biting in conscience, because they go not the right way; but an heretic supposeth that he doth well, and teacheth well, yea, and that no man doth and teacheth so well as he, and so judgeth his way to be right, and, therefore, feeleth he no biting of conscience nor humility in heart. And, soothly, if God of His great mercy sendeth him not humility at the last end, he goeth to hell. And, nevertheless, yet weeneth he to have done well and that he shall get the bliss of Heaven for his teaching.

The hypocrite also sinneth deadly in pride. He is an hypocrite that chooseth vain joy in himself, as the rest and full delight of his heart in this manner.

When a man doth many good deeds bodily and ghostly, and then is put into his mind by the suggestion of the enemy, the beholding of himself and those good deeds, how good, how holy he is, how worthy in men's deem, and how high in God's sight, above other men, he perceiveth this stirring, and receiveth it willingly, for he judgeth it to be good, and from God, forasmuch as it is true (for he doth these good deeds better than other menu). And when it is received thus by consent of his will, there ariseth from it in his heart so great a love and delight in himself, that he hath so much grace, that for the time it ravisheth his mind out of all other thoughts, both corporal and spiritual, and setteth it upon vain joy in himself, as on a rest of his heart. This ravishing in spiritual pride is delectable, and, therefore, he keepeth it, holdeth it, and nourisheth it as much as he can. For this love and delight he prayeth, watcheth, weareth haircloth, and doth other afflictions, and all these trouble him but little. He pretends to love God, and thanketh Him sometimes with his mouth; sometimes wringeth a tear out of his eye, and then he thinketh all safe enough. But soothly, all this is for love of himself which he chooseth, and mistaketh for love and joy in God, and therein lies all his sin. Not that he willingly chooseth sin, as it is sin, but chooseth this delight and joy that he takes for good, as the rest and repose of his soul. Which, because he doth without any striving against it, or displeasure at it in his will, therefore is it sin; for he judgeth it to be a joy in God, and it is not so, and, therefore, sinneth he mortally. Job saith thus of an hypocrite: The joy of an hypocrite is as it were for a moment. If his pride rise up even to the heavens, and his head touch the clouds, at the last end he shall be cast out as a dung-heap. The joy of an hypocrite is but a point, for if he worship himself never so much, and joy in himself never so much, all his lifetime, and bepaint himself with all his good deeds, in the sight and praisings of the world, at the last it will prove right nought but sorrow and pain.

But thou wilt say: Sure there be few or none such that are so blind as to hold and choose vain joy in themselves for joy in God.

As to this I cannot answer, nor will, though I could; only I will tell thee this one thing, that there be many hypocrites, and, nevertheless, they think themselves to be none, and that there be many that dread and fear themselves to be hypocrites, and soothly are none; who is the one, and who is the other, God knows, and none but He. Whoso will humbly dread, shall not be beguiled; and whoso thinketh himself secure, he may lightly fall. For St Paul saith: Whose esteemeth himself to be something, whereas indeed he is nothing, he beguileth himself.

SECTION III: A SHORT EXHORTATION TO HUMILITY AND CHARITY, WITH A CONCLUSION HOW A MAN MAY KNOW HOW MUCH PRIDE HE HATH IN HIM

Now by what hath been said, thou mayest (if thou wilt understand them) conceive comfort for thy degree of living, and also matter of humility. For though it be true, that (in case thou come to Heaven) thou shalt there receive so much reward in special, for thy state of life; nevertheless it may be that there is many a wife, and many a woman, living at large in the world, that shall be nearer God than thou, and shall love God more, and know Him better than thou, for all thy religious state, and that ought to be a shame to thee. Yet if thou labour to get love and charity as fully and as perfectly as those that live in the world (for thou mayest have it by the gift of God, as much as they that live in worldly business), then shalt thou have as much of the Sovereign or Essential reward as they; and, moreover, shalt also have another singular and accidental reward and worship, for thy state of Religion which the others shall not have. If then thou wilt do well, be humble, and forget thy state, as if it were right nought; for in sooth it is so, that is, right nought in itself. And let thy desire and business be to destroy sin, and to get charity, and humility, and other ghostly virtues, for therein lieth all.

I have well-nigh forgotten that image I spake of, but now I turn again thereto. If thou wilt know how much pride is therein, thou mayest try it thus: Look to it wisely, and flatter not thyself; if loving, praising or worshipping, or human favours of worldly men or others, be pleasing to thy heart, and thou turnest them into vain gladness, and well paying of thyself, thinking secretly in thy heart, that men ought to praise thy life, and reward thy speeches more than other men's; and also on the contrary, if it be so, that when men reprove thee, and set thee at nought, hold thee for a fool, or an hypocrite, or slander thee, or speak evil of thee falsely, and in any other way disease thee unreasonably, and for this thou feelest in thy heart a grievous heaviness against them, and a great rising in thy heart, with an unwillingness to suffer any shame or disgrace in the sight of the world; if, I say, it be thus with thee, it is a token that there is much pride in this dark image, seem thou never so holy in the sight of men. For though these stirrings be but little and venial, nevertheless they show well that there is much pride hid in the ground of thy heart, as the fox dareth in his den. These stirrings, with many more, spring so fast out of this image that thou scarcely canst do any good deed but it will be mingled with some pride or vain delight in thyself, and so with thy pride thou defileth all thy good deeds, and makest them loathesome in the sight of thy Lord. I say not that they are lost because they are mingled with this pride. But I say that those good deeds are not so pleasant to thy Lord as they would be if they were simple and truly rooted in the virtue of humility. And, therefore, if thou wilt have cleanness of heart, to come to the love of God, it behoveth thee not only to fly the rest and repose of thy heart in vain-glory, by willingly consenting to pride, and also the wretchless liking therein out of frailty against thy will, but also the very feeling itself of pride, as well as thou canst, which will not be done unless thou be full quick and diligent about the keeping of thy heart, as I shall tell thee hereafter.

CHAPTER VI

SECTION I: OF ENVY AND WRATH AND THEIR BRANCHES, AND HOW, INSTEAD OF SIN, THE PERSON IS OFTEN HATED

TURN this image upside down, and look well therein, and thou shalt find two members or limbs of envy and anger fastened thereto, with several branches springing out of them, which hinder the love and charity which thou oughtest to have toward thy neighbour. The branches of these two sins are these: Hatred, evil suspicion, false and rash or unskilful judging, melancholy, risings of heart against them, despising, unkindness, and backbiting, or other ill-speaking of them, misliking, unskilful or causeless blaming of them, misconstruing their words or deeds, anguish and heaviness against those that despise us, or speak any evil of us, or speak against us, a joy or gladness at their pain, a selfness or bitterness against sinful men and others that will not do as we think they should do, with great desire and eagerness of heart (under colour of charity and justice), that they were well punished and chastised for their sin.

Such motions and stirrings as these seem good; nevertheless, if thou ransack it well, thou shalt find it more fleshly and sensual sometimes against the person than spiritual against the sin; for thou shouldst love the man, be he never so sinful, and hate the sin in every man whatever he be. Many are beguiled in this, for they set the bitter instead of the sweet and take darkness instead of light, contrary to the prophet, saying: Wo to you who call evil good, and good evil; putting darkness for light, and light for darkness; putting bitter for sweet, and sweet for bitter. Thus do all they who, when they should hate the sin of their neighbour and love his person, hate the person instead of the sin, and imagine that they hate the sin. Wherefore it is a special craft and art by itself whoso can do it well.

SECTION II: THAT IT IS A MASTERY AND NOBLE SKILL TO LOVE MEN'S PERSONS, AND YET WISELY TO HATE THEIR SINS, AND HOW

IT is no mastery to watch and fast till thy head ache; nor to run to Rome or Jerusalem on pilgrimage upon thy bare feet; nor for to stir about and preach, as if thou wouldst turn all men by thy preaching. Nor is it any mastery to build churches or chapels, or to feed poor men and build hospitals. But it is a mastery for a man to love his neighbour in charity, and wisely hate his sin, and love the man. For though it be true that all those deeds before said be good in themselves, yet are they common to good men and to bad, for every man may do them if that he would and have wherewith. And for thee to do that which every man may do, I hold it no mastery; but to love thy neighbour in charity and hate his sin can no man do, save only good men, who have it by the gift of God and not by their own travail, as St Paul saith: Love and charity is shed abroad in your hearts by the Holy Ghost, which is given to you. And, therefore, it is more precious and more dainty to come by. All other good deeds without this make not a man good nor worthy of the bliss of heaven, but this alone, and only this, maketh a man good and all his good deeds to be medeful. All other gifts of God and works of man are common to good and bad, to the chosen and the reprobate; but this gift of charity is proper only to good and chosen souls.

And, therefore, for the learning of this hard lesson, thou must understand and consider that a good man for the love of God fasteth, watcheth, goeth on pilgrimage and forsaketh all the pleasures of the world sincerely in his heart, without feigning, and he hath his reward in heaven; and an hypocrite doth the same deeds out of vain-glory and for love of himself, and receiveth his reward here. Also, a true preacher of God's Word, filled with charity and humility, sent of God and received and approved by the Church, if he preach and teach God's Word, shall have a special reward of God; that is the aureola for his preaching. And an hypocrite or an heretic that hath no humility or charity, nor is sent of God nor yet of holy Church, if they preach, they have their reward here. Also a good man living in the world for the love of God buildeth many churches, chapels, abbeys, hospitals and doth other many good deeds of mercy, and he shall have his reward in the bliss of heaven, not for the deed in itself, but for the good will and the charity that he hath in him by the gift of God for to do these good deeds. Another man out of vanity of himself and worship and pleasing of the world and for his own name doth the same good deeds, and hath his reward here. The cause in all these is that the one hath charity and the other none; but which is the one and which is the other, our Lord knoweth, and none but He.

From this, therefore, we are to learn these two lessons. First, that we should love and worship all men in our hearts, and approve and think well of and receive all their deeds that have the likeness of goodness, though the doers be bad in the sight of God, except they be the deeds of known and open heretics, or of open cursed (or excommunicated) men; for of these two we are specially to fly and eschew their company and coming amongst them. And we are also to reprove and refuse their deeds, seem they never so good, as long as they are rebels to God and holy Church. And if a worldly, cursed (or excommunicated) man build a church, or feed poor men, thou mayest safely hold and judge such his doings to be noughts and deem them as they are. Also if an open heretic, who is a rebel to holy Church, preach and teach, though he convert a hundred thousand souls, thou mayest hold the deed, as to himself, right nought; for these men are openly out of charity, without which all is nought that a man doth.

Secondly, that it is a great mastery for a man to know how and to be able to love his neighbour in charity; all which may be plainly proved by St Paul's words, thus: If I speak with the tongues of men and angels, if I have not charity, I am right nought; and if I have so great faith that I can overturn hills and bear them away, and have not charity, I am right nought. And also, though I had all manner of knowledge of all mysteries, and if I give all that I have to the poor, and my body to be burnt, and have not charity, it profiteth me right nought.

Here it seemeth by St Paul's words that a man may do all good deeds bodily without charity, and that charity is nought else but to love God and his neighbour as himself. How should, then, any wretched caitiff upon earth, whatever he be, have any delight or trust or security in himself for anything he doth or is able to do with all his bodily powers or natural wit, sith all this is nought worth without love and charity to his neighbour? And this charity cannot be gotten by his own working, for it is the free gift of God, sent only into an humble soul, as St Paul saith. Who then dare be so bold as to say: I have Christ, or I am charity? Verily no man can say it securely, or of a certainty, but he that is perfectly and truly humble; other men may trow of themselves, and hope that they be in charity by tokens; but he that is perfectly humble feeleth it, and therefore may say it securely. Thus humble was St Paul, and therefore said he thus of himself: Who shall separate us from the love of Christ? Shall tribulation, or anguish, or distress, etc.? And he answereth himself, and saith: I am persuaded that no creature shall be able to separate me from the charity of God in Christ Jesus. Many men do deeds of charity, and have no charity, as I have said. To reprove a sinner for his sin to his amendment, in a convenient time, is a deed of charity; but to hate the sinner instead of the sin, is against charity. He that is verily humble can part the one from the other, and none but he. For though a man had all moral virtues of all the philosophers, he could not do this; he could be able to hate sin in other men (for he hateth it in himself), but he could not be able to love the man in charity, with all his philosophy. Also, if a man had the knowledge of all books and divinity, and be not withal truly humble, he shall lightly stumble and err in this point, and take the one for the other. But humility is worthy to receive a gift from God, which cannot be gotten or learned by cunning of man, and therefore he that is humble can hate the sin and truly love the man.

But now peradventure thou beginnest to be afraid for that which I have said, that charity cannot be gotten by any work that thou canst do; how shalt thou then do

To this I answer, that there is nothing so hard to get as charity; this is truth, as to the getting of it by our own travail and labour. And, on the contrary, I say that there is no gift of God that may so lightly or easily be had as charity, for our Lord giveth no gift so freely, nor so gladly, nor so commonly, as He doth it. How shalt thou, then, have it, sayest thou? Be meek and lowly in spirit and thou shalt have it; and what is lighter to be done than to be humble? Soothingly nothing. Then it followeth that there is nothing so lightly to be had as charity, and, therefore, thou need not be much afraid; be humble, and have it. Thus saith St James: Our Lord resisteth the proud, but giveth grace to the humble. Which grace is properly charity; for according to the measure of thy humility, so shalt thou have charity. If thou have humility imperfectly only in will, not in affection, then hast thou imperfect charity, which indeed is good, for it sufficeth for salvation, as David saith: Lord, with the eyes of mercy thou seest my imperfection. But if thou have humility perfectly, then shalt thou have perfect charity, and this is best. The other we must necessarily have if we will be saved. This we should ever desire and labour for. If thou ask me now who is perfectly humble, I shall tell thee no more concerning humility at this time but this: He is humble that truly knoweth himself as he is.

SECTION III: HOW A MAN SHALL KNOW HOW MUCH WRATH AND ENVY IS HID IN THE GROUND OF HIS HEART, AND HOW HE MAY KNOW WHETHER HE LOVES HIS ENEMIES, AND THE EXAMPLES WE HAVE THEREOF IN OUR SAVIOUR

Now turn we again to this image. If thou wilt, try how much anger and envy is hid in thy heart, which thou feelest and perceivest not. Look well and behold thyself wisely when such stirrings of anger and envy against thy neighbour spring out of thy heart. The more that thou art stirred by melancholy or wicked will against him, the more is this image in thee. For the more thou grudgest by impatience, either against God for any tribulation or sickness, or other bodily disease sent by Him, or against thy neighbour, for aught that he doth against thee, the less is the image of Jesus reformed in thee. I say not that such grudgings or fleshly angriness are deadly sins; but I say that they hinder the cleanness of heart and peace of conscience, that thou canst not have perfect charity, by the which thou shouldst come to life Contemplative. For that end is the purpose of all my saying, that thou shouldst not only cleanse thy heart from deadly sins, but also from venial as much as thou canst; and that the ground of sin might by grace of Jesus Christ be somewhat shaked in thee.

For though it be so that thou feelest no evil against thy neighbour for a time, yet art thou not secure that the ground of anger is quenched in thee; neither yet art thou lord and master of the virtue of charity. For let him but touch thee a little angrily, or by a shrewd word, and thou shalt see presently whether thy heart be yet made whole by perfect charity. The more thou art stirred and evil-willed against his person, the further art thou from charity. And if thou be nothing stirred against his person, neither by any angry carriage or gesture outwardly, nor by any privy hate in thy heart, either to despise or judge him, or undervalue, or set him at nought; but the more shame or villainy he doth to thee by word or deed, the more pity and compassion thou hast of him, as thou wouldst have of a man that were out of his wits, and thinkest that thou canst not find in thy heart to hate him (because love is so good in itself) but pray for him and help him and desire his amendment, not only with thy mouth, as hypocrites can do, but with affection of love in thy heart; then hast thou perfect charity to thy neighbour.

This charity had St Stephen perfectly when he prayed for them that stoned him to death. This charity counselled Christ to those that would be His perfect followers when He said thus: Love your enemies, do good to them that hate you, pray for them that persecute you. And, therefore, if thou wilt be one of Christ's followers, be like Him in this craft. Learn to love thine enemies and sinful men, for all these are thy neighbours. Look and bethink thee how Christ loved Judas, who was both His deadly enemy and a sinful caitiff; how goodly Christ was to him, how benign, how courteous, and how lowly to him whom He knew to be damnable. And nevertheless He chose him to be His apostle, and sent him to preach with His other apostles. He gave him power to work miracles; He showed the same good cheer to him in word and deed as He did to other apostles. He washed his feet, and fed him with His precious Blood, and preached to him as He did to His other apostles. He bewrayed him not openly (for He did it privily); He miscalled him not, despised him not, never spake evil of him; notwithstanding if He had done all these things, He had said nothing but truth. Moreover, when Judas took Him, He kissed him, and called him His friend. All this charity showed Christ unto Judas, whom He knew to be damnable; and this He did in no way of counterfeiting or flattering, but in reality and truth of good love and clean charity. For though it was true that Judas was not worthy to have any gift from God, or any sign of love for his wickedness; nevertheless, it was worthy and seemly that our Lord should show Himself to be that which He is, and that is love and goodness to all His creatures, as He was to Judas. I say not that He loved him for his sin, nor that He loved him as one of His chosen, as He did St Peter; but He loved him inasmuch as he was His creature, and showed him tokens of love, if he would have been mended thereby. Follow thou His example somewhat as much as thou canst; for though thou art shut up in a house as to thy body, nevertheless in thy heart (where the seat of love is) thou mayest have part in such love to thy neighbour, as I have spoken of.

Whoso thinkest himself to be in his life a perfect lover and follower of Christ's teaching (as some men perhaps esteem themselves to be, because they preach and teach, and are poor in worldly goods, as Christ was) and cannot follow Christ in this love and charity, to love their neighbours, even every man, both good and bad, friend and foe, without feigning or flattery, or despising him in his heart, without angriness or malicious reproving, soothly he beguileth himself. The nearer he thinketh himself to be to Christ's example, the further is he off; for Christ said to them that would be His disciples, thus:

This is My bidding, that you should love one another as I have loved you. For if ye love as I have loved, then are ye My disciples.

But now thou wilt say: How shall I love him that is bad as well and truly as him that is good?

To this I say thus: That thou shalt love both good and bad in charity, but not for the same cause as I shall tell how. Thou shalt love thy neighbour as thyself. Now, thou shalt love thyself only in God, or else for God. In God thou lovest thyself, when thou art righteous and virtuous through grace, and lovest not thyself but only for that righteousness and virtues that God giveth thee, then lovest thou thyself in God, for thou lovest not thyself, but God. Also, thou lovest thyself for God, when being in deadly sin thou desirest to be made righteous and virtuous, for then thou lovest not thyself as thou art (for thou art unrighteous), but as thou wouldst be. Right so shalt thou love thy neighbour. If he be good and righteous thou shalt love him by charity in God only; in that he is good and righteous; for then lovest thou God (who is goodness and righteousness) in him, and so thou lovest him more than if he were bad or in deadly sin. As, for example, thy enemies who hate thee, or any other of whom thou hast full evidence they are not in grace; yet notwithstanding shalt thou love them, not as they are, nor as good and righteous men (for they are bad and unrighteous), but thou shalt love them for God, that they may be good and righteous. And so shalt thou hate nothing in them, but that thing which is contrary to righteousness, and that is sin. This is as I understand the doctrine of St Augustine, for to distinguish the love of the man from the hatred of his sin, and the love of thy neighbour. He that is humble, or desires truly to be humble, can thus love his neighbour, and none but he.

CHAPTER VII: OF COVETOUSNESS AND HOW A MAN MAY KNOW HOW MUCH OF IT IS HID IN HIS HEART

HEAVE up this image, and look well about it, and into it, and then shalt thou see covetousness and love of earthly things possess a great part of this image, though it seem little of it. Thou hast forsaken riches and the having much of this world, and art shut up in a cell, but hast thou cleanly forsaken the love of all this? I fear not yet, for it is less mastery to forsake worldly goods than to forsake the love of them. Peradventure thou hast not forsaken thy covetousness, but only hast changed it from great things unto small; from a pound unto a penny, and from a silver dish unto a dish of a halfpenny. This is but a simple change; thou art no good merchant. These examples are childish, nevertheless they signify much more. If thou believe not what I say, put thyself upon the trial. If thou have love and delight in the having and holding of anything that thou hast, how mean soever it may be, with the which love thou feedest thy heart for a time, or if thou have a desire and yearning for to have something that thou hast not, with the which desire thy heart is disquieted and stumbled through unreasonable thinking of the thing, that the pure desire of virtue and of God cannot rest therein; this is a sign that there is covetousness in this image. And if thou wilt put thyself further to the trial, look if anything that thou hast be taken away from thee by violence, or by borrowing, or any other way, so that thou canst not get it again, and for this thou art disquieted, angered, and troubled in thine heart, both for the loss of that thing which thou wouldst have again, and canst not; and also art stirred against him that hath it, to strive and chide with him that may restore it, and will not, this is a token that thou lovest worldly goods. For thus do worldly men when their goods and riches are taken from them; they are heavy, sorry and angry, chiding and striving with them that have them, openly, both by word and deed. But thou dost all this in thy heart privily, where God seeth, and therein thou art in more default than a worldly man; for thou hast forsaken in appearance the love of worldly things, but a worldly man hath not so, and therefore he is excused, though he strive and pursue for his goods by lawful means, for to have them again.

But now sayest thou, that it behoveth thee to have thy necessaries of such things as belong unto thee, as well as a worldly man. I grant well thereto; but thou shouldst not love it for itself, nor have liking in the holding nor in the keeping, nor feel sorrow and heaviness in the losing, or in the withdrawing of it. For as St Gregory saith: As much sorrow as thou hast in losing of a thing, so much love hast thou in the keeping of it. And therefore if so be thy heart made whole, and thou hadst truly felt a desire of spiritual things, and therewith hadst a true sight of the least spiritual thing that is, thou wouldst set at nought all the love and liking of any earthly thing, it would not cleave to thee.

For to love and have more than thou reasonably needest, only for lust and liking, is a great fault. Also, to fix thy love upon the thing which thou needest, for the thing itself, is a fault also, but not so great. But to have and use that thing that thou needest without love of it, more than nature and need requireth, without which the thing cannot be used, is no fault.

Soothly in this point I fear that many who have taken upon them the state and likeness of poverty are much letted and hindered in their pursuit of the love of God; I accuse no man, nor reprove any state, for in each state there be some good, and some otherwise; but one thing I say to every man or woman that hath taken the state of voluntary poverty, whether he be religious or secular, or what degree he be in, as long as his love and his affection is bounden and fastened, and as it were glued with the love of any earthly thing, which he hath, or would have, he cannot have nor feel soothfastly the clean love, and the clear sight of spiritual things. For St Austin said to our Lord thus: Lord, he loveth Thee but little, that loveth anything with Thee, which he loveth not for Thee. For the more love and covetousness of any earthly thing is with thee, the less is the love of God in thy heart. For though it be so, that this love of earthly things putteth them not out of charity; but if it be so much that it strangleth the love of God and of their neighbour, verily it hindereth and letteth them from the fervour of charity, and also from that special reward which they should have in the bliss of heaven for perfect poverty, and that is a great loss if thou couldst see it. For who so could understand the spiritual reward, how good, how precious and how worthy it is (for it is everlasting), he would not for the love of all earthly joy, or having all earthly things (though he might have them without sin) hinder, no, nor lessen the least reward of the bliss of heaven, which he might have if that he would; but God knows I speak more than I do myself. But I pray thee do thus as I say, by the grace of God, if thou canst, or any other man that will, for it would be a comfort to my heart (though I have it not in myself that which I say) that I might have it in thee, or in any other creature, which hath received more plenty of His grace than I.

But see, now then, since covetousness, in the naked ground of it, letteth a man or woman so much from the spiritual feeling of the love of God, how much more, then, doth it let and cumber worldly men and women, who by all their wits and bodily business night and day, study and travail how they may get riches and plenty of worldly goods? They can have no other delight but in worldly things; nay, they will not, for they seek it not. I say no more of them at this time; for in this writing I spake not to them. But this I say, that if they would see, or could see what they do, they would not do so.

CHAPTER VIII

SECTION I Of Gluttony and how a Man shall know when he sinneth not in Eating and Drinking, and when he sinneth venially, and when deadly

STILL mayest thou see more in this image, though it be dark, namely, sensual love to thyself, in gluttony, sloth and lechery. These fleshly likings make a man full beastly, and far from the inward savour of the love of God and from the clear sight of spiritual things. But thou wilt say that thou must needs eat and drink and sleep, which thou canst not do without liking, therefore thou thinkest this liking is no sin.

As unto this I say: That if in eating, drinking and other takings of necessaries for thy body, thou observe and keep measure; which is that thou do but what is needful for nature, and thou receivest or admittest no further pleasure or delight in the taking, than the nature of the thing doth needs bring with it; and all this thou dost not of purpose to please thy sensuality, but for ghostly delight which thou feelest in thy soul, and the upholding of thy body in the service of God, I grant that for a truth thou then sinnest right nought therein, but mayest well eat and sleep in that manner as thou hast mentioned.

Soothly and without doubt I am full far from knowing how to do better in this point, and further from doing of it, for to eat I have by kind or nature, but to skill how to eat, I cannot but by the grace of God. St Paul had this cunning by the grace of God, as he saith himself thus: I am cunning in all things, through Him that strengtheneth me; for I can hunger, and I can eat, I can with plenty, and I can with poverty, I can do all things. St. Austin saith thus to our Lord: Lord, thou hast taught me that I should take meat as a medicine: hunger is a sickness of my nature, and meat is a medicine thereof. Therefore the liking and delight that cometh therewith, and accompanieth eating, inasmuch as it is natural, and followeth of necessity, it is no sin; but when it passeth into lust, and into a voluntary and sought or intended pleasure, then it is sin.

Therefore here lieth all the mastery and skill to be able to distinguish wisely need from lust and voluntary liking, being so knit together that the one cometh with the other. So that it is hard to take the one (which is the meat or drink) as need requireth, and to reject or not to admit the other, namely, the voluntary and willingly admitted lust and liking, which often cometh under the colour of need.

Nevertheless, sith it is so, that need is the ground of this, and that need is no sin; for be a man never so holy, it behoveth him to eat, and drink and sleep; therefore the lust and liking that cometh under the colour of this need, and often exceedeth this need, is the less sin. For it is true that he who chooseth lust and the liking of his flesh, and delight in welfare of meat or drink, as the full rest of his heart that he would never have any other life nor other bliss, but live ever in such lust of his flesh, if he might, it is no doubt but he sinneth deadly; for he loveth his flesh more than God. But he that lieth in deadly sin of pride or envy, or such other, he is so blinded by the devil, that for the time he hath no power of his free will, and therefore he cannot well withstand fleshly likings when they come, but falleth down willingly to them, as a beast doth to carrion; and inasmuch as he hath no general will before to God principally, because that he is in deadly sin, therefore the lust of gluttony into which he falleth easily, is to him deadly sin, for he maketh no resistance either general or special. But another man or woman, who being in grace or charity, hath alway a good general will to God in his soul, whether he sleep or wake, eat or drink, or whatsoever good deed he doth, so that it be not evil in itself; by the which will and desire he chooseth God above all things, and had rather forbear all things in the world, than anger his God for love of Him. This will, though it be but general, is of so great virtue through the grace of our Lord Jesus, that if he fall by frailty in lust and in liking of meat and of drink, or of such other infirmity, either by exercise, in eating too much, or too often, or too greedily, or too lusty and delicately, or too often before the set times of eating, it saveth and keepeth him from deadly sin. And this is truth, as long as he is in charity in his other works, and keepeth his general will in all that he doth; and especially if anon after such his miscarriage he acknowledge his own wretchedness and cry for mercy, and be in purpose specially to withstand such fleshly lusts for the time to come. For our Lord is good and merciful, and forgiveth right soon these venial sins and miscarriages, or excesses about meat and drink (by reason that the occasions of them are hardest to eschew, because of the necessity there is of seeking and taking of them for the upholding of our corporal lives and healths) unto an humble soul.

And these stirrings and likings of gluttony, among all other sins, are most excusable and least perilous. And therefore thou shalt not rise against the ground of this sin as thou shalt against the ground of all other sin, for the ground of this sin is only natural need and necessity, the which thou canst not eschew, unless thou shouldst do worse, namely, slay this need (as many unwise persons do, by destroying their bodies or healths), whereas they should only slay the thief and spare the true man. That is to say, slay unreasonable lust and sensual voluntary liking, and spare and keep natural liking and corporal ability, and they do not so. But against all other sins thou shalt arise to destroy, not only deadly sins and the greater venials, but also against the ground of them by suppressing the stirrings and motions of them, and also avoiding the occasions and motives and incentives to them as much as thou canst; but this thou canst not do here with all thy skill, for thou canst not live without meat and drink, but thou mayest live without lechery or carnal pleasure if thou wilt, and never better than when without it. And therefore thou shalt not fly only the deeds of it (namely, the doing of any external thing against chastity) but also thou shalt suppress and destroy within thee all mere inward and mental desires against the virtue of chastity (the which mental desires or thoughts are sometimes only venial sins, and sometimes mortal); but also thou shalt labour against the ground of the said sin, and seek to destroy the feeling and the rising of fleshly stirrings.

But this travail and labour against the ground of lechery must be spiritual, by prayers and spiritual virtues, and not by bodily penance only; for wot thou well, that if thou fast and watch and scourge thyself, and do all that thou canst, thou shalt never have cleanness and chastity without the gift of God, and without the grace or virtue of humility. Thou shalt sooner kill thyself, than kill fleshly stirrings and feelings of lust and lechery, either in thy heart or in thy flesh, by any bodily penances; but by the grace of Jesus, in an humble soul, the ground may be much stopped and destroyed, and the spring may be much dried, the which will cause true chastity in body and in soul.

The same may be said of pride and of covetousness, and of such other, for thou mayest live though thou wert not proud at all, nor covetous, nor luxurious, and therefore thou shalt labour to destroy the very feelings of them as much as thou canst, and so seek to cleanse and take away the very ground of those sins. But in gluttony it is otherwise, because the ground thereof, which is natural appetite and need, must remain as long as thou livest, therefore must thou only arise and fight against the unreasonable desires of thy natural appetite therein, the which do creep in under pretense, and by occasion of the said just and reasonable need; smite these unreasonable stirrings, and keep the ground whole.

SECTION II: THAT A MAN SHOULD BE BUSY TO PUT AWAY AND HINDER ALL MOTIONS OF SIN, BUT MORE BUSY ABOUT THOSE OF SPIRITUAL SINS THAN THOSE OF BODILY

AND therefore he that riseth against the feeling of fleshly liking in meat and drink, more fully and more sharply than against those of pride, or covetousness, or lechery, or envy (the which because they be more spiritual and less perceivable, seem perhaps less evil, and are less reprehended). I say that he is half-blind, for he seeth not his spiritual uncleannesses (as of pride and envy), how foul they are in God's sight, for, I believe that if a man could see with his spiritual eye how foul pride and covetousness are in God's sight, and how contrary they are to Him, he would more loathe a stirring of pride, and the vain liking of it; and also he would more abhor and rise against that evil will of envy, or anger to his neighbour than many a stirring or liking either of gluttony or of lechery. Nevertheless, all men do not think so, for commonly men are more shy or troubled to feel a stirring of fleshly sin, and have for it more sorrow and heaviness than for great likings in vain-glory or in other ghostly sins. But they are not wise; for if they would understand the holy Scriptures and sayings of doctors they should find it as I say, which I neither may nor will rehearse now.

I will not excuse them that fall in the likings and delights of gluttony and lechery, as if they sinned not; for I wot well that all the kinds of them are sins more or less, according to the measure of the lust and misbehaviour in the sin, and other likings, with consideration of how far voluntary it was with other circumstances. But my desire is, that thou mightest know and esteem all sins according as they are, indeed, the greater to be the greater, as are spiritual sins; and the less to be the less, as are fleshly or sensual sins; and yet nevertheless would I have thee to hate and fly all, both bodily and spiritual, with all thy might. For know thou well, that fleshly desires and unreasonable likings in meat and drink, or any likings that belong to the body, exceeding reasonable needs, though they be not always great sins to him that is in charity. Nevertheless, to a soul that desireth cleanness and purity of heart, and a spiritual feeling of God, they are full heavy, painful and bitter, and greatly to be eschewed; for the spirit cannot feel his kindly savour within, till the flesh hath lost his beastly savour without.

And, therefore, if thou wilt come to cleanness of heart, thou must strive against the unreasonable stirrings of fleshly desires, but against the ground of them thou shalt not rise; for the ground of it is Need, as natural hunger, which thou must necessarily feel, and must attend thereto, and satisfy it in fitting time and manner, and help thyself against it by medicine of meat, as thou wouldst help thyself in a reasonable manner against a bodily sickness, that thou mayest more freely serve God both bodily and spiritually. For know thou well, that what man or woman that shall be occupied spiritually in thoughts, great pain or hunger wilfully undertaken or bodily sickness or pain in the stomach, or in the head, or in other parts of the body for want of good ruling of themselves in too much fasting, or in any other way, will much let the spirit, and much hinder him from the knowing and beholding of spiritual things, unless he have much grace, and be arrived to great abilities in the Contemplative life. For though it be true, that bodily pain either of penance, or of sickness, or of bodily occupation, sometime letteth not the fervour of love to God in devotion, but oft increaseth it, yet I believe that they let the fervour of love in Contemplation, the which may not be had nor felt fully, but in rest and freedom of body and soul from all the aforesaid corporal pains, wants, employments and solicitudes.

SECTION III: WHAT REMEDY A MAN SHOULD USE AGAINST THE FAULTS IN EATING AND DRINKING

THEREFORE, thou shalt behave thyself discreetly about thy body, yielding it necessaries reasonably, and then let God send thee what He pleaseth, either health or sickness; take it gladly, and grudge not willingly against Him.

Do as I say, take thy meat as it cometh, or provide it according to reason, and take it gladly, as a thing that thou needest; but be well aware of lusts that cometh with need, eschew too much as well as too little. And having done, if after it there arise in thee a remorse or biting of conscience, that thou hast eaten too much, and thereupon thou becomest sad and heavy with overmuch bitterness against thyself, lift up the desire of thy heart to thy good Lord Jesus, and acknowledge thyself a wretch, and a beast, and ask Him forgiveness, and say that thou wilt amend it, and pray that he will forgive thee. Leave off then, and think no further of it, nor strive so much with the vice, as if thou wouldst destroy it utterly, for it is not worth the doing so, neither shalt thou be ever able to bring it about that way; but set thyself about some other business bodily or ghostly, according as thou findest thyself best disposed, that thereby thou mayest profit more in other virtues, as in humility and charity. For wot thou well, that he that hath in his desire and in his endeavours no other respect to no other thing but Humility and Charity, always crying after them, how he may have them, he shall through such desire and manner of working profit and increase, not only in those two virtues, but also in all other virtues together with them, as in chastity, abstinence and such other (though he have but a little regard to them in comparison of the other, namely, Humility and Charity) more in one year than he should, without the said desire and manner of working, profit in seven years, though he strive against gluttony, lechery and such other continually, and beat himself with scourges each day from morning to even-song time.

Set thyself, therefore, about Humility and Charity, and using all thy diligence and industry to come by them, yet shalt thou have enough to do in getting of them. And if thou canst get them, they will direct thee, and measure thee privily and secretly, how thou shalt eat, and how thou shalt drink, and succour all thy bodily needs, that there shall no man know of it, unless thou thyself do tell it him, and that thou shalt not be in perplexity, scruples, vexation, anguishment, or heaviness, nor with any lust or adhering to the delights and likings of sensuality, but shalt do all in peace of a glad conscience with all quietness and satisfaction. I have spoken more than I thought to have done in this matter, but nevertheless do (as far as thou canst) as I say, and I hope God shall make all well.

By this that I have said, thou mayest in some measure see into this image of sin, and perceive how much it hinders thee. The Gospel saith, how that Abraham spake to the rich man that was buried in hell, on this wise: There is betwixt us and you a great chaos; that is to say, a thick darkness betwixt thee and us, that we cannot come to thee, nor thou to us. This dark image in thy soul and mine may be in like manner called a chaos, that is, a great darkness, for it letteth us that we cannot come to Abraham, which is Jesus, and it letteth Him, that He will not come to us.

CHAPTER IX: OF THE FIVE WINDOWS OF THIS DARK IMAGE, AND WHAT COMETH IN BY THEM, AND HOW THEY ARE TO BE ORDERED

LIFT up thy lanthorn, and thou shalt see in this image five windows, by which sin cometh into thy soul, as the Prophet saith: Death cometh in by our windows. These are the five senses by which thy soul goeth out of herself, and fetcheth her delight, and seeketh her feeding in earthly things, contrary to the nobility of her own nature. As by the eye to see curious and fair things, and so of the other senses. By the unskilful using of these senses willingly to vanities, thy soul is much letted from the sweetness of the spiritual senses within; and therefore it behoveth thee to stop these windows, and shut them, but only when need requireth to open them.

And this would be little mastery or difficulty for thee to do, if thou didst once see thy own soul by clear understanding what it is, and how fair it is in its own nature, and so is still, were it not so overlaid with a black mantle of this foul image. But because thou knowest it not, therefore leavest thou the inward sight of thyself, and seekest thy food without, abroad, like a brute beast. Thus saith our Lord in a threatening way to a chosen soul in holy Writ: Thou fairest among women, if thou knowest not thyself, go out, and walk after the steps of the flock of thy fellows, and feed thy kids. And it is as much as to say: Thou soul, fair by nature, made after the likeness of God, frail in thy body as a woman, by reason of the first sin, that thou knowest not thyself, nor how that angels' food should be thy delights within, therefore goest thou out by thy bodily senses, and seekest thy meat and thy liking as a beast of the flock, that is as one outcast and rejected, and therewith thou feedest thy thoughts and thine affections, which are unclean as goats. It is a shame for thee to do so.

And, therefore, turn home again into thyself and hold thee within, and beg no more without, namely, swines' meat. For if thou wilt needs be a beggar, ask and crave within of thy Lord Jesus, for He is rich enough, and gladlier would give thee than thou canst ask, and run no more out as a beast of the flock, that is a worldly man or woman, that hath no delight but in his bodily senses. And if thou do thus, thy Lord Jesus will give thee all that thou needest, for He will lead thee into His wine cellar, and make thee to taste and try His wines, which liketh thee best for he hath many tuns. Thus a chosen soul, joying in our Lord, saith of Him in holy Writ: The King brought me into His wine cellar. That is to say: Inasmuch as I forsook the drunkenness of fleshly lusts and worldly likings, which are bitter as wormwood, therefore the King of bliss, the Lord Jesus, led me in; that is, first into myself for to behold and know myself, and after He led me into His cellar; that is to say, above myself by ascending and passing into Him alone, and gave me a taste of His wine; that is for to taste a certainty of spiritual sweetness and heavenly joy. These are not the words of me, a wretched caitiff, living in sin, but they are the words of the spouse of our Lord in holy Writ; and these words I say to thee, to the end that thou mightest draw in thy soul from without, and follow on further as well as thou canst.

I will show thee furthermore (for thy desire draweth more out of my heart than I thought to have said in the beginning) when the use of thy senses be deadly sin, and when venial. Thus, therefore, our Lord saith in the Gospel: A man made a great supper, and called many thereto, and sent his servant at supper-time, after them that were bidden. The first excused himself, and said on this wise, that he could not come, for he had bought a farm. The other also excused himself, that he could not come, for he had bought five yoke of oxen, and went to try them. The third, for that he had married a wife. I forbear to speak of the first and of the last, and will tell ye of the middlemost of them, that had bought the oxen, for he is to our purpose. Five yoke of oxen betoken the five senses, which are beastly as an ox. Now this man that was called to the supper was not rejected because he bought the oxen, but because he went to try them, and so he would not come. Right so say I to thee; for to have thy senses, and to use them in need, it is no sin, but if thou go voluntarily to try them by vain delights in creatures, then it is sin. And if thou choose that delight as a final rest of thy soul, and as a full liking, that thou carest not to have any other bliss but such worldly vanities, then is it deadly, for thou choosest it as thy God, and so shalt thou be put from thy supper; for St Paul forbids us to use our senses in that manner when he said thus: Thou shalt not go after thy lusts, nor voluntarily try thy likings. A man or a woman that is encumbered with deadly sin shall hardly escape deadly sin in this business, though he perceiveth it not; but I hope this toucheth not thee.

Nevertheless, if thou through frailty delight thee in thy senses, and in such vanities, but yet keepest thyself in charity and the grace of God as to other things, and choosest not this delight for a full rest of thy soul, but always settest up God above all things in thy desire, this sin in thee is venial; and that more or less according to its circumstances; nor shalt thou for these venial sins be put from the supper in the bliss of heaven, but thou shalt want the tasting and the assaying of that delicate supper, whilst thou livest here on earth, unless thou be busy with all thy might to withstand and conquer such venial sins, for though it be so that venial sins break not charity, yet soothly they let the fervour and the ghostly feeling of charity.

But thou wilt say again, that thou canst not keep from hearing of vanities, for divers, both those that live in the world and others, come oft to speak with thee, and tell thee some tales of vanity.

As unto this I say thus, that thy communing with thy neighbour is not much hurt to thee, but helpeth thee sometimes, if thou order thy business wisely; for that thou mayest try and find out thereby the measure of thy charity to thy neighbour, whether it be much or little. Thou art bounden (as all other men and women are) to love thy neighbour principally in thy heart, and also in deeds to show him tokens of charity, as reason asketh, according to thy might and knowledge. And since it is so that thou oughtest not to go out of thy house to seek occasion how thou mightest profit thy neighbour by deeds of charity, because thou art enclosed; nevertheless thou art bound to love all men in thy heart, and to show some tokens of true love to them that come to thee. And therefore, whoso will speak with thee, whatsoever he be, or of what degree soever, though thou knowest not what he is, nor why he cometh, yet be thou soon ready with a good will to ask what his will is, be not dainty, nor suffer him long to wait for thee, but look how ready and how glad thou wouldst be if an angel of heaven should come and speak with thee, so ready and so buxom be thou in will for to speak with thy neighbour when he cometh to thee, for thou knowest not what he is, nor why he cometh, nor what need he hath of thee, or thou of him, till thou hast tried. And though thou be at prayer, or at thy devotions, that thou thinkest loth to break off, for that thou thinkest that thou oughtest not leave God for to speak with anyone, I think not so in this case, for if thou be wise thou shalt not leave God, but thou shalt find Him, and have Him, and see Him, in thy neighbour, as well as in prayer, only in another manner.

If thou canst love thy neighbour well, to speak with thy neighbour with discretion shall be no hindrance to thee. Discretion shalt thou have on this manner as me thinketh; Whoso cometh to thee, ask him meekly what he would have; and if he come to tell thee his disease or trouble and to be comforted by thy speech, hear him gladly, and suffer him to say what he will, for ease of his own heart; and when he hath done, comfort him if thou canst, gladly, gently and charitably, and soon break off. And then, after that, if he will fall into idle tales, or vanities of the world, or of other men's actions, answer him but little, and feed not his speech, and he will soon be weary, and quickly take his leave.

If it be another man that cometh to teach thee, as some Churchman, etc., hear him humbly, and with reverence to his order; and if his speeches comfort thee, ask of him more what thou needest, and take not upon thee to teach him, for it falleth not to thy share to teach a priest, but in case of necessity. If his speech comfort thee or profit thee not, answer little, and he will soon take his leave.

If it be another man that cometh to give thee his alms, or else for to hear thee speak, or to be taught by thee, speak gently and humbly to them all, reprove no man for his faults, for that belongeth not to thee, unless he be the more homely or familiar with thee, that thou knowest that he will take it well from thee. And to be short in this matter of thy telling of another of his faults, I say, that when thou conceivest that it will do him good (namely, in his soul) thou mayest tell him thy mind, if thou hast opportunity, and if he is likely to take it well. And above all other things, in this matter of conversing with thy neighbour, keep silence as much as thou canst, and then shalt thou see that by so doing thou shalt in short time be troubled with little press or company that would come to hinder thy devotions. This is my opinion herein; do thou better if thou canst.

CHAPTER X: OF ANOTHER HOLE OR WINDOW THAT IS TO BE STOPPED AS WELL AS THE WINDOWS OF THE SENSES, NAMELY, THE IMAGINATION

BUT thou wilt say that thou hast done all this, namely, stopped the windows of thy five senses, so that thou seest no worldly things, nor hearest them, nor hast any use of thy senses, more than need requireth; and for that end thou art enclosed. And to this I answer: If thou do thus, as I hope thou dost, then hast thou stopped a great window of this image, but yet art thou not secure; for that thou hast not stopped the privy holes of the imaginations of thy heart. For though thou seest me not with thy bodily eye, yet mayest thou see me at the same time in thy soul by imagination; and so mayest thou do of all bodily things. If, then, thou feedest thy soul willingly and wittingly by imaginations of vanities of the world, and desiring of worldly things; as a comfort or pleasure and ease; verily though thy soul be kept within as to thy bodily senses, it is notwithstanding far without by such vain imaginations.

But now thou wilt ask me whether it be any great sin for a soul to busy itself in such vanities, either by the outward senses or by the inward imaginations and thoughts. As unto this I say; that I would never have thee ask any man this question; for he that will truly love God, he asketh not commonly, whether this or that be the greater sin? For he will think that whatsoever letteth him from the love of God is a great sin, and will think nothing sin but that thing which is not good, and letteth him from the love of God. What is sin but a wanting or a forbearing of good? I say not that it will or ought to grieve him so much as a mortal sin would, or a venial sin should, neither say I but that he knoweth and distinguisheth a mortal sin from a venial, and fleeth it more than the other.

CHAPTER XI: A BRIEF REHEARSAL OF WHAT HATH BEEN SAID IN THE FORMER CHAPTERS, WITH A PORTRAITURE OF THIS DARK IMAGE OF SIN

BY this that I have said mayest thou see a little the darkness of this image of sin, not that I have described it fully to thee as it is, for I cannot; nevertheless by this little thou mayest see more if thou look well.

But thou wilt say, how know you that I bear about me such an image as you speak of? To which I answer, that I may take to me a word said by the prophet, which is this: Inveni idolum mihi—I have found an idol in myself; that is, a false image, which some call an idol, very foul, disfigured and misshapen with wretchedness of all those sins which I have spoken of, by the which I am cast down into fleshly or sensual pleasures and worldly vanities, from cleanness of heart, and feeling of spiritual virtues, more than I can or may say: and such fall of mine much grieveth me, and I cry God mercy for it. By this wretchedness which I feel in my own self, more than I have said, may I the better tell thee of thy image, for we all came of Adam and Eve, clothed with clothes of beasts' skins, as the Scripture saith: Our Lord made to Adam and his wife clothes of a beast's hide. In token that by sin they were come to be misshapen like to a beast, in which beastly clothes we all are born, and wrapped, and disfigured from our kingly shape.

This then is an ugly image to look upon; whose head is pride; for pride is the first and principal sin, as the wise man saith: The beginning of all manner of sin is pride. The back and hinder part of it is covetousness, as St Paul saith: I forget that which is behind (vizi, all worldly things) and I stretch forward to that which is before. The breast (in which is the heart) is Envy; for it is no fleshly sin, but it is a devil's sin, as the wise man saith: By envy of the devil death came into the world, for all those that are of his party follow him therein. The arms of it are wrath, inasmuch as a man wreaketh or revengeth himself by his arms, contrary to Christ's bidding in the Gospel: If a man smite thee upon one cheek, thou shalt not smite him again, but offer him the other. The belly of this image is gluttony, as St Paul saith: Meat serveth for the belly, and the belly for meat, but God shall destroy them both; namely, at the last day, when shall be the full reforming of his chosen, and damning of the reprobate, The members of it are lechery, of the which St Paul saith thus: Yield not your members to be instruments of iniquity unto sin; especially to this sin of lechery. The feet of it are sloth; therefore the wise man said to the slow and lazy person (to stir him up to do good deeds), Run, make haste, raise thy friend, that is to say, run quickly about to good works, and make haste, for the time passeth, and raise up thy friend, which is Jesus, by devout Prayer and Meditation. Here hast thou heard the members of this image.

CHAPTER XII: A COMPARING OF THIS IMAGE WITH THE IMAGE OF JESUS, AND HOW IT IS TO BE DEALT WITH

THIS is not the image of Jesus, but it is liker an image of the Devil, for the image of Jesus is made of virtues, with humility and perfect love and charity; but this is made of false fleshly love to thyself, with all those members, spoken of in the former chapter, fastened thereto. This image bearest thou, and every man whatsoever he be, until by grace of Jesus it be somewhat destroyed and broken down. Thus David seemeth to say in the Psalter: Man passeth away as an image, and is troubled in vain. Which is as if he had said: Though it be so that man in the beginning was made after the image of God, stable and stedfast; nevertheless because of sin, he proceedeth far in this image of sin, living in this world, by the which he is unstable and troubled in vain. Also St Paul speaketh of this Image thus: As we have heretofore borne the image of the earthly man, the first Adam, that is, the image of sin, Right so now (if we will come to the love of God) let us bear the image of the heavenly man Jesus, which is the image of virtues.

What shalt thou do with this image? I answer thee by a word that the Jews said to Pilate of Christ—Crucify Him. Take thou this body of sin, and do Him on the Cross; that is to say, break down this image, and slay the false love of sin in thyself; as Christ's body was slain for our sins and trespasses; right so it behoveth thee, if thou wilt be like Christ, slay thy bodily liking and fleshly lusts in thyself. Thus said St Paul: Those that are Christ's followers have crucified and slain their flesh (that is, the image of sin) with all the lusts, and the unreasonable desires and appetites of it. Slay then and break down Pride, and set up Humility; also break down Anger and Envy, and raise up Love and Charity to thy neighbour. Also instead of Covetousness, poverty of Spirit; instead of Sloth, fervour in devotion with cheerful readiness to all good deeds; and instead of Gluttony and Lechery, Sobriety and Charity in body and soul. This considered St Paul, when he said thus: Putting off the old man with all his members, which is rotten according to the desires of error, ye shall shape you and clothe you in the new man, which is the image of God by holiness and righteousness and perfection of virtues. Who shall help thee to break down this image? Verily thy Lord Jesus. In the virtue and in the Name of Him shalt thou break down this mawment (or idol) of sin, pray to Him earnestly, and desire it, and He shall help thee.

Gather then thy heart together, and do after the counsel of the wise man, when he saith thus: With all diligence keep thine heart, for out of it cometh life, and that is when it is well kept, for then wise thoughts, clean affections and burning desires of virtues and of charity, and of the bliss of Heaven come out of it, making the soul to live a blessed life. But on the contrary, if it be not kept, then as our Lord saith in the Gospel, evil thoughts and unclean affections come out of the heart which defile the man. They either benumb and kill the life of the soul by mortal sin, or else they enfeeble the soul and make it sick, if they be venial. For what is a man but his thoughts and his loves? These alone make a man good or bad. So much as thou lovest God and thy neighbour, and knowest Him, so much is thy soul, and if thou love Him little, little is thy soul, and if thou love Him not at all, nothing at all is thy soul. It is nothing as to good, but it is much as to sin. And if thou wilt know what thou lovest, look and observe what thou thinkest upon most, for where our love is, there is our eye; and where our liking is, upon that our heart is thinking most. If thou love God much, thou likest to think much upon Him, and if thou love Him little, then little dost thou think upon Him. Rule well thy thoughts and thine affections, and then art thou virtuous.

Undertake then the breaking down of this image, when thou hast first well bethought thee of thyself, and of thy wretchedness, inwardly, as I have said, how proud, how vain, how envious, how melancholy (or froward), how covetous, how fleshly, and how full of corruption. Also how little knowing, feeling or savour thou hast of God and of spiritual things, how wise, how quick and how much savour thou hast in earthly things. And (that I may say all in one word) how thou art as full of sin as an hide or skin is full of flesh, yet be not thou too much dejected, though thou thinkest thus of thyself. And when thou hast done thus, lift up then the desire of thy heart to thy Lord Jesus, and pray for His help, cry to Him with great desires and sighings that He will help thee to bear this great burthen of this image, or else that He will break it. Think also what a shame it is for thee to be fed with swines' meat of fleshly savours, that oughtest to feel a spiritual savour of heavenly joy.

If thou dost thus, then beginnest thou to rise against the whole ground of sin in thee, as I have said. And it may be that thou shalt feel pain and sorrow, for thou must know that no soul can live without pain, heaviness and sadness, unless that she take delight or have her rest either in her Creator or in some creature. And, therefore, when thou risest against thyself by a fervent desire for to attain to the feeling of thy Lord Jesus within thee, and for to draw away thy love from all bodily things, and from rest in all bodily feelings, insomuch that thou art even a burthen to thyself, and it seems to thee that all creatures are risen up against thee, and all the things, which heretofore thou tookest delight in, do now turn thee to pain and heaviness. And when thou hast thus forsaken thyself, and canst not likely, for all that, as yet find comfort in God, needs must thy soul feel and suffer pain in this case. Nevertheless, I hope that he that will suffer this pain awhile, stedfastly, cleaving to the desire and naked mind after Jesus Christ, and to that his desire, that he will have nothing but his Lord, and will not lightly depart therefrom, nor seek any other comfort from without for a time (for it lasteth not long), our Lord is nigh to him, and soon shall ease his heart, for He will help him to bear his body or sensuality, which is full of corruption; and will, with His merciful power of His gracious presence, break down this false image of love in him; not all at once, but by little and little, till he be in some measure reformed to His likeness.

After such a total rising and resolution made by thee against thyself, when it is passed thou shalt more soberly, more gently and more easily rule thyself, and more charily keep and guard thy thoughts and thine affections, and shalt note and discern them, whether they be good or bad. And thereupon if afterwards thou feel (I put this for an example) a stirring of pride in any manner or spice of it, be then presently well aware, as well and as soon as thou canst, and suffer it not to escape away lightly, but take it in mind, and there rent it, break it and despise it, and do all the shame thou canst unto it; look thou spare it not, nor believe it, though it speak never so fair, for it is false, though it seem to be truth; as the Prophet saith: My people, they who call thee blessed, do deceive thee (by their so saying) and would bring thee into error.

And if thou be diligent to do thus, thou shalt, by the grace of Jesus, within short time, stop much of the spring of Pride and much abate the vain delight thereof, so that thou shalt very early feel any such motion in thee. And when thou feelest it, it shall be so weak and, as it were, half dead, that it shall not much trouble thee. And then shalt thou have a spiritual sight of the virtue of

Humility, and see how good and how fair it is, and thou shalt desire it and love it for its goodness, so that it shall please thee both to behold and see thyself as thou art indeed, and also to be esteemed and held by others to be such a one, that is full of corruption, and (if need be) to suffer gladly despite and reproof for love of righteousness.

In like manner when thou feelest any stirrings of wrath, or anger, or of melancholic risings of heart, or any other evil will against thy neighbour, for any manner of cause, though it seem reasonable, and not to be against charity, beware of it, and be ready with thy thought to restrain it, that it turn not into a further liking or consent; resist it as much as thou canst, and follow it not neither by word nor deed, but as it riseth, smite it down again, and so shalt thou slay it with the sword of the fear of God, that it shall not trouble thee, for know well in all these stirrings of pride, vain-glory, envy, or any other, that as soon as thou perceiveth it, and resistest it with displeasure of thy will and of thy reason, thou slayest it. Though it be so, that it cleave still upon thy heart against thy will, and will not lightly pass away, fear it not, for though it letteth thy soul from peace, yet doth it not defile her.

Right so in like manner shalt thou do against all evil stirrings of Covetousness, Sloth, Gluttony and Lechery; that thou be always ready with thy reason and thy will to reprove them and despise them.

And this mayest thou do the better, and the more readily, if thou be diligent and careful to set thy heart most upon one thing, and that is nought else but a spiritual desire after God, how to please Him, love Him and know Him, to see Him and to enjoy Him by grace here in a little feeling, and in the bliss of Heaven in a full being. This desire, if thou keep it, it will tell thee what is sin, and what is not; and what thing is good and what better; and if thou wilt but fasten thy thoughts to the same desire, it shall teach thee all that thou needest, and it shall procure thee all that thou wantest. And, therefore, whensoever thou risest against the ground of sin in general, or against the ground of any particular sin, hang fast upon this desire, and set the point of thy thoughts more upon God whom thou desirest than upon the sin which thou abhorrest. And if thou do so, then God fighteth for thee, and will destroy sin in thee. And thou shalt much sooner come to thy purpose if thou doest thus, than if thou shouldst leave thy humble desire principally after God, and set thy heart only against the stirrings of sin, as though thou wouldst destroy it by thy own mastering of it, but thou shalt never so bring it about.

CHAPTER XIII: HOW A MAN SHALL BE SHAPEN TO THE IMAGE OF JESUS, AND JESUS SHAPEN IN HIM

Do as I have said, and better if thou canst, and I hope by the grace of Jesus thou shalt make the devil ashamed, and shalt break down all such wicked stirrings, that they shall not much trouble thee. And by this course may the image of sin be broken down in thee and destroyed, by the which thou art misshapen from the kindly shape of Christ's image; and thou shalt be reformed and shapen again to the image of the Humanity of Jesus, by humility and charity, and afterwards shalt thou become full shapen to the image itself of the Godhead, whilst thou livest here, as it were in a shadow of it in contemplation, and hereafter in verity and full reality in the bliss of Heaven.

Of this shaping to the likeness of Christ St Paul speaks thus: My little children whom I travail with again (as a woman that were with child with you) until Christ be shapen again in you. Thou hast conceived Christ within thee by faith, and He liveth in thy soul by grace, inasmuch as thou hast a good will and a desire to serve Him and please Him; but He is not yet fully shapen in thee, nor thou in Him by perfection of charity. And therefore St Paul bare thee and me and others also with travail, as a woman beareth a child, until the time that Christ hath His full shape in us, and we in Him. Of this treateth the second book.

CHAPTER XIV: THE CONCLUSION OF THIS BOOK, AND OF THE CAUSE WHY IT WAS MADE, AND HOW SHE FOR WHOM IT WAS MADE WAS TO MAKE USE OF IT

WHOSO thinkest to attain to the working and to the full use of contemplation and not by this way, that is by perfection of virtues, and taking full heed thereto, cometh not in by the door, and therefore as a thief he shall be cast out. I say not but that a man may have by the gift of God, at by times, a tasting and a glimmering of the contemplative life; some I say at the beginning of their conversion. But the solid feeling of it shall he not have, until he have gotten in him some perfection of virtues. For Christ is the door, and is also the porter, and without His leave and His liberty no man may come in; as He Himself saith: No man cometh to the Father but by Me. That is to say, no man can come to the contemplation of the Godhead but he that is first reformed by perfection of humility and charity, to the likeness of Jesus in His Humanity.

Lo, then, have I told thee a little, as methinketh, first of Contemplative life, what it is; and then of the ways which, by the grace of God, lead thereunto. Not as if I had it myself in feeling and in working, as I have it in talking.

Nevertheless, I would by this writing of mine (such as it is) first stir up my own negligence to do better than I have done; and also my purpose is, to stir thee, or any other man or woman that hath taken the state of life Contemplative, to travail more diligently and more humbly in that manner of life, by such simple words as God hath given me grace for to say. And therefore if there be any word therein that stirreth thee or comforteth thee more to the love of God, thank God, for it is His gift and not of the words written. And if it comforteth thee not, and thou understandest it not readily, study not too long about it, but lay it aside till another time, and go to thy prayers or some other business; take it as it will come, and not all at once.

Also these words which I write, take them not too strictly, but when thou thinkest, upon good consideration, that I write too short, either for lack of English or lack of reason, I pray thee amend it only where need is. Also these words which I write to thee, belong not all of them to one that is of an active life, but to thee or to any other which hath the state of life contemplative.

The Grace of our Lord Jesus Christ be with thee.

BOOK II

PART I

CHAPTER I

SECTION I: THAT A MAN IS THE IMAGE OF GOD AFTER THE SOUL AND NOT AFTER THE BODY; AND HOW HE IS RESTORED AND REFORMED THERETO THAT WAS MISSHAPEN BY SIN

FORASMUCH as thou desirest greatly, and askest it for charity, to hear more of that image of which I have spoken in the former book in part; therefore I shall willingly, with fear, fall to thy desire, and by the help of our Lord's grace, in whom I fully trust, shall open to thee a little more of this image.

I tell thee in truth, that I understand nought else thereby, but thy soul. For thy soul and my soul and every rational soul is an image, and that a worthy one, for it is the image of God, as the Scripture saith: Man is God's Image and made to the image and likeness of Him; not in His bodily shape without, but in his faculties within, as holy Writ saith: Our Lord God shaped man in His soul to His own image and likeness. This is the image that I have spoken of. This image, made after the image of God in its first shaping, was wonderful fair and bright, full of burning love and ghostly light, but through the sin of the first man Adam it was disfigured and misshapen into another likeness, as I have said before, for it fell from that ghostly light and that heavenly feeding into painful darkness and lust of this wretched life, exiled and driven out from the inheritance of Heaven, that it should have had if it had continued, into the wretchedness of this earth, and afterward into the prison of hell, there to have been without end; from which prison it should never return to the heavenly inheritance until it were reformed to the first shape and likeness. But that reforming could not be made by any earthly man, for every man was in the same mischief, and none was sufficient to help himself, and so much less another man. Therefore it needed to be done by Him that was more than man, that is God alone. And it was needful that He should reform and restore man to bliss (if ever he were to be saved) who of His infinite goodness first created him thereto. Now, then, I shall tell thee, how he might be reformed, and how he is reformed to his first likeness by Him that first made and framed him, for that is the intent of this writing. The justice of God requireth that a sin committed be not forgiven, unless that amends be made for it, if it may be done. Now it is certain that mankind that was perfect in Adam the first man (sinning so grievously against God, when he broke His special command, and assented to the false counsel of the devil) deserved justly to be separated from Him, and damned to hell without end, so far forth, that according to God's Justice, he could not be forgiven, unless amends were first made, and full satisfaction given. But this amends could none make that was man only, and proceeded out of Adam by generation; because that the trespass and dishonour done to God was endless great, and therefore it passed man's power to make amends for it. And, secondly, because he that had offended, and would make amends for it, ought to give and pay unto him whom he had offended, all that he owed him, though he had not offended, and over and besides that, to give and pay him something that he owed not, in regard of the same offence and injury done. But mankind had not wherewith to pay God for his trespass, over and above that which he owed him, for what good soever man could do in body or soul was but his debt; for every man ought, as the Gospel saith: For to love God with all his heart, and all his soul, and all his might; and better than this could he not do; and nevertheless this deed was not sufficient to the reforming of mankind, nor could he do this until he was first reformed. Then needed it, that if man's soul should be reformed, and the trespass made good, that our Lord God Himself should reform this image, and make amends for the trespass, since no man could. But that might He not do in His Godhead, for He might not, nor ought not, to make amends by suffering pain in His own nature, therefore it was necessary, that He should take the same nature that had trespassed, and so become man. And that could He not do by the common way of generation, for it was impossible for God's Son to be born of touched woman, therefore must He become man through a gracious generation by the working of the Holy Ghost of a pure gracious virgin our Lady St Mary; and so it was done; for our Lord Jesus, God's Son, became man; and through His precious death which He suffered, made amends to the Father of Heaven for man's guilt. And that could He well do, for He was God, and ought not anything for Himself, but only as He was man, born of the same kind that Adam was that first trespassed, and so though He ought it not for His own person, for that He had not sinned. Nevertheless He ought it of His free will, for the trespass of mankind, having taken upon Him their nature for the salvation of man, out of His endless mercy.

Forsooth it is, there was never any man that could yield to God anything of his own which he owed not, but only this blessed Jesus, for He could pay God something which He owed not, for Himself, which was but one thing, namely, to give His precious life by voluntary undertaking death for love of justice, this He owed not. As much good indeed as He was able to do in this life, for the honour of God was all but due debt; but to undergo death for the love of justice, He was not bound thereto. He was bound to justice, but He was not bound to die: for death is only a pain ordained to man for his own sin. But our Lord Jesus Christ never sinned, neither could sin, and therefore He ought not to die. Since then He ought not to die, and yet died willingly, therefore paid He to God more than He ought. And since that was the best man's deed, and most worthy that ever was done, therefore, was it reasonable that the sin of mankind should be forgiven. Inasmuch as mankind had found a man of the same kind, without spot of sin, that is Jesus; that might make amends for the trespass done, and might pay our Lord God all that He ought; and over and above, that which He ought not. Since, then, that our Lord Jesus, God and man, died thus for the salvation of man's soul, it was just that sin should be forgiven, and man's soul, that was His image, should or might be reformed and restored to the first likeness, and to the bliss of Heaven.

This passion of our Lord, and this precious death is the ground of all the reforming of man's soul; without which man's soul could never be reformed to the likeness of Him, nor come to the bliss of Heaven; but blessed be He for all these His works. Now so it is, that through the virtue of His precious passion, the flaming sword of the Cherubim that drove Adam out of Paradise is now put away; and the endless gates of Heaven are open to every man that will enter in thereto. For the person of Jesus is both God and King of Heaven in the bliss of the Father, and as man, He is porter at the gate, ready to receive every soul that will be reformed here in this life to His likeness. For now may every soul, if he will, be reformed to the likeness of God; since that the trespass is forgiven, and the amends through Jesus is made for the first guilt. Nevertheless though this be true, yet all souls have not the profit nor the fruit of this precious passion, nor are reformed to the likeness of Him.

SECTION II: THAT JEWS AND PAGANS AND ALSO FALSE CHRISTIANS ARE NOT REFORMED EFFECTUALLY THROUGH THE VIRTUE OF THE PASSION THROUGH THEIR OWN FAULTS

TWO manner of men are not reformed by the virtue of this passion. One is of them that know it not; another is of them that love it not. Jews and Pagans have not the benefit, because they know it not. Jews understand not that Jesus the son of the virgin Mary is God's Son. Also the Pagans know it not that the sovereign wisdom of God would become the son of man, and in His manhood would suffer the pains of death. And therefore the Jews held the preaching of the Cross and of the Passion nought but slander and blasphemy; and the Pagans held it nought but fancy and folly. But true Christians hold it the sovereign wisdom of God and His mighty power. Thus saith St Paul: We preach unto you Christ crucified, to the Jews a stumbling block, and to the Gentiles foolishness; but to those that be called, both Jews and Greeks, Christ the Power of God and the Wisdom of God. And therefore these men, through their unbelief, put themselves from the reforming of their own souls, and continuing in this unbelief, shall never be saved nor come to the bliss of Heaven. Forsooth it is, from the beginning of the world to the last ending was there never any man saved, nor shall be, unless he believe generally or specially in Jesus Christ, to come, or already come. For right as all chosen souls, that were before the Incarnation under the Old Testament, believed in Christ that He should come, to reform men's souls; and that either with an open and clear belief, as the Patriarchs and Prophets and other holy men did; or else with a secret and general belief, as children and other simple and imperfect souls had that had no special or explicit clear knowledge of the Mystery of the Incarnation; right so, all chosen souls under the New Testament have belief in Christ already come; either openly and feelingly, as spiritual men and wise men have, or else generally, as children have that are christened, and other simple and unlearned souls have, that are nourished in the bosom of holy Church.

Since this is so, methinks that those men err greatly and grievously who say that Jews and Turks, by keeping of their own law, may be saved, though they believe not in Jesus Christ, as holy Church believeth; inasmuch as they believe that their own faith is good, and secure, and sufficient for their salvation. And in that belief they do as it seems many good deeds of justice and righteousness, and peradventure if they knew that the Christian faith were better than their own, they would leave their own and take it; and therefore they shall be saved. But I say this is not enough, for Christ, God and man, is both the way and the end. And He is the mediator betwixt God and man, and without Him can no soul be reconciled, nor come to the bliss of Heaven, and therefore they that believe not in Him who is both God and man, can never be saved nor come to bliss.

Other men also, that love not Christ, nor His Passion, are not reformed in their souls to His likeness, and these are false Christians, which are out of grace and charity, and live and die in deadly sin. These men know well, as it seemeth, that Jesus is God's Son, and that His passion sufficeth to the salvation of man's soul; and they believe also the other articles of faith. But it is an unshapen and dead faith, for they love Him not, nor choose the fruit of His passion, but lie still in their sins, and in the false love of this world, unto their last end; and so they be not reformed to the likeness of God, but go to the pains of Hell endlessly, as Jews and Turks do, and into much more, and greater pains than they, inasmuch as they had the truth and kept it not; for that makes their sin greater than if they had never known it.

If then thou wilt know what souls are reformed here in this life to the image of God through the virtue of His Passion; verily, only those that believe in Him and love Him; in which souls, the image of God that was misshapen through sin, as it were, into a foul beast's likeness, is restored and reformed to its first shape, and to the worthiness and worship that it had in the beginning; without which restoring and reforming never shall any soul be saved nor come to bliss.

CHAPTER II: OF TWO MANNERS OF REFORMING OF THIS IMAGE, ONE IN FULNESS, ANOTHER IN PART

NOW thou wilt say: How can this be, that the image of God, which is man's soul, should be reformed here in this life to His likeness in any creature? Whereas the contrary seemeth true, nay, it seems that it cannot possibly be so? For if it were reformed, then should it have a stable memory, a clear sight or understanding, a clear burning love to God and spiritual things everlastingly, as it had in the beginning. But these hath no creature living here in this life, as thou perceivest; for as for thyself, thou canst truly say, that thou art far from it. Thy memory, thy reason, and thy love of thy soul, are so much set upon the beholding and loving of earthly things, that of spiritual things thou feelest right little. Thou feelest no reforming in thyself, but art so wrapped about with this black image of sin, for all that thou canst do, that upon what side soever thou turnest, thou feelest thyself defiled and spotted with fleshly stirrings of this foul image; and other changings thou feelest none, fresh fleshliness into spiritualness, neither in the inward faculties of thy soul within, nor in bodily feelings or thy senses without. Wherefore it seems to thee that it cannot be that this image should be so reformed.

Thou askest, therefore, how it can be reformed?

To this I answer, and say thus: There be two manners of reforming of the image of God which is man's soul, whereof one is in fulness, another is in part. Reforming in fulness cannot be had in this life, but is deferred till after, to the bliss of Heaven, where man's soul shall fully be reformed; not to that state that it had at the first by nature, or might have had through grace if it had stood whole; but it shall be restored to much more bliss, and much higher joy through the great mercy and the endless goodness of God, than it should have had if it had never fallen. For then shall the soul receive the whole and the full feeling of God in all its faculties, without any other love or affection to anything else interposing itself. And it shall see mankind in the person of Jesus exalted above the kind or nature of Angels, united to the Godhead, for then shall Jesus, both God and man, be all in all, and only He, and none other but He, as the Prophet saith: Our Lord (Jesus) in that day shall be exalted only. And also the body of man shall then be glorified, for it shall receive fully the rich dowry of immortality, with all that belongeth thereto. This shall a soul have with the body, and much more than I can say; but that shall be the bliss of Heaven, but not in this life. For though it be so that the Passion of our Lord be the cause of all this full reforming of man's soul; nevertheless it was not His will to grant it straightways after passion, to all chosen souls that were living at the time of His Passion, but He delayed it unto the last day, and that for this reason: Manifest it is that our Lord Jesus Christ of His mercy hath ordained a certain number of souls to salvation, which number was not fulfilled in the time of His Passion, and therefore it needed that by length of time through natural generation of men that number should be made up; then if it had so been, that so soon as after the death of our Lord, every soul that would have believed in Him should have been blessed and fully reformed by His life, without any further delay, there would no creature that lived then have been that would not have received the Faith for to have been made blessed, and then should generation have ceased. And so should we that are now chosen souls living, and other souls that come after us, not have been born, and so should our Lord have failed of His number. But that might not be, and therefore our Lord provided much better for us, in that He delayed the full reforming of man's soul till the last end, as St Paul saith; God providing better for us, that they should not be consummate without us. That is, our Lord providing better for us in the delaying of our reforming, than if He had granted it then, for this reason, that the chosen souls should not make a full end without us that come after.

Another reason is this: Since that man in his first creation was set in his free will, and had free choice whether he would have God fully or no, it was therefore reasonable that since he would not choose God then, but wretchedly fell from Him, if he should afterwards be reformed, that he should be set again in the same free choosing that he was first in, as whether he would become reformed or no. And this may be also a cause why man's soul was not fully reformed speedily upon the Passion of Jesus Christ.

CHAPTER III: THAT REFORMING IN PART IS IN TWO MANNERS, ONE IN FAITH, ANOTHER IN FEELING

ANOTHER reforming of this image is in part, and this may be had in this life, and if it be not had in this life, it will never be had, nor the soul ever come to be saved.

But this reforming is on two manners; one is in Faith only, another is in Faith and in Feeling. The first sufficeth to salvation, the second is worthy to have passing great reward in the bliss of Heaven. The first may be had easily and in short time, the second not so, but through length of time and much spiritual pains. The first may be had, and yet the man may have together with it the stirrings and feelings of the image of sin. For though a man feel nothing in himself but all stirrings of sin and fleshly desires, notwithstanding those feelings, if he do not voluntarily assent thereto, he may be and remain reformed in Faith to the likeness of God.

But the second putteth out the liking in, and delight felt in sensual motions and worldly desires, and suffereth no such spots to abide in this image. The first is only of beginning and profiting souls, and of active men. The second is of perfect souls, and of contemplative men. For by the first reforming the image of sin is not destroyed, but it is left, as it were, all whole in feeling. But the second destroyeth the old feelings of this image of sin, and bringeth into the soul new gracious feelings, through the workings of the Holy Ghost. The first is good, the second is better; but the third, that is in the bliss of Heaven, is best of all. First let us speak of that one, and then of that other, and so we shall come to the third.

CHAPTER IV: THAT THROUGH THE SACRAMENT OF BAPTISM (WHICH IS GROUNDED IN THE PASSION OF CHRIST) THIS IMAGE IS REFORMED FROM ORIGINAL SIN

Two manner of sins make the soul to lose the image and likeness of God. The one is called Original, that is the first sin; the other is Actual, that is committed by our own will. These two sins put away a soul from the bliss of Heaven, and damn it to the endless pains of hell; unless, through the grace of God, it be reformed to His likeness, before it pass hence out of this life. Nevertheless, two remedies are there against these two sins, by the which a misshapen soul may be restored again. One is the Sacrament of Baptism against original sin, another is the Sacrament of Penance against actual sin. A soul of a child that is born, as is not christened, by reason of original sin, hath no likeness of God; he is nought but an image of the fiend, and a brand of hell, but as soon as it is christened, it is reformed to the image of God, and through the virtue of the faith of holy Church is suddenly turned from the likeness of the fiend, and made like an Angel of Heaven. Also the same falleth to a Jew or to a Turk, the which before they be christened, are nought but bondslaves of hell; but when they forsake their error, and fall humbly to the truth in Christ, and receive the baptism of water in the Holy Ghost, surely without any further tarrying they are reformed to the likeness of God, so fully that the holy Church believeth that if presently after baptism they should happen to die, they should straight fly up to Heaven without any more letting, though they had before in the time of their unbelief committed never so many or so great sins; nor should they ever feel the pains of hell nor of purgatory, and that privilege should they have by the merit of Christ's Passion.

CHAPTER V: THAT THROUGH THE SACRAMENT OF PENANCE (THAT CONSISTETH IN CONTRITION, CONFESSION AND SATISFACTION) THIS IMAGE IS REFORMED FROM ACTUAL SIN

MOREOVER, Christian men or women that have lost the likeness of God through a deadly sin in breaking God's commandments, if he through the touching of grace in his heart doth truly forsake his sin, with sorrow and contrition of heart, and be in full purpose to amend and turn to a good life; and in this foresaid purpose and will receiveth the Sacrament of Penance, if he may come by it, or if he cannot have a will and desire to come by it, surely, I say, that this man or woman's soul, that was before misshapen to the likeness of the devil through deadly sin, is now by the Sacrament of Penance restored and shapen again to the image of our Lord God.

This is a great courtesy of our Lord, and an endless mercy, who so lightly forgiveth all manner of sin, and so suddenly giveth plenty of grace to a sinful soul that asketh mercy of Him. He requireth not great doing of Penance, nor painful suffering in the flesh, before He forgiveth it. But He requireth a loathing of sin, and a full forsaking in the will for love of Him, and a turning of the heart to Him. This He asketh, for this He giveth. And then when He seeth this, without any further delay He forgiveth the sin, and reformeth the soul to His likeness. The sin is forgiven, that the soul shall not be damned, nevertheless, the pain due to the sin is not yet fully forgiven, unless that the contrition and love be the greater. And therefore shall he go and show himself, and make his confession to his ghostly Father, and receive the penance which he enjoineth him for his trespass, and perform it gladly, so that both the sin and the punishment may be done away before he pass hence.

And this is the wise ordinance of holy Church, to the great benefit of man's soul, that though the sin be forgiven through the virtue of contrition, nevertheless for the exercise of humility, and for to make entire satisfaction, he shall (if he have means for it) show to his priest a plenary confession, for that is his token and warrant against all his enemies, of the forgiveness of his sins, and such a token or warrant will it be needful for him to have. Just as if a man had forfeited his life against a king on earth, it were not enough for him (as to his full security and discharge) to have only forgiveness of the king, unless he have a charter from him, which may be his token and warrant against all other men. Right so may it be said spiritually, if a man through deadly sin have forfeited his life against the King of Heaven, it is not enough for him (as to his full security) to have forgiveness of God only by contrition between God and him, unless he have a charter also made by holy Church (if he may come by it), and this is the Sacrament of Penance, which is his charter and token of forgiveness. For sith it was so, that he had offended and forfeited both against God and His Church, it is skilful that he have forgiveness from that one, and a warrant from that other. And this is one cause why Confession is needful.

Another reason is this: That since this reforming of a soul standeth in Faith only, and not in Feeling (for the forgiveness is only believed and not felt) therefore a fleshly or sensual man, that is at first gross and rude in understanding, and cannot easily judge and conceive, but only outward bodily things, would not easily have believed that his sins had been forgiven him, if he had not received some outward or bodily token of it, and that is Confession, through the which token he is made secure of forgiveness if he do his part and duty in the business. This is the belief of holy Church, as I understand it. Another reason is this: Though the ground of forgiveness stand not principally in Confession, but in contrition of the heart, and in detestation or forethinking of sin; nevertheless, I believe that there is many a soul that would never have felt true contrition, nor had arrived at forsaking of sin, if Confession had not been, for it falleth out oftentimes, that in the time of Confession, grace of compunction cometh to a soul that before never felt grace, but ever was cold and dry, and farther off from feeling of grace. And therefore sith Confession was so profitable to the more party of Christian men, holy Church ordained, for the more security generally to all Christian men, that every man and woman should once in the year, at the least, confess all their sins to their ghostly Father, that come to their mind, though they had never so much contrition before time. Nevertheless, I hope well, that if all men had been as careful about the keeping of themselves and eschewing of all manner of sin; and had arrived at as great knowledge and feeling of God as some men have, holy Church would not have ordained the said token of Confession as an obligation, for it had not been needful. But because all men are not so perfect, and peradventure much or the greater part of Christians are imperfect, therefore holy Church ordained Confession by way of general obligation, to all Christians that will acknowledge holy Church as their Mother, and will be obedient to her laws.

If this be true, as I hope it is, then erreth he greatly that generally saith that Confession of sins to the priest is neither necessary nor profitable, and that no man is bound thereto; for by that which I have said, it is both necessary and profitable to all those souls who in this wretched life are defiled with sin, and namely to those who through deadly sin are misshapen from the likeness of God, who cannot be reformed to His likeness but by the Sacrament of Penance which principally standeth in contrition and sorrow of heart, and secondarily in confession of mouth following after it if it may be had. And thus through this Sacrament of Penance is a sinful soul reformed to the image and likeness of God.

But this reforming standeth in Faith and not in Feeling. For right as Faith's property is to believe that which thou seest not, so also is it to believe that which thou feelest not. For he that is reformed in his soul by the Sacrament of Penance to the image of God, feeleth not any change in himself, neither in his external corporal nature, nor within in the substance of his soul, other than he did before. For as to his feeling, he is as he was, and feeleth the same stirrings of sin, and the same corruption of his flesh in his passions and worldly risings in his heart, as he did before. Yet he ought to believe that through grace he is reformed to the image of God, though he neither feel it nor see it. He may easily feel in himself a sorrow for his sins, and a turning of his will from sin to cleanness of living, if he have grace and take good heed of himself. But he can neither see nor feel the reforming of his soul, how it is wonderfully and unperceivably changed from the foulness of the fiend unto the fairness of an Angel, through a secret gracious working of the Holy Ghost. This cannot he see but only believe it; and if he believe it, then is his soul reformed in truth. For right as Holy Church believeth, a Jew or Saracen, or a child, by the Sacrament of Baptism duly administered, to be reformed in soul to the image of God, through a secret unperceivable working of the Holy Ghost, notwithstanding all the fleshly stirrings of his body of sin, which he feeleth, after his Baptism as well as before; right so, by the Sacrament of Penance humbly and truly received, a bad Christian who hath been encumbered with deadly sin all his lifetime, is reformed within in his soul, unperceivably, saving that he finds a turning of his will to God through a secret power, and a gracious working of the Holy Ghost, which suddenly worketh, and in a moment or the twinkling of an eye, setteth right a froward soul, and turneth it from a spiritual foulness to an invisible fairness, and maketh her, of a servant of the fiend, a son of joy; and of a prisoner of hell, an inheritor of Heaven, notwithstanding all the fleshly feelings of this sinful image, that is the corporal nature.

For thou must know, that the Sacrament of Baptism or of Penance, is not of that virtue to hinder and destroy utterly all the stirrings of fleshly lusts and of inordinate passions, that the soul should never feel any risings nor stirrings of them at any time; for if it were so, then were a soul fully reformed here to the dignity it had at its first creation. But that cannot be fully in this life. But it is of that virtue, that it cleanseth the soul from all sins before done; and if she, being in that case, chance to die, it saveth her from damnation; or if it continue in the body, it giveth her grace to withstand the stirrings of sin, or of the passions of the flesh, so that be they never so grievous, they shall not hurt her, nor separate her from God, as long as she doth not willingly consent thereto. So meant St Paul when he said thus:—There is no condemnation to them that walk not after the flesh. That is, those souls that are reformed to the image of God by Faith, through the Sacrament of Baptism or of Penance, shall not be damned for the feeling of this image of sin, if so be that they go not after the motions of sensuality by deed doing.

CHAPTER VI: THAT WE ARE TO BELIEVE STEDFASTLY THE REFORMING OF THIS IMAGE, IF OUR CONSCIENCE WITNESS TO US A FULL FORSAKING OF SIN, AND A TRUE TURNING OF OUR WILL TO GOOD LIVING

OF this reforming in Faith speaketh St Paul in these words: The just man liveth by Faith. That is, he that is made righteous by Baptism or Penance, he liveth by Faith, which sufficeth to salvation, and also to heavenly peace, as St Paul saith: Being justified by Faith, we have peace with God. That is, we that are made righteous and reformed through Faith in Christ, have peace and accord made betwixt God and us, notwithstanding the vicious motions of our body of sin. For though this reforming be secret, and cannot well be felt here in this life, nevertheless whoso stedfastly believeth it, and is careful to shape his life accordingly, and turns not again to deadly sin, surely when the hour of death cometh, and the soul is departed, then shall he find that true which I say now. St John in comfort of chosen souls that live here in Faith under the feeling of this painful image, saith thus: Little children, now are we the sons of God, and it appeareth not what we shall be; but we know that when Christ shall appear, we shall also appear like Him in glory. That is, we are now, whilst we live here, the sons of God, for we are reformed by Faith in Christ to His likeness, but it appeareth not plainly what we are, but it is kept secret. Nevertheless, we know well, that when our Lord shall appear at the last day, then shall we appear with Him, like to Him in glory.

If then, thou wouldst know if thy soul be reformed to the Image of God or no, thou mayest be resolved by that which I have said, ransack thy conscience and look what thy will is, for; therein consisteth the whole business. If it be turned from all manner of deadly sin, so that thou wouldst not for all the world wittingly and wilfully break the commandments of God; and for what thou hast done amiss heretofore contrary to His bidding, hast humbly made thy confession, with full intent to leave it, and art sorry that thou didst it; I say then, surely that thy soul is reformed in Faith to the likeness of God.

CHAPTER VII: THAT ALL THE SOULS THAT LIVE HUMBLY IN THE FAITH OF HOLY CHURCH, AND HAVE THEIR FAITH ENLIVENED WITH LOVE AND CHARITY, BE REFORMED BY THIS SACRAMENT, THOUGH IT BE SO THAT THEY CANNOT FEEL THE SPECIAL GIFT OF DEVOTION OR OF SPIRITUAL FEELING

IN this reforming, which is only in Faith, the most part of chosen souls lead their lives, setting their wills stedfastly to flee all manner of deadly sin, and keeping themselves in love and charity to their neighbour, and keeping the commandments of God according to their knowledge. And when it is so that wicked stirrings and evil desires of pride, envy, wrath or luxury, or of any other capital sin rise in their hearts, they resist and strive against them, by being displeased at them in their will, so that they follow not those wicked motions in their deeds; and if through frailty they fall, as it were against their will, and through ignorance, their conscience soon after so grieveth and paineth them for it, that they can take no rest till they have made their confession, and had absolution for it.

Surely all these souls that thus live in this state of reforming, and be found therein at the hour of their death, shall be saved, and shall come to a full reforming in the bliss of Heaven though it were so, that they never had spiritual feeling, nor inward taste of devotion, nor any special gift of grace of sweetness or comfort in all their lifetime. For if thou shouldst say, that no soul shall be saved, unless she were here reformed in spiritual feeling, so that she hath felt devotion and spiritual sweetness in God, as some souls through special grace have done; then should very few souls be saved, in comparison of the multitude of the other.

Nay, it is not so to be supposed, that only for the souls that have had such extraordinary devotion, or have through great grace come to a spiritual feeling, and for no more, our Lord Jesus should have taken upon Him the nature of man, and suffered the bitter passion of His death. It had been such a small purchase for Him to have come from so far to so near, and from so high to so low, for so few souls; no, His mercy is spread larger than so. But on the contrary, if thou imaginest the Passion of our Lord to be so precious, and His mercy so great, that there shall no soul be damned, and namely, no Christian, do he never so wickedly, as some fools do imagine, surely thou errest greatly.

Go, therefore, in the middle way, and hold thee there, and believe as holy Church believeth, and that is, that the most sinful man that liveth on earth, if through grace he turn his will from deadly sin by true repentance to the service of God, he is reformed in his soul, and if he die in this state, he shall be saved. Thus hath our Lord promised by His Prophet, saying: At what time soever a sinner shall be converted, and sorry for his sins, he shall live, and not die.

And on the other side, whoso liveth in deadly sin, and will not leave it, nor amend him thereof, nor receive the Sacrament of Penance, or else if he receive it, taketh it not truly, for the love of God (that is, for the love of virtue and cleanness, but only for dread or shame of the world, or only for fear of the pains of hell), he is not reformed to the image of God, and if he die in that state, he shall not be saved, his Faith shall not save him, for it is but a dead faith, because it lacketh love, and therefore it will not serve his turn. But they that have Faith quickened with love and charity, though it be but the least degree of charity, as are simple souls who feel not the gift of special devotion, nor have spiritual knowledge or feeling of God, as some spiritual men have, but believe in general as holy Church believeth, though they know not fully what that is (for it is not necessary that they should know so fully), but in that belief keep themselves in love and charity to their neighbour as well as they can, and eschew all deadly sin according to their best skill, and do deeds of mercy to their neighbours; all these belong to the bliss of Heaven. For thus is it written in the Apocalypse: Ye that fear God, both great and small, praise Him. By great ones are understood souls that are profiting in grace, or that are perfect in the love of God, which are reformed in spiritual feeling. By small, imperfect souls of worldly men and women, and others that have but a childish knowledge of God, and full little feeling of Him, but are brought forth in the bosom of holy Church, and nourished with the Sacraments, as children are fed with milk. All these ought to love God, and thank Him for the salvation of their souls, which proceedeth from His endless mercy and goodness. For holy Church, which is mother of all these, and beareth tender love to all her ghostly children, prayeth and asketh for them all tenderly of her Spouse, that is of Jesus, and getteth them health of soul through virtue of His Passion; and namely for them that cannot speak for themselves by spiritual prayer for their need.

Thus I find in the Gospel that the woman of Canaan asked of our Lord health for her daughter that was troubled with the fiend; and our Lord at first made dainty of the matter, because she was an alien. Nevertheless she ceased not to cry till our Lord had granted her asking, and said to her thus: O woman, great is thy faith, be it unto thee as thou wilt. In the same hour was her daughter made whole. This woman betokeneth holy Church, that asketh help of our Lord for simple ignorant souls, that are encumbered with temptations of the world, and cannot speak perfectly to God by fervour of devotion, nor by burning love in Contemplation. And though our Lord seemeth to make dainty at first, because they are, as it were, aliened from Him, nevertheless, for the great faith and desert of holy Church, He granted to her all that she will. And for these simple souls that believe stedfastly as holy Church believeth, and put themselves wholly upon the mercy of God, and submit themselves under the Sacraments and Laws of holy Church, are saved through the prayers and faith of their holy Mother the Church.

CHAPTER VIII: THAT SOULS REFORMED NEED EVER TO FIGHT AND STRIVE AGAINST THE MOTIONS OF SIN WHILE THEY LIVE HERE. AND HOW A SOUL MAY KNOW WHEN SHE ASSENTETH TO THESE MOTIONS AND WHEN NOT

THIS reforming in Faith is easily gotten, but it is not so easily held. And, therefore, that man or woman that is reformed to the likeness of God in Faith, must use much labour and diligence, if they will keep this image whole and clean, that it fall not down again through weakness of will to the image of sin. He may not be idle or careless; for the image of sin is so near fastened unto him, and so continually presseth upon him by divers stirrings of sin, that unless he be very wary, he shall very easily through consent fall again thereto. And, therefore, he needeth to be ever striving and fighting against the wicked stirring of this image of sin, and that he make no accord with them, nor have friendship with them, to be pliable to their unlawful biddings, for in so doing he beguileth himself. But verily if he strive with them, he need not be much afraid of consenting; for striving breaketh peace and false accord. It is good indeed that a man have peace with all things, save with the fiend and this image of sin, for against them ought he ever to fight in his thoughts and in his deeds, till he hath gotten the mastery, which will never be fully in this life, as long as he beareth and feeleth this image. I say not but that a soul may, through grace, have the upper hand of this image, so far that he will not follow nor assent to the inordinate motions of it, but to be clean delivered from it, so that he shall feel no suggestions nor jangling of fleshly affections or of vain thoughts at any time, that can no man come to in this life.

I trow that a soul that is reformed in feeling, by ravishing of love in contemplation of God, may be far from the sensuality and from vain imaginations, and so far drawn out and parted from the fleshly motions for a time, that she shall feel nothing but God; but such a case lasteth not always. And, therefore, I say, that every man ought to strive against this image of sin, and namely he that is reformed in faith only, who may so easily be deceived by the same. In the person of which men St Paul saith: The flesh lusteth against the spirit, and the spirit against the flesh. That is, a soul reformed to the likeness of God fighteth against the sensual motions of the image of sin, and also this image of sin fighteth against the will of the spirit.

This kind of fighting between these two several images St Paul knew and felt, when he said thus: I find a law in my members fighting against the law of my mind, and leading me captive to the law of sin. By these two laws in a soul I understand this double image: by the law of the spirit I understand the reason of the soul, when it is reformed to the image of God; by the law of the flesh I understand the sensuality, which I call the image of sin. In these two laws a soul reformed leads his life; as Paul saith in these words: With my mind I serve the law of God, but with the flesh the law of sin.

Nevertheless, that a soul reformed should not despair though she serve the law of sin by feeling of the vicious sensuality against the will of the spirit, because of the corruption of corporal nature, St Paul excuseth it, saying thus of his own person: For not that good that I would, do I, but the evil that I hate that I do; but if I do the evil that I hate, it is not I that worketh it, but sin that dwelleth in me. That is, I would feel no fleshly stirrings, but that do I not, but the sinful stirrings of my flesh I hate, and yet I feel them. Nevertheless, since it is so that I have the wicked stirrings of my flesh, and yet I feel them and oft delight in them against my will, they shall not be laid to my charge to my condemnation, as if I had done them. And why? For the corruption of this image of sin doth them, and not I.

Lo St Paul in his own person comforteth all souls that through grace are reformed in Faith, that they should not too much dread the burthen of this image with the inordinate motions thereof, if it be so that they do not willingly and deliberately yield thereto. Yet in this point, many souls that are reformed in truth, are ofttimes much tormented and troubled in vain, as thus: When they have felt fleshly motion of pride, or of envy, of covetousness or luxury, or of any other chief sin, they know not whether they consent thereto or no, and it is no great wonder; for in time of temptation frail man's thoughts are so troubled and so overlaid that he hath no clear sight nor freedom of himself, but is overtaken often with liking unwarily, and so that liking passeth perhaps a good while within him ere he will perceive it, and, therefore, falleth sometime in doubt and dread whether they sinned in time of temptation or no.

As to this point I say, as methinketh, that a soul may discern by this means whether he consent or no. If it be so that he is moved or tempted to any kind of sin, and the liking of it is so great in his fleshly feeling that it troubleth his reason, and, as it were, with mastery possesseth the affection of his soul, and yet he restraineth himself, that he performeth not the sin in deed, nay, nor would not if he might, but is rather pained to feel the liking of that sin, and fain would put it away if he could; and when that stirring is over, is glad and well repaid that he is delivered from it; by this may he gather, that were the liking never so great in his fleshly feeling, yet he consented nor sinned, not especially mortally in the business.

Nevertheless, a good and secure remedy it ere for such simple souls being in such a case, and cannot help it, that they be not too bold in themselves utterly weening that such fleshly stirrings with liking are no sins at all, for so they may fall into carelessness and a false security. Neither on the other side that they be too fearful, or foolish, as to deem them all as deadly sins, or as great venials; for neither is true, but that he hold them all as sins and wretchedness, and that he have sorrow for them, and be not too busy in judging them either deadly or venial. But if his conscience be greatly grieved, that he go speedily, and show to his Confessor in general or in special such stirrings, and, namely, every stirring that beginneth to fasten any root in the heart, and most possesseth it, for to draw it down to sin and worldly vanity. And when he hath thus confessed in general or in particular, let him assuredly believe that they be forgiven, and dispute no more about them that are passed and forgiven, whether they were mortal or venial. But let him be the more careful to carry himself better against such as shall afterwards arise. And if he do so, then may he come to have quiet in his conscience. But some are so unwise and so gross that they would feel or see, or hear the forgiveness of their sins, as clearly and palpably as they might see or feel a bodily thing; and because they cannot, therefore they fall oft into such fears and doubts of themselves, and never come to rest; and in that they are unwise, for Faith goeth before feeling.

Our Lord, when He healed a man sick of the palsy, said thus to him: Trust (my son) that thy sins are forgiven thee; that is, believe steadfastly. He said not to him, See, feel, how that thy sins are forgiven (for the forgiveness of sins is done spiritually and invisibly, through the grace of the Holy Ghost) but believe it. On the same manner, every one that desireth to have peace of conscience, it behoveth him (having done what lay in his power) to believe without spiritual feeling and forgiveness of his sins. And if at first he believe it, he shall afterward, through grace, feel it and understand it that it is so. Thus said the Apostle: Unless ye believe, ye shall not understand. Faith goeth before, and understanding cometh after, and this understanding (which I call the light of grace that cometh from God) a soul cannot have but through great cleanness, as our Lord saith: Blessed are the pure in heart, for they shall see God. Not with their fleshly eye, but their inward eye, that is, their understanding, cleaned and enlightened through grace of the Holy Ghost, to see the truth; the which cleanness a soul cannot feel, unless she have firm faith and belief going before, as the Apostle saith: By faith, purifying the heart; that is, our Lord through faith cleanseth the hearts of His chosen. It is necessary, therefore, that a soul first believe in the reforming of himself made through the Sacrament of Penance, though she see it not; and that he dispose himself fully to live righteously and virtuously, as his Faith requireth; so that afterward he may come to sight, and to the reforming in feeling.

CHAPTER IX: THAT THIS IMAGE IS BOTH FAIR AND FOUL WHILST IT IS IN THIS LIFE HERE, THOUGH IT BE REFORMED; AND OF THE DIFFERENCES OF THE SECRET FEELINGS OF THOSE THAT BE REFORMED AND THOSE THAT BE NOT

FAIR is a man's soul, and foul is a man's soul. Fair, inasmuch as it is reformed in faith to the likeness of God. But foul, inasmuch as it is mingled with sensual feelings and inordinate motions of this image of sin. Foul it is without, like a beast; fair within, like an Angel. Foul in the feeling of sensuality, fair in truth of reason. Foul for the fleshly appetites, fair for the good will. Thus is a chosen soul both fair and foul, according to the saying of Holy Writ: I am black, but beautiful, O daughters of Jerusalem, as the tents of Kedar, and as the curtains of Solomon. That is, O ye Angels of Heaven, that are daughters of the high Jerusalem, wonder not at me, nor despise me for my black shadow. For though I be black without, because of my fleshly nature, as the tents of Kedar, yet am I full fair within, as the Curtains of Solomon, in that I am reformed to the image of God. By Kedar is understood a reprobate soul, which is the tent of the devil. By Solomon is understood our Lord Jesus, for He is peace, or peaceable. By the curtain of Solomon is understood a blessed Angel, in whom our Lord dwelleth, and is hid in him.

Now may a chosen soul with humble trust in God, and joy of heart, say thus: Though I be black, because of my body of sin, like a reprobate soul, that is one of the tabernacles of the fiend; yet within am I fair (through faith and good will) like an Angel of Heaven. For so saith he in another place: Look not upon me, because that I am black, for that the sun hath altered my colour. The sun maketh a skin swarth only without and not within; and it betokeneth this fleshly life. Therefore thus saith the chosen soul: Rebuke me not because I am swarth, for the swartness I have is all without, by the touching and carrying about me this image of sin; but it is nothing within. And, therefore, soothly though it be so that a chosen soul, reformed in faith, dwell in this body of sin, and feel the same fleshly stirrings, and use the same bodily works, as doth a tabernacle of Kedar so far forth that in man's judgement there be no difference betwixt the one and the other, yet within in their souls, and in the sight of God there is a full great difference. But to know this, which is the one, and which is the other, is only kept to God; for it passeth man's judgement and man's feeling. And, therefore, we ought not to judge any man evil, for that thing that may be used both evil and well.

A soul that is not reformed is so fully taken up with the love of the world, and so much over laid with the liking of his flesh in all his sensuality, that he chooseth it as a full rest of his heart, and in the secret desires thereof nothing else would he have, but only that he might ever be sure thereof; he feeleth within him no liquor of grace, moving him to loathe his fleshly life, nor to desire Heaven or bliss. And, therefore, we may say that he beareth not this image of sin, but is borne of it; like a man that is sick and so weak that he cannot bear himself, and, therefore, is laid on a bed, and borne in a litter. Right so, such a sinful soul is so weak and impotent, for lack of grace, that he can neither move hand nor foot to do any good deed, nor to resist (by displeasing of will) the least motion of sin, when it cometh, but falls down thereto, just like a beast upon carrion. But a soul that is reformed, though he use his fleshly senses and feel fleshly stirrings, yet he loatheth them in his heart, for he would not for any good rest in them fully, but fleeth any such rest in them, as the biting of an adder, and had rather have his rest and the love of his heart in God, if he could; and sometimes actually aspireth thereto, and often grudgeth at the fleeing of the pleasures of this life, for love of the life everlasting. This soul is not borne by this image of sin, like a sick man, though he feel it; but he beareth it, for through grace he is made mighty and strong to suffer and bear his body, with all the evil stirrings of it, without hurting or defiling himself, inasmuch as he loveth them not, nor followeth them, nor consenteth to deadly sins, as another doth.

This was bodily fulfilled in the gospel by a man sick of the palsy, who was so feeble that he could not go, and therefore was laid and borne in a litter, and brought to our Lord; and then he saw him in that misery, of His goodness He said to him: Arise, and take up thy bed, and go home to thy house; and so he did, and was whole. And soothly, right as this man bare upon his back, when he was made whole, the bed that before bare him; right so it may be said in the spiritual sense, that a soul, reformed in faith, heareth this image of sin, which bare him before. And therefore be not too much adread of thy blackness that thou hast by bearing of this image of sin; but only for the shame of the discomfort that thou hast from the beholding of it, and also for the upbraiding that thou feelest in thy heart of thy ghostly enemies, when they say to thee thus: Where is they Lord Jesus? What seekest thou? Where is the fairness that thou speakest of? What feelest thou else but blindness of sin? Where is that image of God, that thou sayest is reformed in thee? Comfort thyself, and be faithful stiffly, as I said before, and if thou do so, thou shalt, by this faith, destroy all the temptations of thy enemies. Thus saith St Paul: Take unto you the buckler of faith, with which thou shalt be able to quench all the burning darts of the enemy.

CHAPTER X: OF THREE SORTS OF MEN, WHEREOF SOME BE NOT REFORMED, AND SOME BE REFORMED ONLY IN FAITH, AND SOME BOTH IN FAITH AND FEELING

BY that which I have said, thou mayest perceive, that according to the divers parts of the soul are divers states of men. Some are reformed to the likeness of God, and some are not; and some are reformed only in faith, and some both in faith and feeling. For thou must understand that a soul hath two parts. The one is called sensuality, and that is fleshly feeling by the five outward senses, which is common to man with beasts; of the which sensuality, when it is unskilfully and inordinately ruled, is made up the image of sin. That is, when it is not ruled after reason, for then is the sensuality sin. The other part is called reason; and that is parted also into two, into the superior and inferior part. The superior part is likened to a man, for it should be master and sovereign, and that is properly the image of God, for by that only the soul knoweth God, and loveth Him. And the inferior is likened to a woman, for it should be obedient to the other part of reason, as woman is subject to man. And this consisteth in the knowing and ruling of earthly things, for to use them discreetly according as we have need of them, and to refuse them when we have no need of them, and to have ever with it an eye upwards towards the superior part of reason with dread and reverence, to follow and be guided by it.

Now may I say, that a soul that liveth after the likings and lusts of his flesh, is, as it were, a brute beast; and neither hath knowledge of God nor desire of virtues, nor of good living, but is all blinded in pride, fretted with envy, overlaid with covetousness, defiled with lechery, and other great sins; is not reformed to the likeness of God; for it lieth and resteth fully in the image of sin, that is, in sensuality. Another soul, that feareth God, and resisteth deadly stirrings of the sensual part, and followeth them not but liveth according to reason in ruling and ordering of worldly things, and setteth his intent and his will for to please God by his outward works, is reformed to the likeness of God in faith; and though he feel the same stirrings of sin as the other doth, they shall not disease him, for he resteth not in them as the other doth. But another soul, that through grace fleeth all deadly stirrings of sensuality, and all venials also, so far forth that he feeleth them not, keeping under the very first risings, is reformed in feeling; for he followeth and is led by the superior part of reason, and this he doth by the beholding of God and spiritual things, as I shall tell thee afterwards.

CHAPTER XI: HOW MEN THAT ABIDE AND LIVE IN SIN, MISSHAPE THEMSELVES INTO THE LIKENESS OF DIVERS BEASTS, AND THEY BE CALLED THE LOVERS OF THE WORLD

A WRETCHED man is he then that knoweth not the worthiness of his soul, nor will know it, how it is the most worthy creature that ever God made, except an angel, to whom yet it is like; high above all others, the which nothing can satisfy as its full rest, but only God. And therefore should he not love nor like anything, but Him only, nor covet nor seek anything, but how he may be reformed to His image; for he knoweth not this, therefore seeketh he and coveteth his rest and his liking outwardly in bodily creatures that are worse than himself. Unnaturally doth he, and unreasonably, that leaveth the sovereign Good and everlasting Life (which is God) unsought and unloved, unknown and unworshipped, and chooseth his rest and his bliss in the fading delight of an earthly thing. And yet thus do all the lovers of this world, that have their joy and their bliss in this wretched life. Some have it in pride and vain glory of themselves, that when they have lost the fear of God they travail and study night and day how they may come to the worship and praise of the world, and care not by what means they come thereto, and surpass all other men, either in learning or any other skill, in name or in fame, in riches or in respect, in sovereignty and mastership. Some men have their rest in riches, and in outrageous getting of worldly goods, and set their hearts so fully to get them, that they seek nothing else but how they may come thereto. Some have their liking in fleshly lusts of gluttony and lechery, and other bodily uncleanness, and some in one thing, and some in another.

And thus wretchedly these that do thus, misshape themselves from the worthiness of a man, and turn themselves into the likeness of divers beasts. A proud man is turned into a lion, for pride; for he would be feared and worshipped by all, and that none should withstand the fulfilling of his fleshly will, neither in word nor deed. And if any one contradict his proud will, he becometh angry and wroth, and would revenge himself on him, as a lion wreaketh himself on a little beast. He that doth this is not a man, for he doth unnaturally and unreasonably against the kind of a man, and so is turned and transformed into a lion.

Envious and angry men are turned into hounds, through wrath and envy, that barketh against his neighbour, and biteth him by wicked and malicious words, and with wrongful deeds grieveth them that have not trespassed against him, harming them both in body and soul, contrary to God's bidding.

Some men are misshapen into asses, that are slow to the service of God, and evil willed to do any good deed to their neighbour. They are ready enough to run for worldly profit, and for earthly honour or for pleasing of earthly man. But for procuring reward in heaven, for helping of their own souls, or for the worship of God, they are soon weary, they have no list thereto; and if they must go about any such thing, they go but slowly and with an unwilling mind.

Some are turned into swine, for they are so blind in their understandings and so brutish in their manners that they have no fear of God, but follow only the lusts and likings of the flesh, and have no regard to the virtues and honesty beseeming the noble nature of man, nor to order themselves according to the rules of right reason, nor to refrain the unreasonable motions of sensual nature, but as soon as a fleshly or sensual motion of sin riseth within them, they are ready to fall down thereto, and follow it as swine.

Some men are turned into wolves, that live by ravening; as bad covetous men do that, through violence or might, rob or deceive their neighbours of their worldly goods; and some are turned into foxes, as false and deceiving people that live in treachery and guile.

All these and many more, that live not in the fear of God, but break His commandments, transform themselves from the likeness of God, and make themselves like beasts, yea and worse than beasts, for they are like to the fiend of hell. And therefore verily these men that live thus, if they be not reformed when the hour of death cometh and their souls part from their bodies then shall their eyes be opened, which are now blinded with sin, and then shall they find and feel the torment of their wretchedness that they lived in here. And, forasmuch as the image of God was not reformed through the Sacrament of Penance in them neither in faith nor feeling here in this life, they shall be cast out from the blessed face of our Creator as cursed, and shall be condemned with the devil into the depth of hell, there to remain for ever. Thus saith St John in the Apocalypse: The fearful and unbelievers, the cursed, murderers, fornicators, sorcerers, idolaters, and all that love and make a lie, their portion shall be in the pit that burns with fire and brimstone. If the lovers of this world would often think of this, how all this world shall pass away, and draw to an end, and how that all wicked love shall be most severely punished, they would in a short time loathe all worldly lusts which they now take most delight in, and would lift up their hearts to love God, and would carefully seek and labour how they might be reformed to His likeness ere they pass hence.

CHAPTER XII

SECTION I: HOW LOVERS OF THIS WORLD IN DIVERS WAYS DISENABLE THEMSELVES FROM BECOMING REFORMED IN THEIR SOULS

BUT some now will say thus: I would fain love God, and be a good man, and forsake the love of the world if I might; but I have not grace for it. If I had the same grace that a good man hath, I should do as he doth; but because I have it not, I cannot, and so I need seek to do no more, but am excused.

Unto these men I answer thus: True it is as they say, that they have no grace, and therefore they lie still in their sin, and cannot rise out. But that availeth them not before God, for it is their own fault. They disenable themselves in divers ways, so that the light of grace cannot shine into them, nor rest in their hearts. For some are so froward that they will not have grace, nor be good men at all; for that they know well, if they should turn good men, they must part with the great liking and lust of this world, which they have in earthly things; but that they will not do, for they think they are so sweet that they will not part with them. And they must also do works of penance, as fasting, watching, praying and many other good works, in chastising of their flesh and in withdrawing of their fleshly will, and these may they not do, for they seem so sharp and so terrible to their thinking, that they shrink and loathe to think upon them, and so they cowardly and wretchedly still dwell in their sins.

Some would seem desirous of grace, and begin to dispose themselves for it, but their will is exceedingly weak, for as soon as any stirring of sin cometh, though it be contrary to the command of God, they fall presently thereto, for they are (through former custom of often falling and assenting to sin) so as it were bound and tied to sin, that they think it impossible to withstand it; and so their imagined difficulty of being able to make such resistance maketh their will weak, and smiteth it down again.

Some also feel the stirrings of grace, as when they have bitings of conscience for their evil living, and motions to leave it, but it seems so painful and grievous to them that they will not suffer it nor abide it, but fly from it and forget it if they can, so that they run to seek comfort and contentment outwardly, at such times, in fleshly creatures, to the end that they may not feel such pangs of conscience within their souls. And moreover some men are so blind and so brutish that they think there is no other life but this; nay that there is no soul other than of a beast, and that the soul of a man dieth with the body as the soul of a beast; and therefore they say: Let us eat and drink and make merry here, for of this life we are secure, we see no other heaven.

Verily such are some wretches that say thus in their hearts though they say it not with their mouths. Of which men the Prophet saith thus: The fool hath said in his heart there is no God. Such a fool is every one that loveth or liveth in sin, and chooseth the love of the world as the rest of his soul; he saith there is no God, not with his mouth, for he will speak of Him sometimes, when the world goes well with him, as it were in reverence of Him, saying: Blessed be God. And sometimes in despite, when he is angry against God or his neighbour and sweareth by his blessed body or any of his members. But he saith in his thoughts that there is no God, and that is because he imagineth that God seeth not his sin, or that He will not punish it so severely as the Scripture saith; or that He will forgive him his sin though He see it; or else that there shall no Christian be damned, do he never so ill. Or else, if he fasts the fasts of our Lady, or say every day so many prayers, or hear every day two or three Masses, or do some bodily work, as it were for the honour of God, he thinketh he shall never go to hell, do he never so much sin, and continue in it. This man saith in his heart that there is no God, but is unwise, as the Prophet saith, for he shall one day find and feel in torments that He is a God whom he forgot and set at nought; but set by the wealth of the world, as the Prophet saith: Pain only will give understanding. For he that knoweth not this here, nor will know it, shall know it well when he is in torments.

SECTION II: A LITTLE COUNSEL HOW LOVERS OF THIS WORLD SHOULD DO, IF THEY WILL BE REFORMED IN THEIR SOULS BEFORE THEIR DEPARTURE HENCE

THESE men, though they know well that they are out of grace, and in deadly sin, they have no care nor sorrow nor thought therefore, but give themselves to sensual mirth and worldly solace as much as they can. And the farther they be from grace the more mirth they make, and perchance some of them hold themselves well apaid that they have no grace, that they may as it were the more fully and freely follow the liking of fleshly lusts as though God were asleep and did not see them. And this is one of the greatest faults that can be.

And thus, by their own perverseness, they stop the light of grace from their own soul, that it may not rest therein. The which grace, for its part, is most willing and ready to shine to all creatures, and enter into the souls of men, that will but be willing to receive it, even as the sun shineth upon all creatures bodily, where it is not hindered. Thus saith St John in the Gospel: The light shineth in darkness, and the darkness comprehendeth it not. That is, these blind hearts receive not the gracious light, nor have the benefit of it, but even as a blind man is becompassed with the light of the sun when he standeth in it, and yet seeth it not, nor receiveth any benefit of it, as for going, or walking, or working by it. Even so, spiritually, a soul blinded with deadly sin is all encompassed with this spiritual light, and yet he is never the better, for he is blinded, and will not see nor know his blindness, and this is one of the greatest impediments of grace, that a man so wretched will not, by reason of his pride, be aknown of his blindness; or else, if he know it, careth not for it, but maketh merry, as if he were very secure and safe.

Therefore, unto all these men that are thus blinded and bound with the love of this world, and are fallen from the natural fairness of man, and are become misshapen, I say and counsel that they would think on their souls, and dispose themselves for grace as much as they can; which they may do on this wise, if they will, when they find themselves out of a state of grace, and overlaid with deadly sin, let them first think with themselves what a miserable and dangerous thing it is to be out of the state of grace and separated from God; for there is nothing that holdeth them from falling into the pit of hell presently, save the bare single thread of this bodily life, whereby they hang; and what may more easily be broken in two than a single thread? For, were the breath stopped in their body (and that may easily happen) their soul would presently pass out, and would instantly be in hell, there to remain everlastingly. And if they would but thus think with themselves for some time, they would shake and tremble at the righteous judgements of God and at His severe punishing of sins, and they would begin to grieve and sorrow for their sins, and for their want of God's grace and favour, and then would they cry and pray that they might have grace, and if they did thus, then would grace enter in and put out darkness and hardness of heart and weakness of their will, and give them might and strength to forsake the false love of this world, so far at least as it is deadly sin; for there is no soul so far from God through wilfulness of deadly sin (I except none that liveth in this body of sin) that may not, through grace, become righteous, and be restored to cleanness of living, if he will but bow and submit his will to God with humility, for to amend his life, and heartily ask grace and forgiveness of Him, and excuse our Lord and wholly accuse himself.

For holy Writ saith: I will not, saith the Lord, the death of a sinner, but rather that he be converted and live, for our Lord's will is that the most froward man that liveth, and who through sin is misshapen in soul, if he will but change his will and ask grace, may be reformed to His likeness.

PART II

CHAPTER I: OF REFORMING IN FAITH AND FEELING ALSO: THAT THIS REFORMING CANNOT BE SUDDENLY GOTTEN, BUT IN LENGTH OF TIME, BY GRACE, AND MUCH SPIRITUAL AND CORPORAL INDUSTRY

THE reforming in Faith, which I have before treated of, may easily be gotten. But after this cometh reforming in Faith and Feeling, which will not easily be gotten, but by much pains and industry. For reforming in Faith is common to all chosen souls, though they be in the lowest degree of charity. But reforming in Feeling is only in those souls that are coming to the state of perfection, and that cannot be attained unto suddenly, but after great plenty of grace, and much and long spiritual exercising, and thereby shall a man attain thereto, and that will be after that he is first healed of his spiritual sickness, and after that all bitter passions and fleshly lusts and other old feelings are burnt out of the heart by the fire of desire: and new gracious feelings are brought in with burning love and spiritual light. Then doth the soul draw very near to perfection, and to reforming in feeling.

And here it is no otherwise then, as when a man through bodily sickness is brought near to death, though he receive a medicine, by the which he is restored, and is freed from the danger of death, yet cannot he, therefore, presently rise up, and go to work as a sound man may; for the feebleness of his body keeps him down, so that he must rest, and follow the use of medicines, and use a good diet, by measure, according to the advice of a physician, till he hath fully recovered his health. Right so in this spiritual business, he who through deadly sin is brought to a spiritual death, though through the medicine of the Sacrament of Penance he be restored to life, so that he shall not be damned, nevertheless he is not presently whole, and cured of all his passions and of all his fleshly desires, nor is apt for contemplation; but he must abide a great while, and take good heed to himself and order himself so, that he may recover perfect health of soul; for he shall linger a great while, ere he be fully whole. Yet if he take medicines, by the counsel of a good spiritual Physician, and use them in time with measure and discretion, he shall much the sooner be restored to his spiritual strength, and come to reforming in feeling. For reforming in Faith is the lowest state of all chosen souls, for beneath that they cannot well be.

But reforming in feeling is the highest state in this life that the soul can come to. But from the lowest to the highest a soul cannot suddenly start, no more than a man that would climb upon a ladder that is high, and setteth his foot on the lowest stave, can at the next step get up to the highest, but must go by degrees from one to another till he come to the highest.

Even so it is spiritually, no man becometh suddenly supreme or high in grace, but through long exercise and cunning working of the soul may he come thereto, namely when He (in whom all grace lieth) helpeth and teacheth a wretched soul, for without His special help and inward teaching can no soul arrive thereto.

CHAPTER II

SECTION I: THE CAUSES WHY SO FEW SOULS IN COMPARISON OF THE MULTITUDE OF OTHERS, COME TO THIS REFORMING THAT IS BOTH IN FAITH AND FEELING

BUT now thou wilt say, Since our Lord is so courteous of His goodness, and so free of His gracious gifts, it is a wonder that so few souls (as it seems) in comparison of the multitude of others come to this reforming in feeling. It would seem that either He is unwilling, but that is not so; or that He hath no regard of His creatures, who by receiving of Faith are become His servants.

Unto this I answer that one occasion is this: Many that are reformed in Faith, set not their hearts to profit in grace, nor to seek a higher estate of good living, through much industry in praying and thinking, and other bodily and spiritual exercises; but think it enough for them to keep themselves from deadly sins, and to stand still in the plight they are in. For they say it is enough for them to be saved, and have the least degree in Heaven, they will covet no more.

Thus perchance, do some souls, who are in the state of grace, and lead an active life in the world, say or think; and it is no wonder, for they are so busied with worldly things that are needful to be done that they cannot fully set their hearts to profit in spiritual exercises. But nevertheless, such proceeding is perilous to them, for they fall daily, and are now up, and now down, and cannot come to the stability of good living, yet are they somewhat excusable, by reason of their condition of life. But other men and women who are free from worldly businesses if they will, and may have their needful sustenance without much solicitude about it, especially religious men and women, who have bound themselves by entering into religion to the state of perfection, and other men also in secular estate that have good abilities and understanding, and may (if they will dispose themselves) come to much grace; these men are more to blame. These persons, I say, are more to blame, for they stand still, as idle, and will not profit in grace, nor in further seeking to come to the love and knowledge of God.

For verily it is perilous for a soul to be reformed only in Faith, and will not seek to make any further progress, nor give himself diligently to spiritual exercises, for so he may easily lose that he hath, and fall again into deadly sin. For a soul cannot stand still always in one state, for it is either profiting in grace, or decaying through sin. For it fareth with him, as it doth with a man that were drawn out of a pit, and when he is up, would go no further than the pit's brink, surely he were a very fool, for a little puff of wind, or an unwary moving of himself, might soon cast him down again, and that worse than he was before. But if he fly as far as he can from the brink and go forward, on further ground, then, though there come a great storm, he is the more secure from falling into the pit. Right so is it in this spiritual business; he that is drawn out of the pit of sin through reforming of Faith, and when he is out of deadly sin thinketh himself secure enough, and therefore will not profit, but remaineth still at the pit's brink, as near as he may, he is not wise; for upon the least temptation of the enemy, or of his flesh, he falleth into sin again. But if he flee from the pit, that is, if he set his heart fully to come to more grace, and to use his best industry to come thereto, and give himself heartily to prayer, meditating and other good works, though great temptations rise against him, he falleth not easily to deadly sin again.

And verily it is a wonder to me, that seeing grace is so good and so profitable, why a man, when he hath but a little thereof, yea so little that he can scarce have less, should say: Ho, I will have no more of this, for I have enough. When yet I see a worldly man, though he have of worldly goods much more than he needeth, yet will he never say: Ho, I have enough, I will have no more of this; but will covet more and more, and bestir all his wits and might, and will never set a stint to his covetousness to get more. Much more, then, should a chosen soul covet spiritual good, which is everlasting, and which maketh a soul blessed, and never should cease from coveting, if he did well, to get what he might get. For he that most coveteth, most shall have; and surely if he do thus, he shall profit and grow in grace greatly.

Another cause of such fewness of souls reformed in feeling is this: Some men that are reformed in Faith, in the beginning of their turning to God, set themselves in a certain manner of working, whether it be spiritual or corporal, and think ever to hold on in that manner of working, and not to change it for any other that cometh through grace, though it were better, imagining the first course to be best for them to hold on in, and therefore they rest therein, and through custom so bind themselves thereto that when they have fulfilled it they find themselves wonderfully well satisfied, for they imagine they have done a great good thing therein for God. And if it chance that they be at any time hindered from their said custom, though it be by a just occasion, they are sad and troubled in conscience, as if they had done a great deadly sin.

These men hinder themselves somewhat from feeling of more grace, for they set their perfection in a corporal work, and so they make an end in the midst of the way, where no end is. For those corporal or sensible customs, which men use in their beginnings, are good, but they are but means and ways to lead a soul forward to perfection.

And therefore he that setteth his perfection in any bodily or spiritual exercise, which he feeleth in the beginning of his turning to God, and will seek no further, but ever rest therein, he hindereth himself greatly. For it is but a silly way of trading, wherein an apprentice is ever in the same degree of skill, and can do as much in it on the first day as he can thirty years after. Or else, if the trade be good and subtle, he is but of a dull wit, or an evil will that profiteth not therein.

Now it is certain, that of all crafts the service of God is most sovereign and most subtle, and the highest and hardest to come to perfection in it, and also the most profitable and gainful to them that faithfully prosecute it; and therefore it seemeth that the apprentices to it that are ever alike in learning are either dull witted or evil willed.

I do not reprove those customs that men use in their beginnings, whether they be corporal or spiritual, but say that they be full good and profitable for them to use. But I would that they should hold them only as a way and an entry towards spiritual feeling, and that they use them as convenient means till better come; and that while they use them they covet after better. And then if better come that are more spiritual, and more drawing in of the thoughts from fleshliness and sensuality, and vain imaginations, if that same better thing should be hindered by cleaving still to their former customs, that then they leave such their custom (when it may be left without scandal or harm to others) and follow that which they feel. But if neither hinder the other, that then they use both if they may. I mean not of leaving customs necessary through bond of law, or of rule, or of penance, but of others voluntarily undertaken. Thus saith the Prophet in the Psalms: Surely the lawgiver will give His blessing, they shall go from strength to strength, and the God of Gods shall be seen in Sion. That is, our Saviour will give His grace to chosen souls, calling them from sin and making them righteous through good works to His likeness; through which grace they shall profit and grow from virtue to virtue till they come to Sion, that is, till they come to contemplation in which they shall see the God of gods, that is they shall see well that there is but one God.

SECTION II: HOW THAT WITHOUT GREAT CORPORAL AND SPIRITUAL INDUSTRY, AND WITHOUT MUCH GRACE AND HUMILITY, SOULS CANNOT COME TO REFORMING IN FEELING NOR KEEP THEMSELVES THEREIN AFTER THEY COME THERETO

BUT now thou wilt say, since it is so, that reforming in Faith only is so low, and so perilous to rest in, for fear of falling again; and reforming in Feeling is so high, and so secure for them that can arrive thereto, therefore covetest thou to know what kind of exercises and industries were most convenient to be used for it, by the which thou mayest profit and come thereto; or whether there be any one certain exercise or special work by which a man may come to that grace and that reforming in feeling.

To this I answer thus: Thou knowest well that what man or woman that will dispose himself to come to cleanness of heart and to feeling of grace, it behoveth him to use much industry and great striving both in will and in deeds continually against the wicked stirrings of all chief sins. Not only against pride or envy, but against all other, with all the kinds that come out of them, as I have said before in the First Book. For why? Passions and fleshly desires hinder the cleanness of heart and peace of conscience. And it behoveth him also to labour to get all virtues, not only chastity and temperance, but also patience and mildness, charity and humility, and all the other. And this cannot be done by one manner of work, but by divers works, according to the divers and sundry dispositions of men, as now praying, now meditating, now working some good works, now proving and exercising themselves in divers ways, in hunger, in thirst, in cold, in suffering of shame and despite, if need be, and bodily pains and labours, for the love of virtue and justice. This thou knowest full well, for this thou readest in every book that treateth of good life; thus saith every man that would stir up men's souls to the love of God. And so it appeareth that there is no one special exercise, no certain work by which only a soul can come to that grace, but principally through the grace of our Lord

Jesus, and by many and great deeds, in all that he is able to do, and yet all is little enough.

And one reason why there must be such painstaking is this: That since our Lord Jesus Himself is the special master and teacher of this art, and the special Physician of spiritual sicknesses; for without Him all is nought; it is therefore reasonable, that as He teacheth and stirreth, so a man should follow and work. But he is a simple master that cannot teach his scholar whilst he is learning but only one lesson, and he is an unskilful physician, that by one medicine would heal all sores. Therefore our Lord Jesus, that is so wise and so good, to show His wisdom and goodness teacheth divers lessons to His scholars, after that they profit in their learning, and giveth to divers souls divers and several medicines according to the nature of their sickness.

Another reason also is this: If there were one certain work by which a soul might come to the perfect love of God, then might a man fancy that he might come thereto by his own endeavours, and through his own travail only; as a merchant cometh to his riches only by his own industry and travail. But it is not so in this spiritual business, concerning the love of God, for he that will serve God wisely and come to the perfect love of God, he will covet to have none other reward but Him only. But then for to have him may no creature deserve by his own travail or industry; for though a man could labour both corporally and spiritually as much as could all the creatures that ever have been, yet could he not, for all that, only by his own working deserve to have God for his reward; for He is the sovereign bliss and endless goodness, and surpasseth without comparison all men's deserts; and therefore He cannot be gotten by any man's special working, as a temporal reward may, for He is free and giveth to whom He will, and when He will, neither for this, nor for that, nor in this time, nor after that time. For though a soul work all that he can and may all his lifetime, yet shall he never have the perfect love of Jesus till our Lord will freely give it.

Nevertheless, on the other side, I say that God useth not to give such grace unless a man do work and travail all that he can and may; yea, till it seem to him that he can work no more, or else be in full will and desire to do more if he could. And so it seemeth, that neither grace only, without the full working of the soul so far as it can, nor the man's working alone, without grace, bringeth the soul to the reforming in feeling (the which reforming consisteth in perfect love and charity). But that both joined together, that is grace joined to working, bringeth into a soul the blessed feeling of perfect love. The which grace cannot rest fully, but only on humble souls that be full of the fear of God.

Therefore I may affirm that he that hath not humility, nor doth use his industry and labour, cannot come to this reforming in feeling. And he hath not full humility, that understandeth and perceiveth not himself truly as he is. As thus: He that doth all the good deeds that he can, as fasting, watching, wearing hair-cloth, and all other sufferings of bodily penance, or doth all the outward works of mercy to his neighbour, or else internal works, as praying, weeping, sighing, meditating, if he always rest in them, and lean so much on them, and so greatly regardeth them in his own sight and esteem that he presumeth on his own deserts, and thinketh himself ever rich and good, holy and virtuous, verily as long as he feeleth himself thus, he is not humble enough. No; though he say or think that all that he doth is of God's gift, and not of himself, he is not yet humble enough; for he doth not as yet make himself naked of all his good deeds, nor truly poor in spirit, nor feels himself to be nothing, as indeed he is. And verily, till a soul through grace is come sensibly to annihilate herself and strip herself of all the good deeds that she doth, through the sight and beholding of the truth of Jesus, she is not perfectly humble; for what is humility but truth? Verily nothing else. And therefore he that through grace can see Jesus, how that He doth all, and himself doth just nothing, but suffereth Jesus to work in him what He pleaseth, he is humble. But this is very hard, and as it were impossible, and unreasonable (to a man that worketh all by human reason, and seeth no further) for to do many good deeds, and then to attribute all to Jesus and set himself at nought. But whoso can have a spiritual sight of the truth, he shall think it full true and full reasonable to do so. And verily he that hath this sight shall do never the less, but shall be stirred up to travail corporally and spiritually, much the more, and with a better will. And this may be one cause why some men peradventure labour and travail, and pine their wretched bodies with outrageous penance all their lifetime, and are ever saying prayers and psalms and many beads, and yet cannot come to the spiritual feeling of the love of God, as it seems some do in short time, with less pains, for they have not that humility I spake of.

Also on the other side I say: He that useth not his industry, but thinketh thus with himself, to what end should I take pains? Why should I pray, or meditate, or watch, or fast, or do any other bodily penance to attain to such grace, seeing it cannot be gotten or had but only by the free gift of Jesus? Therefore I will continue in my sensuality as I am, and do even nothing of any such corporal or spiritual works; but expect till He give it, for if He be pleased to give it, He asketh no working of me, how much soever or how little I do, I shall have it, and if He be pleased not to give it, labour I never so hard, I shall get it never the sooner. He that saith thus shall never come to this reforming, for he draweth himself wilfully to idleness of the flesh, and disenableth himself for the receiving of the gift of grace, inasmuch as he layeth aside and putteth from him both inward working, which consisteth in a lasting desire and longing after Jesus, and outward working, by exercising his body in outward deeds, so that he shall never receive the said grace.

Therefore I say that he that hath not true humility, nor is very serious and diligent, either only in internal exercises and continual desire towards God by prayer, and devout affections and thoughts of Him, or else both inward and outward, he cannot come to this spiritual forming of His image.

CHAPTER III: AN ENTRY OR GOOD BEGINNING OF A SPIRITUAL JOURNEY, SHOWING HOW A SOUL SHOULD BEHAVE HERSELF IN INTENDING AND WORKING THAT WILL COME TO THIS REFORMING, BY EXAMPLE OF A PILGRIM GOING TO JERUSALEM

NEVERTHELESS, for that thou covetest to know some manner of working by which thou mayest the sooner attain to this reforming, I shall show thee, as well as I can, the shortest and readiest help that I know in this working. And how that may be I shall tell thee by an example of a good pilgrim in this wise. There was a man that would go to Jerusalem and because he knew not the way he came to another man, who he believed knew the way thither better, and asked him whether he might come to that city, who answered that he could not come thither without great pains and travail, for the way is long and perilous, and full of great thieves and robbers and many other hindrances there be that befall a man in his going, and also there be many several ways as it seemeth leading thitherward. And many men travelling thitherward are oftentimes killed or robbed, and so may not come to that place which they desire. Nevertheless, there is one way, the which whosoever taketh and holdeth to it, I will undertake (saith he) he shall come to that city of Jerusalem, and shall never lose his life, nor be slain, nor die by default, though he should oft be robbed and well beaten, and suffer much pain in the going, yet his life shall be safe. Then said the pilgrim, so I may have my life saved, and come to the place that I covet, I care not what mischief I suffer in going. And therefore, tell and advise me what you think necessary, and I promise you on a certainty that I will follow your counsel. That other man answered and said thus: Lo, I set thee in the right way; this is the way, and see that thou bear in mind that which I tell thee. Whatsoever thou seest, hearest, or feelest, that would stay or hinder thee in the way, stick not at it, willingly consent not to it, abide not with it, behold it not, like it not, fear it not, but still go forward holding on thy way, and ever think and say with thyself that thou fain wouldst be at Jerusalem for that thou covetest and that thou desirest; and nought else but that, and if men rob thee and spoil thee, beat thee, scorn thee, despise thee, do not thou strive against such their doings, if thou mean to have thy life safe, but be content with the harm thou receivest, and hold on thy way, as if all that were nothing, lest thou receive more harm. Also if men would seek to stay thee by telling tales, and feed thee with lies or conceits to draw thee to merriment, or to forsake or prolong thy pilgrimage, give them a deaf ear and answer them not again, and say naught else but that thou wouldst fain be at Jerusalem. And if men proffer thee gifts, and would make thee rich with worldly goods, listen not to them, but think ever on Jerusalem. And if thou wilt hold this course and do that which I have said, I will undertake for thy life, that thou shalt not be slain, but that thou shalt come to that place that thou desirest.

Now to apply this spiritually to our purpose: Jerusalem is, as much as to say, a sight of peace; and betokeneth contemplation in perfect love of God; for contemplation is nothing else but a sight of God, which is very peace. Then if thou covet to come to this blessed sight of very peace, and be a true pilgrim towards Jerusalem, though it be so that I was never there, nevertheless, as far forth as I can, I shall set thee in the way towards it.

The beginning of the high way, in which thou shalt go, is reforming in Faith, grounded humbly on the faith and on the laws of holy Church as I have said before, for trust assuredly, though you have sinned heretofore, if you be now reformed by the Sacrament of Penance, after the law of holy Church, that thou art in the right way. Now then, since thou art in the safe way, if thou wilt speed in thy going and make a good journey, it behoveth thee to hold these two things often in thy mind: humility and Love; and often say to thyself, I am nothing, I have nothing, I covet nothing, but one. Thou shalt have the meaning of these words in thine intent, and in the habit of thy soul perpetually, though thou have them not always expressly in thy thought (for that is not necessary). Humility saith, I am nothing, I have nothing; Love saith, I covet nothing, but one, and that is Jesus. These two stirrings well fastened, with the minding of Jesus, make good music in the harp of the soul, when they be cunningly struck upon with the finger of reason; for the lower thou smitest upon the one, the higher soundeth the other. The less thou feelest that thou art, or that thou hast of thyself, through Humility, the more thou covetest for to have of Jesus, through desire of love. I mean not only that Humility which a soul feeleth by the sight and sense of his own sin, for frailness and wretchedness of this life, or of the wretchedness of his neighbour; for though this kind of Humility be true and wholesome, nevertheless it is boisterous and fleshly in comparison of that other, not so clean, nor soft, nor lovely. I mean that Humility which a soul feeleth through grace, in the sight and beholding of the endless being, and the wonderful goodness of Jesus, and if thou canst not see it with thy spiritual eye, yet that thou believe it; for through this sight of his being, either in full faith or in feeling, thou shalt esteem thyself not only the most wretched creature that is, but also as nothing in the substance of thy soul, though thou hadst never done any sin. And this is lovely Humility; for in respect of Jesus (who is truly all) thou art just nothing, and so must thou think that thou hast just nothing, but art as a vessel that standeth ever empty, and as if nothing were therein, as of itself; for do thou never so many good deeds outward or inward, until thou have and feel that thou hast the love of Jesus, thou hast just nothing. For with that precious liquor only may thy soul be filled, and with none other. And forasmuch as that thing alone is so precious and noble, therefore whatever else thou hast, or what thou dost, hold and esteem it as nothing as to rest in, without the sight and the love of Jesus. Cast it all behind thee, and forget it, that thou mayest have this, which is the best of all. Just as a true pilgrim, going towards Jerusalem, leaveth behind him house and land, wife and children, and maketh himself poor and bare from all things that he hath, that he may go lightly without letting. Right so, if thou wilt be a spiritual pilgrim, thou shalt strip thyself naked of all that thou hast, that are either good deeds or bad, and cast them all behind thee, that thou be so poor in thy own feeling that there be nothing of thy own working that thou wilt restingly lean on; but ever desiring more grace and love, and ever seeking the spiritual presence of Jesus. And if thou dost thus, then shalt thou resolve in thy heart fully and wholly that thou wilt be at Jerusalem, and at no other place but there; that is, thou shalt purpose in thy heart wholly and fully that thou wilt nothing have but the love of Jesus and the spiritual sight of Him in such manner as He shall please to show Himself; for to that end only art thou made and redeemed, and He it is that is thy beginning and thy end, thy joy and thy bliss. And therefore whatsoever thou hast, be thou never so rich in other deeds spiritual or corporal (unless thou have this love that I speak of, and know and feel that thou hast it) hold and esteem that thou hast right nothing. Imprint this well in the desire of thy soul, and cleave fast thereto, and it shall save thee from all perils in thy going, that thou shalt never perish, and it shall save thee from the thieves and robbers which I call unclean spirits, that though they spoil thee and beat thee by divers temptations, thy life shall ever be safe; and in brief, if thou keep it, as I have said, thou shalt escape all perils and mischiefs, and come to the city of Jerusalem in a short time.

Now then, since thou art in the way, and knowest the name of the place, and whither thou tendest, begin therefore to go thy journey. Thy setting forth is naught else but spiritual working, and bodily also, when there is need, which thou shalt use according to discretion in this wise. What work soever it is that thou shalt do (according to thy degree, and the estate thou art in), corporally or spiritually, if it help and further this gracious desire that thou hast to love Jesus, and make it more whole, more easy, and more mighty to all virtues and to all goodness, that work I hold the best, be it preaching, be it meditating, reading, or working; and as long as that work strengtheneth most thy heart and thy will to the love of Jesus, and draweth thy affections and thy thoughts farthest off from worldly vanities, it is good to use it; and if so be that through use the savour or good taste thereof groweth less, and thou thinkest of some other work that savoureth more, and thou feelest more grace in that other, take the other, and leave that. For though thy desire and the yearning of thy heart to Jesus ought ever to be unchangeable, nevertheless thy spiritual works that thou art to use, in praying or thinking, for the feeding and nourishing thy desire, may be divers, and may well be changed, after that thou feelest thyself disposed through grace severally to apply thy heart to them; for it fareth with works and this desire as it doth with sticks and a fire, for the more sticks are laid to the fire, the greater is the fire. Right so, the more several spiritual works that a man hath in his design, to keep entire this desires the mightier and more burning shall his desire be to God.

And therefore consider wisely what work thou canst best do, and which most helpeth to keep whole this desire of Jesus (if so be thou be free, and not bound by any obligation), and that do. Bind not thyself to voluntary customs unchangeably, which may hinder the liberty of thy heart to correspond or answer the motion or invitation of Jesus, if His grace at any time should specially visit thee. And I shall tell thee what customs are ever good and necessary to be kept, that is, such as consist in the getting of virtues, and in hindering or resisting of sin, such customs should never be left; for thou shouldst ever be humble, patient, sober and chaste, if thou do as thou shouldst. But the customs of other things, if they hinder a better good, are good to be laid aside, giving place to that which would be better for us. As thus, if a man have a custom to say so many beads or prayers, or to meditate of such or such a subject, for so long a time, or to watch, or kneel thus long, or any other such bodily deed, these customs are to be left sometimes when reasonable cause requireth, or when more grace cometh otherwise, or in some other exercise.

CHAPTER IV: OF CERTAIN TEMPTATIONS AND LETTINGS WHICH SOULS FEEL FROM THEIR SPIRITUAL ENEMIES, IN THEIR SPIRITUAL KNOWING AND GOING TOWARDS JERUSALEM, AND THE REMEDIES AGAINST THEM

NOW that thou art in the way, and knowest how thou shouldst go, beware of thy enemies, that will be busy to let thee if they can. For their intent is to put out of thy heart that desire, and that longing that thou hast to the love of Jesus, and to drive thee home again to the love of worldly vanities; for that nothing grieveth them so much as this desire. These enemies are principally fleshly desires, and vain fears, which rise out of thy heart, through the corruption of thy fleshly nature, and would hinder thy desire of the love of God, that they may fully and peaceably possess thy heart; these are thy nearest enemies. Also other enemies there are, as unclean spirits, which are busy with slights and wiles to deceive thee. But one remedy hast thou, which I mentioned before, and that is, that whatsoever they say, believe them not; but hold on thy way, and only desire the love of Jesus. Answer them ever on this wise: I am nothing, I have nothing, I covet nothing only the love of our Lord Jesus.

If thy enemies, by suggestions in thy soul, say unto thee that thou hast not made thy Confession aright, or that there is some old former sin hid in thy heart that thou knowest not, nor never madest thy Confession aright of it, and therefore thou must turn home again, and leave off thy desire, and go confess thyself better; believe not this saying, for it is false, for thou art rightly confessed, and so do thou surely hope and trust; and that thou art in the right way, and that thou needest no further to ransack thy soul for confession of that which is past, hold on thy way, and think only on Jerusalem.

Also, if they say that thou art not worthy to have the love of God, and therefore why shouldst thou covet that which thou wilt not be able to attain, nor art not worthy of; believe them not but go on, and say thus: Not because I am worthy, but because I am unworthy, therefore would I love God; for if I had His love, that would make me worthy; and since I was created to that end, though I should never have it, yet will I covet it, and therefore will I pray and think that I may get it. And then if thy enemies see that thou beginnest to wax bold, and well-willed to thy work, they will begin to be afraid of thee, yet will they not cease to seek to stay and hinder thee as much as they can, as long as thou art going in the ways what with affrighting and threatening thee on one side, and what with flattering and vain pleasing thee on the other side, to make thee break thy purpose and turn home again. And they will say thus: If thou hold on thus thy desire to Jesus, travailing so fervently as thou now beginnest, thou wilt fall into bodily sickness, or thou wilt craze thy head and fall into fancies or melancholy, as thou seest some do; or thou wilt fall into poverty, or bodily mischief, and none will be able to help thee, or thou wilt fall into secret temptations and illusions of the devil, that thou shalt not be able to help thyself; for it is very dangerous for any man to give himself over to the love of God, and leave all the world, and covet nothing but only the love of Him. For that many perils may fall out that a man knows nothing of, and therefore turn home again, and leave off this desire, for thou shalt never bring it to pass, and do as other worldly men do.

Thus will thy enemies say, but believe them not, but hold on thy desire, and say naught else; but that thou wouldst have Jesus, and be Jerusalem; and if they perceive that thy will is so strong, that thou wilt not give over, neither for fear of sin, nor of sickness, for fancies nor for frenzies, for doubts nor for dreads of spiritual temptations, for mischiefs nor for poverty, for life nor for death, but ever seekest and longest after one thing, and nothing else but that one thing, and turnest a deaf ear to them, as though thou heardest them not, and holdest thee on stiffly and constantly in thy course of prayer, and in thy other spiritual exercises without stinting, but yet with discretion, after the counsel and directions of thy Superior, or of thy ghostly Father, then begin they to be wroth, and to come a little nearer to thee. Then they begin to rob thee and beat thee, and do thee all the shame that they can, and that is, when they make that all the deeds that thou doest, be they never so well done, are judged by others to be evil, and turned into the worse part. And whatsoever thou wouldst do, or have done for the help or comfort of thy body or soul, it shall be letted or hindered by other men, so that thou shalt be put from thy will in everything which thou reasonably desirest. And all this they do, that thou mayest be stirred up to anger, or melancholy, or evil will against thy neighbour. But against all these diseases, and all other that thou mayest feel, use this remedy. Take Jesus into thy mind, and trouble not thyself with them, nor be angry; tarry not with them, but think on thy lesson: That thou art nothing, that thou hast nothing, that thou canst nothing lose of earthly goods, that thou covetest nothing but the love of Jesus; and hold on thy way, with thy exercises, to Jerusalem. And though thou be sometimes tarried and letted in thy way, through thy frailty, with such inconveniences as befall thy bodily life, through evil will of man, or malice of the enemy; as soon as thou canst, come again to thyself, leave off the thinking of thy inconveniences, and go on with thy exercise. Abide not long upon the thinking of those thy defects for fear of thy enemies.

And after this, when they see that thou art so well willed, that thou art not angry, nor heavy, nor wroth, nor much moved against any creature for aught that they can do or say against thee, but settest thy heart fully to suffer all that may fall, ease or unease, praise or dispraise, and that thou dost esteem or regard nothing so that thou mayest keep thy thought and thy desire whole to the love of God, then are they much abashed. But then will they set upon thee with flattery and vain pleasing, and that is when they set before thee all thy good deeds and virtues, and tell thee that all men praise thee and speak well of thy holiness, and how all men love thee and worship thee for thy holy living. Thus will thy enemies do, that thou mayest believe them, and take delight in this vain joy, and rest therein. But if thou do well thou shalt esteem all such janglings and suggestions to be false flatterings of thy enemy, that proffereth thee to drink venom tempered with honey, and therefore refuse it, and say thou wilt have none of it, but thou wouldst be at Jerusalem.

Such lettings shalt thou feel, or the like, what from thy flesh, and what from the world, and what of the fiend, more than I can rehearse. Now for as long as a man suffereth his thoughts willingly to run about the world in beholding of sundry things, he perceiveth few lettings. But as soon as he draweth all his thoughts and his yearnings to one thing only, to have it, to know it, and to love it, which is Jesus; then shall he feel many painful lettings; for whatsoever thing he feeleth which is not that which he coveteth, that same thing is a letting to him. Therefore I have set down some of them for examples in particular. And moreover in general, I shall now tell thee that whatsoever stirring thou feelest of the flesh, or of the fiend, either pleasant or painful, bitter or sweet, lovely or dreadful, gladsome or sorrowful, that would draw down thy thoughts or thy desires from the love of Jesus to worldly vanities, and would hinder or cool thy spiritual covetousness that thou hast to the love of Him, and would have thy heart to be occupied with that stirring and rest upon it, set it at naught, entertain it not willingly, tarry not therewith too long. But if it be any worldly thing that is necessary to be done, for thyself or thy neighbour, dispatch it, and quit thee soon of it, and bring it to an end that it hang not on thy heart. But if it be another thing that may be spared and is not very needful, or else concerns thee not, heed it not, jangle or dally not therewith, nor trouble or vex thyself about it, fear it not, like it not, but cast it out of thy heart speedily, and say thus: I am nothing, I have nothing, I seek nor covet nothing but the love of Jesus. Fasten thy thoughts to this desire and strengthen it, and maintain it by prayer and other spiritual exercises that thou forget it not, and it shall lead thee in the right way, and save thee from all dangers; that though thou feel them thou shalt not perish, and I hope that it shall bring thee to the perfect love of our Lord Jesus.

Nevertheless on the other side, I say also, what work or what stirring it is that may help or strengthen or nourish thy desire, and draw thy thoughts farthest from lust and the minding of the world, more entire and more burning to the love of God, whether it be praying, meditating, reading or hearing, solitariness or being in company, silence or talking, going or sitting, hold to it for the time, and exercise thyself therein as long as any savour or relish therein lasteth, if it be so that thou take therewith meat, and drink, and sleep, as a pilgrim doth, and use discretion in thy exercises, after the advice and directions of thy superior. For a pilgrim, though he be in never so great haste in his journey, yet will he eat and drink and sleep. Do thou likewise; and though it hinder and stay thee at one time, it shall further thee at another time.

CHAPTER V: OF AN EVIL DAY AND A GOOD NIGHT, AND WHAT THEY MEAN, AND HOW THE LOVE OF THE WORLD IS LIKENED TO AN EVIL DAY, AND THE LOVE OF GOD TO A GOOD NIGHT

IF thou wouldst know then what this desire is, verily it is Jesus, for He worketh this desire in thee, and giveth it thee; and He it is that desireth in thee, and He it is that is desired; He is all, and He doth all, if thou couldst see Him. Thou dost nothing, but sufferest Him to work in thy soul, and assentest to Him with great gladness of heart, that He will vouchsafe to do so in thee. Thou art nothing else but a reasonable instrument by which and in which He worketh; and therefore when thou feelest thy thoughts, through the touching of grace, taken up with the desire of Jesus, with a mighty devout will for to please Him and love Him, then think that thou hast Jesus, for He it is that thou desirest. Behold Him well, for He goeth before thee, not in bodily shape, but insensibly, by secret presence of His power. Therefore see Him spiritually if thou canst, and fasten all thy thoughts and affections to Him, and follow Him wheresoever He goeth; for He will lead thee the right way to Jerusalem, that is to the sight of peace and contemplation. Thus prayed the Prophet to the Father of Heaven, saying: Send out Thy light and Thy truth (that is Thy Son Jesus), and He shall lead me (by desire in me) to Thy holy hill and to Thy tabernacles. That is, to the feeling of perfect love and height of Contemplation.

Of this desire the Prophet Isaias speaketh thus: Memoriale tuum, &c. Lord Jesus, the remembrance of Thee is imprinted in the desire of my soul, for my soul hath desired Thee in the night, and my spirit hath coveted Thee in all its thoughts. The Prophet saith he desired God all in the night, being a space betwixt two days; for when one day is ended another day beginneth not presently, but first cometh night which parteth the days, being sometimes long and sometimes short, and then after that cometh another day. The Prophet meaneth not only of this manner of night, but he meaneth a spiritual night. Thou shalt understand that there be two days or two lights. The first is a false light, the second a true light. The false light is the love of this worlds which a man hath in himself through the corruption of nature. The true light is the perfect love of Jesus felt through grace in a man's soul. The love of this world is a false light, for it passeth away and lasteth not, and so it performeth not that which it promiseth. This light did the enemy promise to Adam when he stirred him to sin, and said thus: Your eyes shall be opened, and ye shall be as gods. And therein he said truth. For when Adam had sinned, forthwith his inner eye was shut, and spiritual light withdrawn, and his outward eye was opened, and he felt and saw a new light of fleshly liking and worldly love which he saw not before. And so saw he a new day, but this was an evil day, for this was it that Job cursed, when he said thus: Let the day perish wherein I was born. He cursed not the day running on in the year which God made, but he cursed this day which man made, that is the concupiscence and the love of this world in the which he was born, though he felt it not. That day and that light he asked of God that it might perish and last no longer. But the everlasting love of Jesus is a true day and a blessed light; for God is both love and light, and He is everlasting, as St John saith: He that loveth God dwelleth in the light. And now, what man perceiveth and seeth the love of this world to be false and failing, and therefore will forsake it and seek the love of Jesus, yet may he not for all that presently feel the love of Him, but he must abide awhile in the night, for he cannot suddenly come from that one light to that other, that is from the love of the world to perfect love of God. This night is nought else but a forbearing and a withdrawing of the thought and of the soul from earthly things by great desire and yearning for to love and see and feel Jesus and spiritual things. This is the night; for even as the night is dark, and doth hide all bodily things, and a time of ceasing from all bodily works; even so a man that setteth himself fully to think on Jesus, and to desire only the love of Him, is careful to hide his thoughts from vain beholding and perceiving, and his affections from fleshly liking and loving of all bodily creatures, whereby his thoughts may become free and not be subject, nor his affections bound or pinned to, or troubled with anything lower or worse than himself. And if he come to this pass then is it night with him, for then he is in darkness. But this is a good night and a light darkness, for it is a stopping out of the false love of this world, and it is an approaching of the true day. And verily the darker that this night is the nearer is the true day of the love of Jesus; for the more that a soul can, through longing after God, be hid from the noise and stirrings of fleshly affections and unclean thoughts, the nearer is she to feel the light of the love of Him, for it is even at her. Thus seemeth the Prophet to mean, when he saith: When I sit in darkness our Lord is my light. That is, when my soul is hid from all stirrings of sin as it were in sleep, then is our Lord my light, for then approacheth He by His grace to show me His light, nevertheless this night is sometime painful. As first, when a man is very foul, and is not used through grace to be often in this darkness, but would fain have it, and be in it, and therefore he setteth his thoughts and his desires to Godward as much as he can, he would not feel nor think but only of Him, and because he cannot easily have it, therefore it is painful for the custom and familiarity that he hath formerly had with the sins of the world, and of fleshly affections and earthly things; and his daily fleshly deeds press so upon him, and continually strike in, and through force draw down the soul to them, that he cannot well be hid from them so soon as he would. Therefore this darkness is painful to him, and especially when grace toucheth him not abundantly, instilling some extraordinary devotion into him. Nevertheless if it be so with thee, be not too sad or heavy for it, nor strive much as though thou wouldst by force drive them out of thy thoughts, for thou canst not do so; but do thou rather expect grace, suffer quietly, and force not thyself too much. But slyly (if thou canst) draw thy desire and spiritual eye to Jesus, as if thou didst not care for them. For be thou assured, when thou wouldest desire Jesus, and think only of Him, and thou art not able freely to do so, for the pressing in of such worldly thoughts, thou art certainly coming out of the false day and art entering into this darkness. But thy darkness is not restful, not quiet to thee by reason of thy uncleanness and unacquaintedness with it, and therefore use it often, and in process of time through feeling of grace it will be more easy and more restful to thee, and that is when thy soul through grace is made so free, and so able and so good and so gathered into itself that it listeth to think on just nothing, then is it in a good darkness. This nothing I mean thus: that a soul may through grace be gathered into itself freely and wholly, and not be driven against its will, nor drawn down by force for to think, or like, or love with cleaving of affection to any sin, or any earthly thing vainly, then thinketh the soul just nought, for then it thinketh of no earthly thing cleavingly. This is a rich nought, and this nought and this night is a great ease to the soul that desireth the love of Jesus, it is in ease as to the thoughts of any earthly thing, nevertheless it is full busy to think on Him.

What thing then maketh this darkness? Verily nought else but a gracious desire to have the love of Jesus, for that desire and that longing that it hath at that time to the love of God, for to see Him and have Him, driveth out of the heart all worldly vanities and fleshly affections, and gathereth the soul into itself, and busieth it only in thinking how it may come to the love of Him. And at that time she may freely and devoutedly behold Jesus, whether she would pray or meditate, and so it bringeth her to this right nothing; and verily it is not altogether dark nor nothing when it thinketh thus; for though it be dark from false light, it is not altogether dark from the true light. For Jesus, that is both love and light, is in this darkness, whether it be painful or restful. If it be painful, then is Jesus in the soul, as travelling in the desire and longing after light, but He is not yet as resting in love, nor as showering His light. And therefore it is called night and darkness, inasmuch as the soul is hid from the false light of the world, and hath not yet a full feeling of true light, but is in expecting of that blessed love of God which it desireth.

Therefore if thou wouldst know when thou art in this secure darkness, and when not, thou mayest try it thus, and seek no further. When thou feelest thy intent and thy will fully set for to desire God, and think only on Him, thou mayest, as it were, at first ask thyself in thy own thoughts whether thou covetest to have anything of this life for love of the thing itself, or for to have the using of any of thy bodily senses in any creature. And then if the eye answer then thus: I would see just nothing, and thy mouth: I would savour just nothing, and thine ear: I would hear just nothing; and thy body: I would feel just nothing; and after that, thy heart say: I would think just nothing of earthly things, nor of bodily deeds, nor would have my affections fastened fleshly to any creature but only in God and to Godwards, if I could; and when they all answer thus to thee, and do it full readily being touched by grace, then art thou entered somewhat into this darkness. For though withal thou feel and perceive within thee the presentations and profferings of vain thoughts, and pressing in of fleshly affections; nevertheless thou art in this profitable darkness, if it be so that thy thoughts be not fixed to them; for such vain imaginations that fall into the heart unadvisedly, they trouble indeed this darkness, and somewhat molest the soul because it would be hid from them, but cannot; but they do not take away the profit of this darkness, for the soul shall by this means in time come to restful darkness. And then is this darkness restful when the soul is hid for a time from the painful feeling of all such vain thoughts, and is rested only in the desire and longing after Jesus, with a spiritual beholding of Him, as it shall be said hereafter; but this lasteth whole and entire but a short time, yet though it be but for a short time, yet it is full profitable.

CHAPTER VI: HOW THAT THE DESIRE OF JESUS FELT IN THIS LIGHTSOME DARKNESS SLAYETH ALL MOTIONS OF SIN, AND ENABLETH THE SOUL TO PERCEIVE SPIRITUAL LIGHTNINGS FROM THE HEAVENLY JERUSALEM, THAT IS, JESUS

SEEING then this darkness and this night consisting only in the desire and longing after the love of Jesus with a blind thinking on Him, is so good and so restful, though it be but short, how good then, and how blessed it is to feel His love, and to be illuminated with His blessed invisible light thereby to see the truth, the which light a soul receiveth when the night passeth, and the day springeth.

This I conceive was the night that the Prophet meant when he said: My soul hath desired Thee in the night, as I have said before. It is much better to be hid in this dark night from beholding of the world, though it were painful, than to be out in false liking of this world, which seemeth so shining, and so comfortable to them that are blind in the knowledge of spiritual light; for when thou art in this darkness, thou art much nearer Jerusalem than when thou art in the midst of the false light. Therefore apply thy heart fully to the stirrings of grace, and use thy self to dwell in this darkness, and by often essaying to be acquainted therewith, and it shall soon be made restful to thee, and the true light of spiritual knowing shall spring up to thee, not all at once, but secretly by little and little, as the Prophet saith: To them that dwell in the country of the shadow of death light is sprung up. That is, light of grace springeth, and shall spring to all them that can dwell in the shadow of death; that is in this darkness which is like to death; for as death slayeth a living body and all its fleshly senses, right so the desire of the love of Jesus felt in this darkness slayeth all sins, all fleshly affections, and all unclean thoughts for the time, and then dost thou hasten to draw near to Jerusalem. Thou art not there yet, but by some small sudden lightnings that glide out of small caves from that city, shalt thou be able to see it afar off ere thou come to it, for know thou well, though that thy soul be in this restful darkness without the trouble of worldly vanities, it is not yet clothed all in light, nor turned all into the fire of love. But it perceiveth full well that there is somewhat above itself that it knoweth not, nor hath not yet, but would have it, and burningly yearneth after it, and that is nought else but the sight of Jerusalem outwardly, which is like to a city which the Prophet Ezechiel saw in his visions. He saith that he saw a city upon a hill towards the south, that to his sight when it was measured was no more in length and breadth than a reed, that is six cubits and a palm of length. But as soon as he was brought into the city, and looked about him, then he saw that it was wondrous great, for he saw many halls, and chambers both open and secret; he saw gates and porches without and within, and many more buildings than I now speak of, and it was in length and breadth many hundred cubits, that it seemed a wonder to him that this city was so long and so large within, that seemed so little to his sight when he was without.

This city betokeneth the perfect love of God set upon the hill of Contemplation, which to the sight of a soul that without the feeling of it travelleth in desire towards it seemeth somewhat, but it seemeth but a little thing, no more than a rood, that is, six cubits and a palm of length. By six cubits are understood the perfection of man's work; and by the palm, a little touch of Contemplation. He seeth well that there is such a thing that passeth the deservings of all the workings of man, like as a palm is surpassed by six cubits, but he seeth not within what it is, yet if he can come within the city of Contemplation, then seeth he much more than he saw at first.

CHAPTER VII: HOW A MAN SHALL KNOW FALSE ILLUMINATIONS THAT ARE FEIGNED BY THE ENEMY, FROM THE TRUE LIGHT OF KNOWING THAT COMETH OUT OF JESUS, AND BY WHAT TOKENS

BUT now beware of the midday fiend that feigneth light as if it came out of Jerusalem, and is not so; for the fiend seeth that our Lord Jesus showeth light to His lovers of truth; therefore for the deceiving of them that are unwise, he showeth a light that is not true under colour of a true light, and cozeneth them. Nevertheless, how a soul may know the true light when it shineth from God, and when it is feigned by the enemy shall I declare (as methinketh) by an example of the firmament.

Sometime the firmament showeth a light from the sun, which seemeth to be the sun and is not; and sometimes showeth the true sun truly. To know the one from the other is thus: the feigned sun showeth himself only betwixt two black rainy clouds; and then because the sun is near, there shineth out from the clouds a light as if it were a sun, but is not. But the true sun showeth itself when the firmament is clear, or much cleared from black clouds. Now to our purpose. Some men, as it seems, forsake the love of the world and would come to the love of God, and to the light of understanding Him, but they would not come through that darkness which I spake of before. They will not know themselves truly and humbly what they have been heretofore, or what they are yet through sin, nor how naught they are in their nature against God. They are not busy to enter into themselves, all other outward things being left and flee all wicked stirrings that rise in their hearts of Pride, Envy, Anger, or other sins through a lasting desire to Jesus in praying and meditating, in silence, and in weeping, and in other corporal and spiritual exercises as devout and holy men have done. But as soon as they have forsaken the world, as it were outwardly in appearance, or else soon after, they imagine that they are holy and able to have the spiritual understanding of the Gospel and of holy Writ, and, namely, if they can literally fulfil the commandments of God and keep themselves from corporal sins, then they imagine that they love God perfectly. And therefore they will presently preach and teach all other men, as if they had received grace of understanding in perfection of charity through special gift of the Holy Ghost. And also they are much more stirred, forasmuch as they feel sometimes much knowledge as it were suddenly given to them without great study before had, and also much fervour of love as it seemeth for to preach truth and righteousness to their neighbour. Therefore they hold it as a grace of God that visiteth them with His blessed light above other souls. Nevertheless, if they will look well about them, they shall find that this light of knowledge and that fervour which they feel cometh not from the true Sun, which is our Lord Jesus, but cometh from the midday fiend that feigneth light, and likeneth him to the Sun, and therefore shall he be known by the foresaid example.

Light of knowledge, that is feigned by the fiend to a dark soul, is showed betwixt two black rainy clouds. Whereof the upper cloud is presumption and exalting of himself, and the lower cloud is the down-putting and disdaining of his neighbour. Then whatsoever light of knowing or feeling of fervour it be that shineth to a soul with presumption and exalting of itself, and disdain of his neighbour felt at the same time, it is not the light of grace given of the Holy Ghost; although the knowledge in itself be true, but it is either from the fiend, if it come suddenly, or else from a man's own wit if it come by study, and so it may easily be known that this feigned light of knowing is not the light of the true Sun.

Therefore, they that have this knowing on this manner are full of spiritual pride, and see it not; they are so blind with this feigned light that they hold the exalting of their own heart and their disobedience to the laws of holy Church as it were perfect humility to the Gospel and to the laws of God; and imagine that the following of their own will to be freedom of spirit. And thereupon they begin to rain, like black clouds, waters of errors and heresies; for the words that they utter in preaching tend all to backbiting, and to strife and discord, reproving of States and of Persons; and yet they say that all this is charity and zeal of the truth. But it is not so; for St James the Apostle saith thus: Ubi zelus est et contentio, &c.—Where envy is and contention, there is unstableness and every evil work. And therefore that knowledge that bringeth forth such sins cometh not from the Father of lights, that is God, but is earthly, beastly and devilish. And so by these tokens, namely, pride, presumption, disobedience, indignation, backbiting and other such sins (for these follow after) may the feigned light be known from the true. For the true Sun shineth not nor breaketh forth by special visitation to give light of understanding or perfect charity to a soul, unless the firmament be first made bright and clear from clouds; that is, unless the conscience be made clean through the fire of burning desire to Jesus in this darkness which wasteth and burneth up all wicked stirrings of pride, vain-glory, wrath, envy and all other sins in the soul. As the Prophet saith: Ignis ante ipsum procedet, &c.—A fire shall go before him; that is, desire of love shall go before Jesus in man's soul, and it shall burn all his enemies; that is, it shall waste all sins. For except a soul be first smitten down from the height of itself by fear and humility, and be well tried and burnt in this fire of desire, and as it were purified from all spiritual filth, through long time in devout prayers and other spiritual exercises, it is not able to bear the shinings of spiritual light nor to receive the precious liquor of perfect love of Jesus. But when it is purified and made subtle through this fire, then may it receive the gracious light of spiritual knowing and the perfection of love, which is the true Sun.

Thus saith holy Writ: Vobis qui timetis Deum, &c.—The true Sun of Righteousness, that is, our Lord Jesus, shall spring to you that fear Him; that is, to humble souls that humble themselves to their neighbour, through knowing of their own wretchedness, and cast themselves down under God by annihilating themselves in their own substance through reverent fear and spiritual beholding of Him lastingly, for that is perfect humility. Unto these souls the true Sun shall spring, and enlighten their reason to the knowing of Truth, and kindle their affections in the fervour of love, and then shall they both burn and shine, namely, burn in perfect love through the virtue of this heavenly Sun, and shine in the knowledge of God and spiritual things, for then be they reformed in feeling.

Therefore, he that would not be deceived, I think it is good for him to draw down himself and hide himself in this darkness. First, from intermeddling with other men, as I have said, and forget all the world if he can; and follow Jesus with constant desire offered up in prayers and meditating on Him. And then I believe the light that cometh after this darkness is secure and true, and that it shineth out of the city of Jerusalem from the true Sun to a soul that travelleth in darkness, and crieth after light for to show her the right way and comfort her in travel. For I believe that after true darkness going before feigned light never cometh. That is, if a man truly and fully set himself to forsake the love of the world, and can through grace come to the feeling and knowing of himself, and hold himself humbly in that feeling, he shall not be deceived with any errors nor heresies nor fancies; for all these come in by the gate of pride. If then pride can be stopped out, there shall no such sin rest in a soul, and though they come and proffer themselves, they shall not enter; for grace which the soul feeleth in this humble darkness shall teach the soul truth, and show it that all such proffering are from the enemy.

CHAPTER VIII: HOW GREAT PROFIT IT IS TO THE SOUL TO BE BROUGHT THROUGH GRACE INTO LIGHTSOME DARKNESS, AND HOW A MAN SHALL DISPOSE HIMSELF IF HE WILL COME THERETO

THERE be many devout souls that through grace come into this darkness and feel the knowledge of themselves, and yet know they not fully what it is, and that ignorance is partly a hindrance to them. They feel well often their thoughts and their affections drawn out and separated from the minding of earthly things, and brought into great rest of a delectable softness, without painful troubling of vain thoughts or of their bodily senses, and they feel that time so great a freedom of spirit that they can think on Jesus peaceably and offer up their Psalms and Prayers mightily, savourly and sweetly to Him, as long as frailty of bodily nature will suffer them. They understand well that this feeling is good, but they know not what it is. Therefore unto all such souls I say, as methinketh, that this manner of feeling, though it be but short and but seldom, it is really this darkness that I speak of. For it is a feeling of themselves first, and a rising above themselves through burning desire to the sight of Jesus; or else, if I shall say more truly, this gracious feeling is a spiritual sight of Jesus. And if they can keep themselves in that rest, or bring it through grace into a custom, so that they can lightly and freely have it when they list, and hold themselves in it, they shall never be overcome by temptation of the fiend, nor of the flesh, nor by errors or heresies; for they are set in the gate of Contemplation, able and ready to receive the perfect love of Jesus. Therefore he that hath it, it is good that he know it humbly, keep it tenderly, and pursue it fervently that no creature let him utterly from it, but that he follow it when he may. And that he forget and set at nought all things that may put him from this, if so be, he be at his own liberty, and may do what he will without scandal or offence to his neighbour. For I think that he cannot come to this rest lightly, unless he hath great plenty of grace and set himself to follow the motions of grace, and that ought he to do; for grace would ever be free, namely from sin and worldly business, and all other things that let the working of it, though they are not sins.

Nevertheless, another soul that hath not yet received this plenty of grace, if he desire to come to this spiritual knowing of Jesus, he must, as much as in him lieth, enable himself to it, and put away all lettings that obstruct grace as much as he can. He must truly learn to die to the world, and truly forsake the love of it. First, pride, both spiritual and corporal, that he desire no worship, worldly knowledge, nor worldly craft, profits, nor riches, nor precious clothing, nor worldly array, nor anything by which he may be honoured above other men; he shall covet none of all these. But if they be put upon him take them with fear, so that he be poor both outwardly and inwardly, or at least fully inwardly in his heart. And that he covet to be forgotten of the world, and men regard him no more, though he be never so rich or so wise, than the poorest man living. Also that he suffereth not his heart to rest in the beholding of his own deeds, or in his virtues, imagining that he doth better than another, in that he forsaketh the world, which others do not, and therefore he setteth well by himself. Also he must leave all risings of heart, and evil will of anger and envy against his neighbour. And that he offend no man, nor anger him indiscreetly by word or deed; nor give any man occasion whereby he may reasonably be angered, or moved, so that he may be free from every man. And also that he forsake covetousness, that he covet right naught of earthly goods, but only crave his bodily sustenance which he needeth, and hold himself well apaid, when God stirreth up other men to give it him. And that he put no manner of trust in the possession of any worldly goods, nor in the help or favour of any worldly friends, but principally and fully in God; for if he doth otherwise, he bindeth himself to the world, so that he cannot be free to think on Jesus. And also gluttony, and lechery, and all other fleshly uncleanness must he utterly leave, that his affections be bound to no woman by fleshly familiarity; for it is no doubt but that such blind love as is sometime betwixt a man and a woman, and seemeth good and honest, forasmuch as they would not sin in act, is in the sight of God full unclean and very great sin. For it is a great sin for a man to suffer his affections, which should be fastened to Jesus and to all His virtues, and to all spiritual cleanness, to be bound by any fleshly love willingly to any creature, especially if it be so much that it beareth down his thoughts, and maketh them unrestful that he cannot have favour in God. And this I hold to be done willingly, when a man doth it, though he confess it to be a sin, or else when he is so blinded with it that he will not see it. And also that a man covet not delights of meats and drinks only for lust of his flesh, but be contented with such as he can easily have without great trouble; namely, if he be in health with what meat will put away hunger, and keep his body in ordinary strength for the service of God. And that he grudge not, nor strive not, nor vex himself for his meat, though sometime he be served not as his flesh desires. All these sins and all other must he forsake utterly in his will, and in deed when he can; and all other things that hinder him, so that he may dispose himself to think freely on Jesus. For as long as these lettings and such other hang upon him, he cannot die to the world, nor come into this darkness of knowing of himself. And therefore that he may come thereto, he must do all these things, as St Paul did, saying thus: This world is slain and crucified to me, and I to the world. That is, he that hath forsaken the love of the world in honours and riches and in all other worldly things abovesaid, for the love of God, and loveth it not, nor pursueth it, but is well satisfied that he hath right nought of it, nor verily would have though he might, verily to him the world is dead, for he hath no favour nor delight therein. And if the world set him at nought, and hath no regard to him, nor favour, nor worship, and set no price by him, but forgetteth him as a dead man, then is he dead to the world. And in this plight was St. Paul set perfectly, and so must every other man in part that would come to the perfect love of God; for he cannot live to God fully, unless he die first to the world. This dying to the world is this darkness, and it is the gate to Contemplation, and to reforming in feeling, and none other than this. There may be many sundry ways, and several works letting and leading sundry souls to Contemplation; for according to divers disposings of men, and after divers states as are religious and seculars, according as they are in, are there divers exercises in working. Nevertheless there is but one gate; for whatsoever exercise a soul useth, unless thereby he come to this knowing, and to an humble feeling of himself, and that is, that he be mortified and dead to the world, as to his love of it, and that he may feel himself sometime in this restful darkness, by the which he may be hid from the vanities of the world, as to the love of them, and that he may feel himself what he is indeed, he is not yet come to the reforming in feeling, nor hath he Contemplation fully. He is full far from it, and if he will come to it by any other gate, he is but a thief and a breaker of the wall, and therefore shall be cast out as unworthy.

But he that can bring himself first to nought by the grace of humility, and die on this manner, he is in the gate; for he is dead to the world, and he liveth to God. Of the which St Paul speaketh thus: Ye are dead. That is, ye that for the love of God forsake all the love of the world, are dead to the world, and Your life is hid with Christ in God. That is, ye live spiritually in the love of Jesus. But your life is hid from worldly men, as Christ liveth, and is hid in His Godhead from the love and the sight of fleshly lovers.

This gate our Lord Himself showed in the Gospel, when He said thus: Every man that forsaketh for My love Father or Mother, Sister or Brother, or any earthly good, he shall have an hundredfold in this life, and afterward the bliss of Heaven. This hundredfold which a soul shall have, if he forsake the world, is nought but the profit of this lightsome darkness, which I call the gate of Contemplation. For he that is in this darkness, and is hid through grace from worldly vanity, he coveteth nothing of worldly goods, he seeketh it not, he is not hindered therewith, he looketh not after it, he loveth it not, and therefore hath he an hundredfold more than the King, or than he that coveteth most of worldly goods, for he that coveteth nought but Jesus hath an hundredfold, for he hath more rest, more peace in heart, more true love and delight in soul in one day, than he that most coveteth of this world, and hath all the wealth of it in his full possession, hath all his life-time.

This is, then, a good darkness, and a rich nought, that bringeth a soul to so much spiritual ease, and so quiet softness. I suppose David meant of this night, or this nought, when he said thus: Ad nihilum redactus sum, et nescivi—I was brought to nought, and I knew it not. That is, the grace of our Lord Jesus sent into my heart hath slain in me, and brought to nought all the love of the world, and I knew not how, for not through any working of my own, nor by my own wit had I it, but by the grace of our Lord Jesus. And therefore methinketh that he that would have the light of grace, and sweetly feel the love of Jesus in his soul, he must forsake all the false light or worldly love, and abide in this darkness. And, nevertheless, if he be fearful, at first to continue therein, he must not turn again to the love of the world, but suffer awhile, and put all his hope and his trust in Jesus, and he shall not be long without some spiritual light. Thus the Prophet commandeth: Qui ambulat in tenebris, &c.—He that walketh in darkness and hath no light, let him hope in our Lord, and let him rely upon his God. That is, whoso would hide himself from the love of the world, and cannot readily feel the light of spiritual love, let him not despair, nor turn again to the world, but hope in our Lord, and rely upon Him; that is, trust in God, and cleave to Him by desire, and abide awhile, and he shall have light. For it falleth out therein as it doth when a man hath been a great while in the sun, and after that cometh suddenly into a dark house where no sun shineth, he will be as it were blind, and see just nought. But if he will abide awhile, he shall be able presently to see about him; first great things, and then small things, and afterwards all that is ever in the house. Just so is it spiritually: he that forsaketh the love of the world, and cometh to himself into his own conscience, at first it is somewhat dark and blind to his sight; but if he stand still, and hold out by serious praying, and often meditating in the same will to the love of Jesus, he shall be able afterwards to see both great and small things which he knew not before. This it seemeth the Prophet promiseth when he saith thus: Orietur in tenebris lux tua, &c.—In darkness shall thy light spring up, and thy darkness shall be as noon-day, and thy Lord God shall give thee rest, and shall fill thy soul with lights. That is, thou that truly forsaketh the light of all worldly love, and hidest thy thought in this darkness, light of blessed love and spiritual knowing of God shall spring up to thee, and thy darkness shall be as midday; that is, thy darkness of painful desire, and thy blind trust in God, that thou hast at first, shall turn into clear knowledge, and into security of love, and thy Lord God shall give rest to thee; that is, thy fleshly desires, and thy painful fears and doubts, and wicked spirits that have before time vexed thee, all these shall grow weak, and lose much of their might, and thou shalt be made so strong that they shall not trouble thee, for thou shalt be hid in rest from them. And then shall our Lord fulfil thy soul with shinings; that is, when thou art brought into this spiritual rest, then shalt thou more easily attend to God, and do nought else but love Him, and then shall He fill all the powers of thy soul with beams of spiritual light. Wonder not that I call the forsaking of worldly love a darkness, for the Prophet calleth it so, saying thus to a soul:—Intra in tenebras tuas filia Chaldaeorum—Go into thy darkness, thou daughter of Chaldee. That is, thou soul that art as a daughter of Chaldee through love of this world, forsake it, and go into thy darkness.

CHAPTER IX: THAT THE WORKING OF OUR LORD JESUS IN THE REFORMING OF A SOUL, IS DIVIDED INTO FOUR TIMES, WHICH ARE: CALLING, JUSTIFYING, MAGNIFYING AND GLORIFYING

LO, I have told thee a little, how, if thou covet to be reformed in feeling, thou shalt dispose thyself towards thy forthgoing. Nevertheless I do not say that thou canst do thus of thyself; for I know well that it is our Lord Jesus that bringeth all this to the end where He pleaseth. For He only, through His grace, stirreth up a soul, and bringeth it first into this darkness and then into light, as the Prophet saith: Sicut tenebrae ejus ita et lumen ejus. That is, just as the light of knowing and the feeling of spiritual love is from Jesus, just so the darkness, that is, the forsaking of worldly love, is from Him, for He doth all. He formeth and reformeth. He formeth only by Himself, but He reformeth us with us; for grace given, and the applying our will to grace doth work all this. And in what manner this is done, St Paul rehearses thus: Quos Deus praescivit, &c.—Those whom God foreknew should be made conformable to the Image of His Son, those He called; and whom He called those He justified; and whom He justified those He glorified. Though these words may be understood of all chosen souls in the lowest degree of charity, who are reformed only in faith; nevertheless they may be understood more especially of those souls that are reformed in feeling, to whom our Lord God showeth great plenty of grace, and is much more busy about them; for they are in a special manner His own children, who bear the full shape and the likeness of His Son Jesus. In these words St Paul divideth the working of our Lord into four times.

The first is the time of calling of a soul from worldly vanity, and that time is often easy and comfortable; for in the beginning of turning such a man that is disposed to much grace, is so quickly and so feelingly inspired, and feeleth often so great sweetness of devotion, and hath so many tears in compunction that he thinketh sometimes that he is half in Heaven; but this ease passeth away after for a time. And then cometh the second time, namely, the time of justifying, which is laborious. For when he beginneth to go forth mightily in the way of righteousness, and setteth his will fully against all sin outward and inward, and stretcheth out his desires to virtues and to the love of Jesus, then feeleth he much letting both within himself from the frowardness and hardness of his own will, and from without through the temptation of his enemy, that he is oft in full great torment, and that is no wonder: for he hath so long been crooked towards the false love of the world, that he cannot be made straight, as a crooked staff cannot be made even, unless it be cast and wrought by the fire. Therefore our Lord Jesus, knowing what is fit for a froward soul, suffereth it to be tormented and letted by sundry temptations, and to be tried soundly by spiritual tribulations that all the rust of uncleanness may be burnt out of it. And this shall be done both inwardly with fears and doubts and perplexities that it shall almost fall into despair, and shall seem as it were forsaken of God, and wholly left in the hands of the fiend (saving only a little secret trust that it shall have in the goodness and mercy of God, for that secret trust our Lord leaveth in such a soul, though he go never so far from it, by the which the soul is borne up from despair, and saved from spiritual mischief), and outwardly also it shall be mortified and pained in the sensuality, either by divers sicknesses, or by feeble tormentings of the enemy; or else by a secret working of God the silly soul through feeling and bearing of the wretched body shall be so pained that it shall despair almost of suffering or continuing in the body, unless our Lord Himself keep it therein. And yet, notwithstanding, the soul had rather be in all this pain than to be blinded with the false love of the world, for that would be hell to such a soul; but the suffering of this manner of pain is only Purgatory, and therefore he suffereth it gladly. And he would not put it away though he might, because it is so profitable. All this doth our Lord in great profit to a soul to drive it out of its sensuality, that it may receive spiritual light; for after this, when a soul is thus mortified, and brought from worldly love into this darkness, that it hath no more savour nor delight of worldly liking than of a straw, but thinketh it bitter as wormwood, then cometh the third time of Magnifying: and that is, when a soul is reformed in feeling in part, and receiveth the gift of perfection, and the grace of Contemplation, and that is a time of great rest; for then is Jesus more familiar with a soul.

And after this cometh a fourth time of Glorifying; that is, when a soul shall be fully reformed in the bliss of heaven. For these souls that are thus called from sin, and thus Justified, or else on any other manner by divers trials both through fire and water, and afterwards are thus magnified, they shall be glorified. For our Lord shall then give them fully what they coveted here; and more than they could covet; for He shall raise them above all other chosen souls, to be equal with cherubim and seraphim, seeing they passed all other in knowing and loving of God here in this life.

Therefore he that will come to this magnifying must not be afraid of this justifying, for that is the way; for our Lord saith by His Prophet a word of great comfort to all such souls that are tried with the fire of tribulation thus: Puer meus noli timere, &c.—My child, if thou pass through fire fear not, for the flame shall not hurt thee. It shall cleanse thee from all fleshly filth, and make thee able to receive spiritual fire of the love of God, and this must first be done; for as I said before it cannot otherwise be reformed in feeling.

CHAPTER X: HOW IT FALLETH OUT SOMETIMES THAT SOULS THAT ARE BUT BEGINNING OR PROFITING IN GRACE SEEM TO HAVE MORE LOVE, AS TO OUTWARD TOKENS THEREOF, THAN SOME HAVE THAT BE PERFECT, AND YET IT IS NOT REALLY SO IN THEIR INTERIOR

BUT now thou wilt say, how can this be true? For there be many souls newly turned to God that have many spiritual feelings; some have great compunction for their sins, and some have great devotions and fervours in their prayers, and often have sundry teachings of spiritual light in understanding, and some men have other kind of feelings of comfortable heat and great sweetness; and yet these souls never come fully into this restful darkness, which I speak of, with fervent desire and lasting love and thought on God. And hereupon thou askest whether these souls be reformed in feeling or no. And it seemeth yes, inasmuch as they have such great spiritual feelings, which other men who stand only in faith feel not.

Unto this I answer, as methinketh, that these spiritual feelings, whether they stand in compunction or devotion, or in spiritual imagination, are not the feelings which a soul shall have and feel in the grace of Contemplation. I say not but that they are true and graciously given of God. But these souls that feel such are not yet reformed in feeling, nor have as yet the gift of perfection nor the spiritual burning love of Jesus as they may arrive to. And nevertheless, it often seemeth otherwise that such souls feel more of the love of God than others that have the gift of perfection, inasmuch as the feeling showeth more outwardly by great fervour of bodily tokens in weeping, praying, kneeling and speaking, and other bodily stirrings, so far forth that it seemeth to another man that they were even ravished in love. Though I, for my part, do not think them so, for I will understand that these kind of feelings and fervours of devotion and compunction that these men feel are gracious gifts of God sent into chosen souls to draw them out of worldly love and fleshly lust, which hath long time been rooted in their hearts, from the which love they would not be drawn out but by such feeble motions of great fervours.

And the reason why this fervour is so much in outward showing is not only from the greatness of that love which they have, but from the littleness and weakness of their soul, that cannot bear a little touching of God; for it is yet, as it were, fleshly, fastened to the flesh, and never was yet parted from it by spiritual mortification; and therefore the least touching of love, and the least sparkle of spiritual light sent from Heaven into such a soul is so much and so comfortable and so delectable above all the likings that ever it felt before in fleshly love of earthly things, that she is, as it were, overcome with it. And also it is so new and so sudden and so unaccustomed to her that she is not able to bear it, but bursteth and breaketh out into weeping, sobbing and other bodily stirrings. Just as a barrel that is old, when it receiveth new wine that is fresh and strong, the barrel swelleth out and is ready to cleave and burst until the wine hath boiled and purged out all uncleanness; but as soon as the wine is fined and cleared, then it standeth still and the barrel whole; just so a soul that is old through sin, when it receiveth a little of the love of God, which is so fresh and strong that the body is in point to cleave and to break were it not that God keepeth it whole. But yet it bursteth out at the eyes by weeping, and at the mouth by speaking, which is more for weakness and feebleness of the soul than through greatness of love. For afterward, when love hath boiled all uncleanness out of the soul by such great fervours, then is the love clear and standeth still. And then is both the body and the soul much more in peace. And yet hath the soul much more love than it had before, though it show less outwardly; for it is now all whole in rest within, and but little in outward showing of fervour. And therefore I say that these souls that feel such great bodily fervours, though they be in much grace, are not yet reformed in feeling, but they are greatly disposed towards it. For I trow that such a man, namely, that hath been greatly defiled in sin, shall not be reformed in feeling, unless he be first burnt and purified with such great compunctions going before.

Another soul that never was much defiled with the love of the world, but hath ever been kept from great sins in innocency, may lightlier and more privily, without great fervour showed outwardly, come to this reforming. Then is this true, as I hope, that such comforts and fervours that a soul feeleth in a state of its beginning, or of its profiting, are, as it were, his spiritual food sent from Heaven for to strengthen him in his journey. Even as a Pilgrim travelleth all day meatless and drinkless, and is near-at-hand overcome with weariness, falleth at last to a good inn, and there hath he meat and drink, and is well refreshed for the time, right so is it spiritually. A devout soul, that will forsake the love of the world, and would fain love God and setteth all her business thereto, prayeth and exerciseth all day bodily and spiritually, and sometimes feeleth no comfort nor savour in devotion; then our Lord, having pity on all His creatures, that they should not perish for want, nor fall into heaviness or grudging, sendeth to it, among other things, His spiritual food, and comforteth it in devotion as He pleaseth. And when the soul feeleth any comfort, then doth she hold herself well paid for all her travail and all the suffering it had on the day, when it fareth well at night by feeling of any grace.

Also in the same manner falleth it out with other souls that are profiting and proceeding well forward in grace. These feel oftentimes gracious touchings of the Holy Ghost in their soul, both in understanding and sight of spiritual things and in affection of love. But yet be they not reformed in feeling, nor are they yet perfect, for why? All such feelings come to them in that state as it were unawares, for they come to them ere they think of them, and go from them before they think; and they cannot come by such things again, nor wot they where they may find them; for they have not as yet any familiarity with them, of thought and lasting desire in Jesus. Nor is the eye of their soul opened to the beholding of spiritual things, but they draw well toward it; and therefore they are not yet reformed in feeling nor have yet the full gift of Contemplation.

CHAPTER XI: AFTER WHAT MANNER A MAN SHALL COME TO KNOW HIS OWN SOUL, AND HOW A MAN SHOULD SET HIS LOVE IN JESUS, GOD AND MAN IN ONE PERSON

A SOUL that would know spiritual things needs first to have the knowledge of itself; for she cannot have the knowledge of a thing that is above herself, unless she have first the knowledge of herself. And that is when the soul is so gathered into herself, and separated from beholding of all earthly things and from the use of her bodily senses, that she feeleth herself as she is in her own kind, which is without a body. Then, if thou covet for to know and see thy soul what it is, thou shalt not turn thy thought with imagination into thy body, to seek it and feel it as it were hid within thy heart, as thy heart is hid and holden within thy body. If thou seek in that manner, thou shalt never find it in itself. The more thou seekest for to find and feel it as thou wouldst feel a bodily thing, the farther thou art from it. For thy soul is no bodily thing, but a life invisible, not hid and holden within thy body, as a less thing is hidden and holden within a greater; but it holdeth and quickeneth thy body, and is much greater in might and virtue than is thy body. If then thou wilt find it, withdraw thy thoughts from all bodily things outward, and from minding of thy own body, also from all thy five senses, as much as thou canst, and think on the nature of a reasonable soul spiritually, as thou wouldst think for to know any virtue, as justice, humility or any other. Right so think that a soul is a life immortal, invisible, and hath in itself a power to know the sovereign verity, and for to love the sovereign goodness, which is God; when thou seest this, then feelest thou somewhat of thyself. Seek thyself in none other place, but the more fully, the more clearly that thou thinkest of the nature and the worthiness of a reasonable soul, what it is and what is the kindly working of it, the better seest thou thyself.

It is full hard for a soul that is rude and much in the flesh for to have sight and knowledge of itself or of an angel or of God. It falleth presently to the imagining of a bodily shape, and it weeneth thereby to have the sight of itself, and in like manner of God, and of spiritual things. And that may not be, for all spiritual things are seen and known by the understanding of the soul, not by the imagination. Right as a soul seeth by her understanding, that the virtue of righteousness is to give to everything that which he ought to have; right so, and on such a manner may the soul see itself by the understanding.

Nevertheless, I say not that thy soul should rest still in this knowing, but it shall by this seek a higher knowledge above itself, and that is the nature of God, for the soul is but a glass, in the which thou shouldst see God spiritually. And therefore thou shalt first find thy glass and keep it bright and clean from fleshly filth and worldly vanity, and hold it well up from the earth, that thou mayest see it and our Lord therein also. For to this end do all chosen souls travail in this life, in their meaning and in their intent, though they have not the special feeling of this. And therefore it is said before that many souls beginning and profiting have many great fervours, and much sweet devotion, and as it seemeth are all burning in love, and yet have they not love perfectly nor spiritual knowledge of God. For be thou well assured that though a soul feel never so much fervour, even so much that he thinketh his body cannot bear it; or though he melt all into weeping, as long as his thinking and his beholding of God is for the most part or all in imagination and not in the understanding, he is not yet come to perfect love nor to Contemplation.

For thou shalt understand that the love of God is in three manner of ways; all of which are good, but each one is better than the other. The first cometh only through Faith, without gracious imagination or spiritual knowing of God. This love is in the least soul that is reformed in Faith, in the lowest degree of charity; and it is good, for it sufficeth to salvation. The second is that which a soul feeleth through faith and imagination of Jesus in His Manhood. This love is better than the first, when the imagination is stirred by grace, for then the spiritual eye is opened in beholding of our Lord's humanity. The third love that a soul feeleth through spiritual sight of the Godhead in the humanity, as it may be seen here, is the best and most worthy, and that is perfect love. This love a soul feeleth not, until it be reformed in feeling. Souls beginning and profiting have not this love, for they cannot think on Jesus nor love Him spiritually, but, as it were, all manly and fleshly after the conditions and likeness of a man; and accordingly they frame all their working in their thoughts and in their affections. They fear Him as a man, and worship Him and love Him principally by the imagination of His humanity, and go no further.

As thus: If they have done amiss and trespassed against God, they think then that God is angry with them, as a man would be if they had trespassed against him; and therefore they fall down, as it were, at the feet of our Lord with sorrow of heart, and cry Him mercy. And when they have done thus, they have a good trust that our Lord of His mercy will forgive them their trespass. This manner of doing is right good, but it is not spiritual as it might be. Also when they would worship God, they present themselves in their thoughts, as if they were before our Lord's face in a bodily likeness, and imagine a wonderful light there where our Lord Jesus is, and then they reverence Him, and worship Him, and fear Him, and fully put them into His mercy for to do with them what He will. Also when they would love God, they behold Him, worship Him, and dread Him as a man (not yet as God in the humanity), either in His Passion, or in some other thing in His humanity, and in that beholding they feel their hearts much stirred to the love of God.

This manner of working is good and gracious, but it is much less and lower than is the working of the understanding; that is, when the soul graciously beholdeth God in man, for in our Lord Jesus are two natures, the Humanity and the Divinity. And as the Divinity is more sovereign and more worthy than the Humanity, right so the spiritual beholding of the Divinity in Jesus Man is more worthy, and more spiritual, and more meritorious than the beholding of the Humanity alone, whether he behold the Humanity as mortal or as glorified. And right so by the same reason the love which a soul feeleth in thinking and beholding of the Divinity in the Manhood, when it is graciously showed, is more worthy, more spiritual, and more meritorious than the fervour of devotion, that the soul feeleth by the imagination only of the humanity, show it never so much outwardly; for in regard of that of the Divinity, this of the Humanity is but a human thing. For our Lord showeth not Himself in the imagination as He is, nor that He is, for the soul cannot at that time for frailty of the flesh suffer it so.

Nevertheless unto such souls that cannot meditate on the Divinity spiritually, that they may not err in their devotion, but that they should be comforted and strengthened by some manner of inward beholding of Jesus to forsake sin and the love of the world, wherefore our Lord Jesus tempereth this invisible light of His Godhead, and clotheth it under bodily likeness of His Manhood, and showeth it unto the inner eye of the soul, and feedeth it with the love of His precious flesh spiritually. The which love is of so great might, that it slayeth all wicked love in the soul, and strengthens it for to suffer bodily penance and other bodily difficulties in the time of need for the love of Jesus. And this is the shadowing of our Lord Jesus over a chosen soul, in which shadowing the soul is kept from the burning of worldly love; for as a shadow is made of a light and of a body, even so this spiritual shadow is made of the blessed invisible light of the Godhead, and of the Manhood united thereto, showed to a devout soul. Of the which shadow the Prophet saith thus: Spiritus ante faciem nostram, &c.—Our Lord Christ before our face as a Spirit, under His shadow we shall live among folks. That is, our Lord Jesus in His Godhead is a spirit, that cannot be seen of us living in the flesh as He is in His blessed light, therefore we shall live under the shadow of His Manhood as long as we are here.

But though that this be true that this love in imagination is good; nevertheless a soul should desire to have spiritual love in understanding of the Godhead; for that is the end and the full bliss of the soul, and all bodily beholdings are but means leading a soul to it. I say not that we should refuse the Manhood of Jesus, and separate God from man; but thou shalt in Jesus Man, behold, fear, admire and love spiritually the Godhead, and so shalt thou, without separating them, love God in man, and both God and man spiritually and fleshly. Thus our Lord taught Mary Magdalen to do like a Contemplative, when He said thus: Noli me tangere, &c.—Touch me not: I am not yet ascended to My Father. The meaning is this: Mary Magdalen loved our Lord Jesus well before the time of His Passion, but her love was much bodily and little spiritual. She understood well that He was God, but she loved Him but little as God; for she could not then, and therefore she suffered all her affection and all her thoughts to fall on Him as He was in form of man. And our Lord blamed her not then, but praised it much. But after when He was risen from death, and appeared to her, she would have worshipped Him with the same manner of love as she did before, and then our Lord forbade her, and said thus: Touch Me not. That is, set not thy rest nor the love of thy heart on that form of man which thou seest with thy fleshly eye, for to rest therein only, for in that form I am not ascended up to My Father; that is, I am not equal to the Father, that is, the form of the Godhead; and love Me, know Me and worship Me as God and Man, godly, not as a man, manly, so shalt thou touch Me. For since I am both God and Man, and all the reason why I am to be beloved and worshipped is, for that I am God, and for that I took the nature of man; and therefore make Me a God in thy heart and in thy love, and worship Me in thine understanding as Jesus, God and Man, the sovereign verity and the sovereign goodness, and blessed life; for I am so. And thus our Lord taught her, as I understand, and also all other souls that are disposed to Contemplation, and enabled thereto that they should do so. Nevertheless other souls are not so skilful, nor are yet made spiritual through grace, it is good for them that they keep on their own working in imagination, with affections towards our Saviour's Humanity, until more grace come freely to them. It is not safe for a man to leave any good thing utterly, until he see and feel a better.

In like manner may it be said of other kind of feelings that are like to bodily, as hearing of delectable songs, or feeling of comfortable heat in the body, seeing of light, or sweetness of bodily savour. These are not spiritual feelings; for spiritual feelings are felt in the powers of the soul, principally in the understanding, and in love, and little in the imagination. But these feelings are felt in the powers of the body in the imagination, and therefore are not spiritual feelings. But when they are even at best, and most true, yet are they but outward tokens of the inward grace which is felt in the powers of the soul. This may be plainly proved out of Holy Writ, saying thus: Apparuerunt Apostolis, &c.—The Holy Ghost appeared to the Apostles on the day of Pentecost in the likeness of burning tongues, and inflamed their hearts, and sat upon each of them. Now it is true that the Holy Ghost, which is God in Himself invisible, was not that fire nor those tongues that were seen, nor that burning which was felt bodily, but He was invisibly felt in the powers of their souls, for He enlightened their reason and enkindled their affections through His blessed presence so clearly and so burningly, that they had suddenly the spiritual knowledge of truth, and the perfection of love, as our Lord promised them, saying thus: Spiritus Sanctus docebit vos, &c.—The Holy Spirit shall teach you all truth. That fire and that burning then was nought else but a bodily token showed outwardly in witnessing of that grace which was felt inwardly. And as it was in them, so is it in other souls that are visited and lightened within of the Holy Ghost, and have withal such outward feelings for comforting them and witnessing of their inward grace. But yet I do not think that such grace is in all souls that are perfect, but only where our Lord pleaseth.

Other imperfect souls that have such feelings outwardly, and have not yet received inward grace, it is not good for them to rest in such outward feelings, but only inasmuch as they help the soul to more love, and to more stableness of thought in God; for some may be true and some may be feigned, as I have said before.

PART III

CHAPTER I: IN WHAT SENSE THIS MANNER OF SPEAKING OF REFORMING OF A SOUL IN FEELING IS TO BE UNDERSTOOD; AND IN WHAT MANNER IT IS REFORMED, AND HOW IT IS FOUND IN ST PAUL'S WRITINGS

I HAVE heretofore told thee somewhat of reforming in Faith, and also I have touched concerning thy proceeding from that reforming to a higher reforming which is in feeling. Not that I would by these discourses limit God's working by the law of my speaking, as to say that God worketh thus in a soul and no other wise. No, I mean not so, but I speak after my simple feeling that our Lord worketh thus in some creatures as I conceive. And I hope well, also, that He worketh otherwise, which passeth my wit and my feeling. Nevertheless, whether He worketh thus or otherwise by several ways, in longer time or shorter, with much travail or little, if all come to one end, that is, the perfect love of Him, then is it good enough. For if He will give one soul on one day the full grace of Contemplation, and without any travail, as He well may; as good is that to that soul as if he had been tried, pained, mortified and purified twenty years. And therefore in this manner take my sayings as I have said, and namely as I meant to say them. For now by the grace of our Lord Jesus shall I speak a little as methinketh more plainly of reforming in feeling, what it is, and how it is made, and what are spiritual feelings which a soul receiveth. Yet in the first place, that I may not be understood to make this manner of speaking of reforming of a soul in feeling as a fiction or fancy of my own, I shall ground it on St Paul's words, where he saith thus: Nolite conformari huic saeculo, &c. That is, ye that are through grace reformed in Faith, conform not yourselves henceforward to the manner of the world, in pride, in covetousness and in other sins, but be ye reformed in newness of feeling. Lo, here thou mayest see that St Paul speaketh of reforming in feeling; and what that newness of feeling is he expoundeth in another place thus: Ut impleamini in agnitione, &c. That is: We pray God that ye may be fulfilled in knowing of God's will in all understanding and in all manner of spiritual wisdom. This is reforming in feeling; for thou must understand that the soul hath two manners of feelings, one without by the five bodily senses; another within of the spiritual senses, which are properly the faculties of the soul—memory, understanding and will. When these faculties are through grace fulfilled in all understanding of the will of God and spiritual wisdom, then hath the soul new gracious feelings. That this is so he showeth in another place, thus: Renovamini spiritu mentis vestri, &c.—Be ye renewed in the spirit of your soul. That is, ye shall be reformed, not in bodily feeling nor in imagination, but in the upper part of your reason. And be clothed with the new man, that is shapen after God in righteousness, holiness and truth. That is, your reason, which is properly the image of God, through grace of the Holy Ghost, shall be clothed in a new light of truth, holiness and righteousness, and then is it reformed in feeling. For when the soul hath perfect knowledge of God, then is it reformed. Thus saith St Paul: Expoliantes veterem hominem, &c.—Spoil yourself of the old man with all his deeds. That is, cast from you the love of the world with all worldly manners, and clothe you with the new man. That is, you shall be renewed in the knowing of God, after the likeness of Him that made you.

By these words thou mayest understand that St Paul would have men's souls reformed in perfect knowledge of God, for that is the new feeling which he speaketh of generally. And therefore upon his words I shall speak more plainly of this reforming as God shall give me grace. For there be two manners of knowing of God.

One is had principally in imagination, and little in understanding. This knowing is in chosen souls beginning and profiting in grace, who know God, and love Him humanly (not spiritually) with human affections, and with a corporal image of His Humanity, as I have spoken before.

This knowing is good, and is likened to milk, by which they are tenderly nourished as children until they be able to come to the Father's table, and take from His hand substantial bread.

Another knowing is principally felt in the understanding, and little in imagination; for the understanding is the lady, and the imagination is the maid, serving the understanding when need is. This knowing is solid bread meet for perfect souls, and is reforming in feeling.

CHAPTER II: HOW GOD OPENETH THE INWARD EYE OF THE SOUL TO SEE HIM, NOT ALL AT ONCE, BUT BY DIVERS TIMES, AND OF THREE MANNERS OF REFORMING OF A SOUL EXPLAINED BY A FAMILIAR EXAMPLE

A SOUL that is called from the love of the world, and after that is righted, tried and mortified and purified, as I have said before, our Lord Jesus of His merciful goodness reformeth it in feeling when He pleaseth. He openeth the inner eye of the soul, when He enlighteneth her reason through the touching and shining of His blessed light for to see Him and know Him, not all fully at once, but by little and little, by divers times, as the soul is able to bear it. He seeth Him not what He is, for that can no creature do in Heaven nor in earth. Nor seeth he Him as He is, for that sight is only in the bliss of Heaven. But he seeth Him that He is an unchangeable being, a supreme power, a sovereign truth, supreme goodness, a blessed life, an endless bliss. This seeth a soul, and much more that cometh withal not blindly and nakedly and unsavourly, as doth a learned man, that knoweth and seeth Him only by his learning, through might of his naked reason; but he seeth Him in understanding, that is, comforted and lighted by the gift of the Holy Ghost, with a wonderful reverence, and a secret burning love, and with a spiritual savour and heavenly delight, more clearly and more fully than can be written or spoken.

This sight, though it be but short and little, is so worthy and so mighty that it draweth and ravisheth all the affections of the soul from be holding and minding of all earthly things to itself, for to rest therein evermore if it could. And upon this kind of sight and knowing the soul groundeth all its working inward in all the affections; for then she worshippeth God in the humanity, as verity; wondereth at Him, as power and might; loveth Him, as goodness. This sight and this goodness, and this knowing of Jesus, with the blessed love that cometh out of it, may be called reforming of a soul in feeling and in faith, which I have spoken of. It is in faith, for it is dark yet in comparison of that full knowing of Jesus, with the blessed love that cometh out of it, that shall be in Heaven. For then shall we see Him, not only that He is, but as He is, as St John saith: Tunc videbimus eum sicut est—Then shall we see Him as He is. Nevertheless it is in feeling also, as in regard of that blind knowing that a soul hath standing only in faith, for this soul knoweth somewhat of the very nature of Jesus as God through this gracious sight, which that other in faith knoweth not, but only believeth it to be truth.

Nevertheless, that thou mayest the better conceive what I mean, I shall show these three manners of reforming of a soul by example of three men standing in the light of the sun. Of the which one is blind, another can see, but hath his eyes stopped, the third looketh forth with full sight. The blind man hath no manner of knowledge that he is in the sun, but he believeth it if an honest man tell him so; and he betokeneth a soul that is only reformed in Faith, that believeth in God as holy Church teacheth, and understandeth not what. This sufficeth as to salvation. That other man seeth a light of the sun, but he seeth it not clearly what it is, for his eyelid letteth him that he cannot see; but he seeth through the lids of his eyes a glimmering of great light. And this man betokeneth a soul that is reformed in Faith and in feeling, and so he is Contemplative, for he seeth somewhat of the Godhead of Jesus through grace, not clearly nor fully; for the lid, that is, his bodily nature, is yet a wall betwixt his nature and the nature of Jesus God, and letteth him from the clear sight. But he seeth through this wall, after that grace toucheth him more or less, that Jesus is God, and that Jesus is sovereign goodness, and sovereign being, and a blessed life, and that all other goodness cometh from Him. Thus seeth the soul by grace, notwithstanding its bodily nature, and the more clean and subtle that the soul is made, and the more it is separated from sensuality, the sharper sight it hath and the greater love of the Divinity of Jesus. This sight is so mighty that though no other man living should believe in Jesus, nor love Him, yet would he never believe the less, nor love Him the less, for he seeth it so certainly that he cannot but believe it.

The third man that hath full sight of the sun, he believeth it not, for he seeth it fully. And he betokeneth a full blessed soul, that without any wall of his body or of sin, seeth openly the face of Jesus in the bliss of Heaven. There is no faith, and therefore he is fully reformed in feeling. There is no state above the second reforming that a soul can come to here in this life, for this is the state of perfection and the way to heavenward. Nevertheless, all the souls that are in this state are not all alike in degrees; for some have it little, short and seldom; and some longer, clearer and oftener; and some have it best of all, clearest and longest, according to the abounding of grace, and yet all these have the gift of Contemplation. For the soul hath not perfect sight of Jesus all at once, but at first a little and a little, and after that it profiteth and cometh to more feeling; and as long as it is in this life it groweth more in knowing, and in this love of Jesus. And verily I know not what can be more desirable to such a soul that hath felt a little of it, than utterly to leave it and set at nought all other things, for to hold only thereto, to have a clearer sight and clearer love of Jesus, in whom is all the Blessed Trinity.

This manner of knowing of Jesus, as I understand, is the opening of Heaven to the eye of a clean soul, of which holy men speak in their writings. Not as some imagine, that the opening of Heaven is as if a soul could see by imagination through the skies above the Firmament, how our Lord Jesus sitteth in His

Majesty, in a bodily light, as much as an hundred suns. No, it is not so; no, though he see never so high on this manner, verily he seeth not the spiritual Heaven. The higher he soareth up above the sun for to see Jesus God, thus by such imagination the lower he falleth beneath the sun. Nevertheless, this kind of sight is tolerable in simple souls that can seek no better for Him that is invisible.

CHAPTER III: HOW JESUS IS HEAVEN TO THE SOUL, AND WHY HE IS CALLED FIRE

WHAT then is Heaven to a reasonable soul? Verily nought else but Jesus God. For if that be Heaven only that is above all things, then is God only Heaven to man's soul, for He alone is above the nature of a soul. Then if a soul can through grace have knowledge of that blessed nature of Jesus, verily he seeth Heaven, for he seeth God. Therefore there be many men that err in understanding of some words that are spoken of God, for that they understand them not spiritually.

Holy Writ saith, that a soul that will find God must lift her inward eye upward, and seek God above itself. Then some men that would do after this saying, understand this word above themselves to signify the placing or setting of a thing in place and worthiness above another, as one element or planet is above another in situation and worthiness of a bodily place. But it is not so taken spiritually; for a soul is above each bodily thing, not in place, or sight, but in purity and worthiness of nature. Right so in the same manner God is above all bodily and spiritual creatures, not in place and sight, but in purity and worthiness of His unchangeable blessed nature.

And therefore he that will wisely seek God, and find Him, he must not run out with his thoughts as if he would climb above the sun, and part the firmament, and imagine the Majesty like to a hundred suns. But he must rather draw down the sun, and all the firmament, and forget it, and cast it beneath him where he is, and set all this and all bodily things also at nought; and then, if he can, think spiritually both of himself and of God also. And if he do thus, then seeth the soul above itself, then seeth it into Heaven.

Upon this same manner shall this word within be understood. It is commonly said that a soul should see our Lord within all things and within itself. True it is, that our Lord is within all creatures, but not on that manner that a kernel is hid within the shell of a nut; or as a little bodily thing is contained within a greater. But He is within all creatures, as holding and preserving them in their being, through the subtlety and power of His own blessed nature, and purity invisible. For even as a thing that is most precious and most clean is laid innermost, right so by the same likeness it is said that the nature of God, which is most precious, most clean, most goodly, most remote from bodily substance, is hid within all things. And therefore he that will seek God within, he must first forget all bodily things, for all such things are without; and also his own body; and he must forget thinking of his own soul, and think on the uncreated nature; that is, Jesus, who made him, quickeneth him, holdeth him, and giveth him reason, memory and love, the which is within him through His power and sovereign subtlety.

Upon this manner must the soul do, when grace toucheth it, or else it will but little avail to seek Jesus, and to find Him within itself, and within all creatures as methinketh.

Also it is said in Holy Writ, that God is light. So sayeth St John: God is light. This light we must not take for a bodily light; but it must be understood thus: God is light; that is, God is truth and verity itself, for verity is spiritual light. He then that most graciously knoweth verity, best seeth God. And nevertheless it is likened to corporal light, for this reason: Right as the sun showeth to the bodily eye both itself and all bodily things thereby; even so verity, that is, God, showeth to the reason of the soul itself first, and by itself all other spiritual things that are needful to the knowing of a soul. Thus saith the Prophet: Domine in lumine tuo videbimus lumen.—Lord, we shall see Thy light by Thy light. That is, we shall see Thee, who art verity, by Thyself.

In like manner, it is said that God is fire. Our God is wasting fire. That is to say, God is not elementary fire, that heateth and burneth a body, but God is love and charity. For as fire wasteth all bodily things, that can be wasted, even so the love of God burneth and wasteth all sin out of the soul and maketh it clean, as fire cleanseth all manner of metals. These words and all other that are spoken of our Lord in Holy Writ by bodily similitude, must needs be understood spiritually, else there is no savour in them. And the reason why such words are said of our Lord in Holy Writ is this, for that we are so carnal, that we cannot speak of God nor understand anything of Him, unless we be first entered by such words. But when the inner eye is open through grace to have a little sight of Jesus, then will the soul easily enough turn all such words of bodily things into spiritual understanding. This spiritual opening of the inner eye into knowing of the Divinity, I call reforming in faith and feeling. For then the soul feeleth somewhat in understanding of that thing that it had before, in naked believing, and that is the beginning of Contemplation. Of the which St Paul saith thus: Non Contemplantibus nobis quae videntur, &c.—Our Contemplation is not on things that are seen, but on things unseen. For things that are seen are passing, but things unseen are everlasting. To which sight every soul should desire to come. both here in part, and in the bliss of Heaven fully. For in that sight, and in that knowing of Jesus fully, consisteth the bliss of a reasonable soul and endless life. Thus saith our Lord: Haec est autem vita aeterna, &c. —This is eternal life, that they know Thee the true God, and Thy Son whom Thou hast sent.

CHAPTER IV: OF TWO MANNER OF LOVES, CREATED AND UNCREATED, AND HOW WE ARE BOUND TO LOVE JESUS MUCH FOR OUR CREATION; BUT MORE FOR OUR REDEMPTION; AND MOST OF ALL FOR OUR SALVATION, THROUGH THE GIFTS OF HIS LOVE

BUT now perhaps thou wonderest why, since this knowing of God is the bliss and end of a Soul, why I have said heretofore that a soul should covet nought else but only the love of God, and speak nothing of this sight that a soul should covet it.

Unto this I may answer, that the sight of Jesus is the full bliss of a soul; but not only for the sight, but also for the blessed love that cometh out of that sight. And because that love cometh out of knowing, and not knowing out of love; therefore it is said, that in knowing, and in sight principally of God with love is the bliss of a soul; and the more He is known, the better He is loved. But forasmuch as a soul cannot arrive to this knowing, and the love that cometh out of it, without love, therefore I say that thou must covet love; for love is a cause why a soul cometh to this knowing, and to the love that cometh out of it. And in what manner that is, I shall tell thee more plainly.

Holy writers say, and true it is, that there be two sorts of spiritual love: One is called Created, and the other Uncreated. Love uncreated is God Himself, the Third Person in the Trinity, that is the Holy Ghost. He is love uncreated, and unmade; as St John saith: God is love. That is, the Holy Ghost. Love created is the affection of the soul produced by the Holy Ghost out of the sight and the knowing of Verity; that is, God stirred up, and set upon him. This love is called created, for it is made by the Holy Ghost. This love is not God in Himself, for it is made: but it is the love of the soul felt by the sight of Jesus, and stirred up towards Him only. Now may you see that created love is not the cause why a soul cometh to the spiritual sight of Jesus. And some men think that they could love God so fervently, as it were by their own strength, that they might be worthy to have the spiritual knowing of Him. No, it is not so; but love uncreated, that is, God Himself, is cause of all this knowing. For a blind wretched soul is so far from the clear knowing, and the blessed feeling of His love, through sin and frailty of its corporal nature, that it could never come to it, if it were not for the endless greatness of the love of God. But because He loveth us so much, therefore giveth He us His love, that is the Holy Ghost. He is both the giver and the gift, and maketh us then by that gift for to know and love Him.

Lo, this is the love that I spake of, that thou shouldst only covet and desire this uncreated love, that is, the Holy Ghost; for verily a less thing or a less gift than He is cannot avail us, to bring us to the blessed sight of Jesus. And therefore ought we fully to desire and ask of Jesus only this gift of love, that He would for the greatness of His so blessed love touch our hearts with His invisible light to the knowledge of Himself, and make us partakers of His love; that as He loveth us, so we might love Him again. Thus saith St John: Nos diligamus Deum, &c.—Let us love God now, for He loved us first. He loved us much when He made us after His likeness; but He loved us more when He bought us with His precious Blood, by voluntary undertaking of death in His Humanity from the power of the enemy and the pains of Hell; but He loveth us most when He giveth us the gift of the Holy Ghost, that is, love, by the which we know Him and love Him, and are made secure that we are His sons chosen to salvation. For this love are we more bound to Him than for any other love that ever He showed to us, either in our making or redeeming. For though He had made us and bought us, if He did not save us withal, what would our making or redeeming profit us? Verily right nought.

Therefore the greatest token of love showed to us, as methinketh, is this: That He giveth Himself in His Godhead to our souls. He gave Himself, first, in His manhood to us for our ransom, when He offered Himself to the Father of Heaven upon the altar of the Cross.

This was a right fair gift, and a right great token of love. But when He giveth Himself in His Godhead spiritually to our souls for our salvation, and maketh us to know Him and to love Him, then loveth He us fully; for then giveth He Himself to us, and more cannot He give us, nor could less suffice us. And for this cause it is said that the justifying of a sinful soul through forgiveness of sins is attributed and appropriated principally to the working of the Holy Ghost; for the Holy Ghost is love. And in the justifying of a sinner, our Lord Jesus showeth to a soul most of His love, for He putteth away all sin, and uniteth it to Him and that is the best thing that He can do to a soul; and therefore it is attributed to the Holy Ghost. The making of the soul is attributed to the Father, as to the sovereign might and power that He showeth in making of it. The redeeming of it is attributed to the Son, as to the sovereign skill and wisdom that He showed in His Manhood; for He overcame the enemy principally through wisdom, and not through strength. But the justifying and full saving of a soul through forgiveness of sins is appropriated to the Third Person, that is, the Holy Ghost, for therein showeth Jesus most love unto man's soul, and for that thing should He be most loved of us again. His making is common to us and all unreasonable creatures; for as He made us of nought, so made He them, and therefore this is a work of greatest might, but not of greatest love. Also the Redemption is common to us and all reasonable souls, as to Jews and Saracens, and to false Christian men; for He died for all souls alike, and bought them if they would have the perfect love of it. And also it is sufficient for the restoring of all, though it be so that all have it not. And this work had most of wisdom, not most of love. But the justifying and sanctifying of our souls through the gift of the Holy Ghost, that is only the work of love, and is not common, but a special gift only to chosen souls. And verily that is most the working of love to us that are His chosen children.

This is the love of God that I spake of, which thou shouldst covet and desire; for this love is God Himself and the Holy Ghost. This love uncreated, when it is given to us, it worketh in our souls all that good is, and all that belongeth to goodness. This love loveth us before we love Him, for it cleanseth us first from our sins, it maketh us to love Him, and maketh our wills strong to withstand all sins, and stirreth us up to exercise ourselves through divers exercises both bodily and ghostly in all virtues. It stirreth us up also to forsake sin and carnal affections and worldly fears. It keepeth us from malicious temptations of the enemy, and driveth us out from business and vanities of the world, and from the conversation of worldly lovers. All this doth the uncreated love of God, when He giveth Himself to us; we do right nought but suffer Him and assent to Him; for that is the most that we do to assent willingly to His gracious working in us. And yet is not that will from and of ourselves but of His making, so that methinketh He doth in us all that is well done, and yet we see it not.

And He not only doth all thus, but afterwards this love doth more; for He openeth the eye of the soul, and showeth to the soul the sight of Jesus wonderfully, and the knowledge of Him as well as the soul can suffer it by little and little; and by that sight He ravisheth all the affections of the soul to Him, and then beginneth the soul to know Him spiritually and to love Him burningly. Then seeth the soul somewhat of the nature of the blessed Divinity of Jesus, how that He is all, and that He worketh all, and that all good deeds that are done and good thoughts are only of Him; for He is all-sovereign might and all-sovereign verity and all-sovereign goodness. And therefore every good deed is done of Him and by Him. And He alone shall have the worship and the thanks for all good deeds, and nothing else but He; for though wretched men steal His worship here for a while, yet at the last end shall verity show full well that Jesus did all, and man did right nought of himself. And then shall the thieves of God's goods that are not reconciled to Him here in this life be judged to death for their sins. And Jesus shall be fully worshipped and thanked of all blessed creatures for His working. This love is nothing else but Jesus Himself, that for love worketh all this in man's soul and reformeth it in feeling to His likeness, as I have said before, and somewhat more shall say. This love bringeth into the soul the perfection of all virtues, and maketh it all clean and true, soft and easy, and turneth it all into love and into liking. And in what manner He doth that I shall tell thee a little hereafter. This love draweth the soul from vain beholding of worldly things into Contemplation of spiritual creatures and of the secrets of God, from sensuality into spirituality, from earthly feeling into heavenly savour.

CHAPTER V: HOW THAT SOME SOULS LOVE JESUS BY BODILY FERVOURS, AND BY THEIR OWN HUMAN AFFECTIONS THAT ARE MOVED BY GRACE AND BY REASON. AND HOW SOME LOVE HIM MORE QUIETLY BY SPIRITUAL AFFECTIONS ONLY MOVED INWARDLY THROUGH SPIRITUAL GRACE OF THE HOLY GHOST

THEREFORE I may truly say, that he that hath most of this love here in this life, most pleaseth God, and shall have most clear sight of Him, and most fully love Him in the bliss of Heaven, for that he hath the greatest gift of love here in earth. This love cannot be had by a man's own travail, as some imagine. It is freely had by the gracious gift of Jesus after much bodily and spiritual pains going before. For there are some lovers of God that make themselves to love God as it were by their own might; for they strain themselves through great violence, and pant so strongly, that they burst into bodily fervours, as if they would draw God down from Heaven to them. And they say in their hearts and with their mouth: Ah, Lord! I love Thee, and I will love Thee, and I will suffer death for the love of Thee. And in this manner of working they feel great fervour and much grace. And true it is, I think, this working good and meritorious, if it be well tempered with humility and discretion. But yet these men love not, nor have the gift of love on that manner that I speak of, neither do they ask it so. For a soul that hath the gift of love through gracious beholding of Jesus, as I mean, or that soul that hath it not yet, but would have it, she is not busy to strain herself above her strength, as it were by bodily might, for to have it by bodily fervours, and so far to feel the love of God, but thinketh herself to be right nought, and that she can do right nought of herself; but as it were a dead thing, only depending and borne up by the mercy of God. She seeth well that Jesus is all, and doth all, and, therefore, asketh she nought else but the gift of love; for since the soul seeth that her own love is nought, therefore she desireth His love, for that is enough. Therefore she prayeth and desireth that the love of God should touch her with His blessed light, that she may see a little of Him by His gracious presence, for then should she love Him; and so by this way cometh the gift of love, which is God, into a soul. The more that a soul noughteth itself through grace by sight of this verity, sometime without any fervour showed outwardly, and the less that it thinketh that it loveth or seeth God, the nearer it approacheth for to perceive the gift of this blessed love; for then is love master, and worketh in the soul, and maketh it forget itself, and for to see and look on only how love worketh; and then is the soul more suffering than doing, and that is pure love. Thus St Paul meant when he said thus: Quicumque spiritu Dei aguntur, &c.—They that are wrought by the spirit of God are God's sons. That is, souls that are made so humble, and so pliable to God, that they work not of themselves, but suffer the Holy Ghost to stir and work in them the feelings of love with a sweet chord to His stirrings. These are in a special manner God's sons most like unto Him.

Other souls that cannot love thus, but travail themselves by their own afflictions, and stir themselves through their own thinking of God and bodily exercise, for to draw out of themselves, by mastery, the feeling of love, by fervours and other bodily signs, these love not spiritually. They do well and meritoriously, if so be they understand humbly that this their working is not the kindly gracious feeling of love, but is a human acting of the soul at the bidding of reason. And, nevertheless, through the goodness of God, because the soul doth as much as in it is, these human affections of the soul stirred into God by man's working are turned into spiritual affections, and are meritorious, as if they had been done spiritually in the first beginning. And this is a great courtesy of our Lord showed to humble souls, which turneth all these human affections of natural love into the affection and into the reward of His own love, as if He had wrought them all fully by Himself. And so these human affections thus turned may be called affections of spiritual love through purchase, not through kindly bringing forth of the Holy Ghost. I say not that a soul can work such human affections only of itself without grace; for I wot well that St Paul saith that we can do just nought, nor think anything that is good of ourselves without grace. Non enim quod sumus sufficientes, &c.—Not as if we were sufficient of ourselves to think anything as of ourselves, but all our sufficiency is of God. For God worketh in all both good work and good will, as St Paul saith: It as God that worketh in us both to will and to do, according to His good pleasure. But I say that such affections are good, being made by the will and endeavours of a soul according to the general grace that He giveth to all chosen souls, not of special grace made spiritually by the touching of His gracious presence, as He worketh in His perfect love, as I said before; for in unperfect lovers love worketh at a distance by human affections; but in perfect lovers love worketh nearly by her own spiritual affections, and killeth in a soul, for the time, all other affections, both carnal, natural and human; and that is properly the working of love by itself. Thus love may be had in some measure, in part, here in a pure soul through the spiritual sight of Jesus; but in the bliss of Heaven it is fulfilled by clear sight in His Godhead; for there shall no affections be felt in a soul but such as are divine and spiritual.

CHAPTER VI: THAT THE GIFT OF LOVE, AMONGST ALL OTHER GIFTS OF JESUS, IS MOST WORTHY AND MOST PROFITABLE. AND HOW JESUS DOTH ALL THAT IS WELL DONE IN HIS LOVERS, ONLY FOR LOVE. AND HOW LOVE MAKETH THE EXERCISE OF ALL VIRTUES AND ALL GOOD DEEDS LIGHT AND EASY

ASK, then, of God nothing but this gift of love, which is the Holy Ghost. For among all the gifts that our Lord giveth there is none so good, nor so profitable, so worthy nor so excellent as this is. For there is no gift of God that is both the giver and the gift, but this gift of love; and, therefore, it is the best and the worthiest. The gift of prophecy, the gift of working miracles, the gift of great knowledge and counsel, and the gift of great fasting, or of great penance doing, or any other such, are great gifts of the Holy Ghost, but they are not the Holy Ghost, for a reprobate and damnable soul may have all these gifts as well as an elect soul. And, therefore, all these kinds of gifts are not greatly to be desired or cared for much. But the gift of love is the Holy Ghost, God Himself, and Him can no soul have and withal be damned; for that gift alone saveth from damnation, and maketh it God's son, and a receiver of the heavenly heritage. And that love, as I have said before, is not the affection of love that is created in a soul, but it is the Holy Ghost Himself, that is, love uncreated, that saveth a soul. For He first giveth Himself to that soul before the soul loveth Him, and He formeth the affection in the soul, and maketh the soul to love Him only for Himself. And not only so, but also by this gift the soul loveth itself, and her neighbour as herself only for God. And this is the gift of love that maketh the distinction betwixt chosen and reprobate souls. And this gift maketh perfect peace betwixt God and a soul, and uniteth all blessed creatures wholly in God; for it maketh Jesus for to love us, and us Him also, and each of us to love one another in Him.

Covet this gift of love principally, as I have said; for if He please out of His grace to give it thee on that manner, it shall open and enlighten the reason of thy soul, to see verity, that is God, and spiritual things. And it shall stir up thy affections wholly and fully for to love Him. And it shall work in thy soul only as He will, and thou shalt behold Jesus reverently, with softness of love, and see how He worketh. Thus commanded He by His Prophet that we should do, saying thus: Vaacaate et videte quoniam ego sum Deus.—Cease ye, and see that I am God. That is, ye that are reformed in feeling, and have your inner eye opened into sight of spiritual things, cease ye sometime from outward working, and see that I am God. That is, see only how I, Jesus, God and Man, do; behold ye Me, for I do all, I am love, and for love I do all that I do, and ye do nought. And that this is truth, I shall show you, for there is no good deed done by you, nor good thought felt in you, but what is done by Me. That is, through power and wisdom and love mightily, wisely and lovely, else it is no good deed. But now it is true that I, Jesus, am both power and wisdom and blessed love, and ye are naught, for I am God. Therefore may you easily see that I do all your good deeds, and all your good thoughts, and all your good loves in you, and ye do right nought. And yet, nevertheless, be all these good deeds called yours. Not because ye work them principally, but for that I give them unto you for love that I bear to you. And, therefore, since I am Jesus, and for love do all this, cease then ye from beholding of yourselves, and set yourselves at nought, and look on Me, and see that I am God, for I do all this. This is somewhat of the meaning of that verse of David before said.

See then and behold what love worketh in a chosen soul, which he reformeth in feeling to his likeness, when the reason is enlightened to the spiritual knowing of Jesus, and to the feeling of His love. Then bringeth love into the soul the perfection of virtues, and turneth them all into quietness, and into liking, as it were, without working of the soul; for the soul striveth not much for the getting of them, as it did before; but it hath them easily, and feeleth them restfully, only through the gift of love, that is, the Holy Ghost. And that is a very great comfort, and gladness unspeakable, when she feeleth suddenly in herself (and scarce knows how) the virtues of humility and patience, sobriety and staidness, chastity and purity and love to her neighbour. And all other virtues which were sometimes travaillous, painful and hard for to keep, are now turned into easiness, and liking, and into wonderful lightness, insomuch that she thinketh it no mastery nor difficulty to keep every virtue, but it is most pleasing to him to keep it, and all this is made by love.

Other men that stand in the way of common charity, and are not yet got so far in grace, but work under the command of reason, they strive and fight all day against sins for the procuring of virtues; and sometimes they be above, and sometimes beneath as wrestlers are.

These men do full well, they have virtues in reason, and will, not in savour, nor in love. For they fight with themselves as it were by their own might for them; therefore cannot they fully have rest, nor perfectly the higher hand. Nevertheless they shall have great reward, but they are not yet humble enough. They have not yet put themselves altogether into God's hand, for they see Him not yet. But a soul that hath spiritual sight of Jesus taketh no great care of striving for virtues for that time. He is not busy about them particularly, but he maketh it all his business to keep that sight, and that beholding of Jesus which it hath for to hold the mind stably thereto, and bind his love only to it, that it fall not from it, but forget all other things as much as it can. And when it doth thus, then is Jesus verily Master against all sins, and overshadoweth it with His blessed presence, and getteth it all virtues. And the soul is so comforted and so borne up with the restful feeling of love that it hath of the sight of Jesus, that it feeleth no great disease outwardly. And thus doth love generally slay all sins in a soul, and reformeth it in the new feelings of virtues.

CHAPTER VII: HOW LOVE THROUGH GRACIOUS BEHOLDING OF JESUS SLAYETH ALL STIRRINGS OF PRIDE; AND MAKETH THE SOUL TO LOSE THE SAVOUR AND DELIGHT IN ALL EARTHLY HONOURS

NEVERTHELESS I shall tell thee more particularly how love killeth sins in a soul, and reformeth virtues. And first of Pride, and the virtue contrary thereto, namely, Humility. Thou must understand that there be two kinds of Humility; one is had by working of reason; another is felt by the special gift of love. Both are of love, but the former love worketh by, and with the reason of the soul, and the latter love worketh by herself. The first is imperfect, the other is perfect. The first a man feeleth from the beholding of his own sins and wretchedness, through the which beholding he thinketh himself unworthy to have any gift of grace, or any reward of God, but thinketh it enough that He would of His great mercy, grant him forgiveness of his sins. And also he thinketh himself, because of his sins, to be worse than the greatest sinner that liveth, and that every man doth better than he. And by such beholding thrusteth he himself down in his thoughts under all men. And he is busy to withstand the stirrings of pride as much as he can, both bodily and spiritual pride, and despiseth himself so that he assenteth not to the feelings of pride. And if his heart be taken sometimes with it, that it be defiled with vain joy of worship and praise from others; or from the conceit of his wit, or of any other thing, as soon as he perceiveth it he is displeased with himself, and hath sorrow for it in heart, and asketh forgiveness for it of God, and showeth himself to his confessor, and accuseth himself humbly, and receiveth his penance. This is good humility, but it is not yet perfect humility; for it is of souls that are beginning and profiting in grace caused by the beholding of their sins. Love worketh this humility by reason.

Perfect humility a soul feeleth from the sight and spiritual knowing of Jesus; for when the Holy Ghost lighteneth the reason into the sight of verity, how Jesus is all, and that He doth all, the soul hath so great love and so great joy in that spiritual sight (for it is really so indeed) that it forgetteth itself, fully leaneth to Jesus with all the love that it hath to behold Him. It taketh no heed of any unworthiness of itself, nor of sins aforedone, but setteth at nought itself, with all the sins, and all the good deeds that ever it did, as if there were nothing but Jesus. Thus was David humble when he said thus: Et substantia mea tanquam nihilum ante Te.—And my substance is as nothing before Thee. That is, Lord Jesus, the sight of why blessed uncreated substance and of Thine endless Being showeth well unto me that my substance and being of my soul is as nought in regard of Thee.

Also, such a soul in respect to his neighbour hath no regard to him, nor judging of him, whether he be better or worse than himself; for he esteemeth himself and all other men to be all alike, and to be just nought of themselves in regard of God (and this is very so). For all the goodness that is wrought in himself, or in others, is only of God, whom he beholdeth as all in all. And therefore setteth he all other creatures at nought, as he doth himself. Thus humble was the Prophet when he said thus: Omnes gentes quasi non sint sic sunt coram eo, &c.—All nations are before our Lord as if they were not, and are reputed as nothing, and as a vain thing. That is, in comparison of the endless Being, and the unchangeable nature of God, mankind is as nought; for of nought was it made, and to nought shall it return, unless He keep it in its being that made it of nought. This is truth, and this should make a soul humble, if by grace it could see this truth. Therefore when once love openeth the inner eye of the soul, for to see this truth, with other circumstances that attend it, then beginneth the soul to be really humble; for then through the sight of God it feeleth and seeth itself as it is; and then doth the soul forsake the beholding and leaning upon itself; and fully falleth to the beholding of Jesus. And when it doth so, then setteth the soul nought by all the joy and worship of the world, for the joy of worldly worship is so little, and so nought, in regard of that joy and of that love that it feeleth in the spiritual sight of Jesus and knowledge of the truth that, though it might have it without any sin, he would have nothing to do with it. No, though men would worship him, praise him, and favour him, or set him in great state, it would nothing at all please him. No, though he had great skill in all the seven liberal sciences, and of all skill under the sun, or had power to work all manner of miracles, yet would he take no more delight in all this, nor no more savour than to gnaw on a dry stick. He had rather forget all this, and to be alone out of the sight of the world, than to think of them and be worshipped of all men; for the heart of a true lover of Jesus is made so much, and so large through a little sight of Him, and a little feeling of His spiritual love, that all the liking and all the joy of all the earth cannot suffice to fill a corner of it. And then appeareth it well that these wretched worldly lovers, that are, as it were, ravished with the love of their own worship, and pursue after it to have it with all the might and all the wit they have, they have no taste of this Humility, but are wondrous far from it. But the lover of Jesus hath this humility lastingly, and that not with heaviness and striving for it, but with liking and gladness. The which gladness he hath not therefore, because he forsaketh the worship of the world, for that were a proud humility belonging to an hypocrite; but because he hath a sight and a spiritual knowing of the verity and worthiness of Jesus through the gift of the Holy Ghost. That reverend sight, and that lovely beholding of Jesus comforteth his love so wonderfully, and beareth it up so mightily and so easily, that verily it cannot like, nor fully rest in any earthly joy, nor would he if he could. He maketh no matter whether men praise him or dispraise him, worship him or despise him, as to himself he sets it not to heart, neither to be well pleased (for his greater humiliation) when men despise him, nor to be displeased when men worship him or praise him. He had rather forget both the one and the other, and only think on Jesus, and get humility by that way. And that is much the securer way whosoever can attain to it. Thus did David when he said: Oculi mei semper ad Dominum, &c.—My eyes are always to the Lord, for He shall pluck my feet out of the net. For when he doth so, then forsaketh he utterly himself, and casteth himself wholly under Jesus, and then is he in a secure guard; for the shield of Truth which he holdeth keepeth him so well that he shall not be hurt through any stirring of pride, as long as he holdeth himself within the shield. As the Prophet saith: Scuto circumdabit te veritas ejus, &c.—Verity shall compass thee with a shield. And that is, if thou, leaving all other things, only beholdest Him; for then shalt thou not dread for the night's dread; that is, thou shalt not fear the spirit of pride, whether he come by night or by day, as the next verse saith thus: A sagitta volante in die—From the arrow that flieth by day. Pride cometh by night to assail a soul when it is despised and contemned of other men, that thereby it should fall into heaviness and into sorrow. It cometh also as an arrow flying on the day, when a man is praised and worshipped of all men; whether it be for wordly doing or spiritual, that he should have vain joy in himself, and to rest therein, and false gladness in a thing that is passing. This is a sharp arrow and a perilous, it fleeth swiftly, and it striketh softly, but it woundeth deadly. But the lover of Jesus, that stably beholdeth by devout prayers, and busy thinking on him, is so encompassed with the safe shield of Truth that he dreadeth it not; for this arrow cannot enter into his soul. Nay, though it come it hurteth him not, but glanceth away and passeth forth.

And thus is the soul made humble, as I understand, by the working of the Holy Ghost, that is, the gift of love; for He openeth the eye of the soul to see and love Jesus, and He keepeth the soul in that sight restfully and securely; and He slayeth all the stirrings of pride wonderfully and privily and softly, and the soul knoweth not how. And also He bringeth in by that way verily and lovely the virtue of humility. All this doth love, but not in all lovers alike fully; for some have this grace but short and little, as it were in the beginning of it, and a little assaying toward it; for the conscience is not yet cleansed fully through grace. And some have it more fully, for they have clearer sight of Jesus, and they feel more of this love. And some have it most fully, for they have the full gift of Contemplation. Nevertheless, he that hath the least on this manner that I have said, I hope verily he hath the gift of perfect humility, for he hath the gift of perfect love.

CHAPTER VIII: HOW LOVE SLAYETH ALL STIRRINGS OF WRATH AND ENVY EASILY; AND REFORMETH IN THE SOUL THE VIRTUES OF PEACE AND PATIENCE, AND OF PERFECT CHARITY TO HIS NEIGHBOUR, AS HE DID SPECIALLY IN THE APOSTLES

LOVE, where it worketh, worketh wisely and easily in a soul; for he slayeth mightily anger and envy, and all passions of wrath and melancholy in it, and bringeth into the soul the virtues of patience and mildness, peaceableness and amity to his neighbour. It is full hard and a great mastery for a man that standeth only in working of his own reason to keep patience, holy rest and softness in heart and charity to his neighbour, when they use him hardly and do him wrong, that he do not through motion or rising of anger or bitterness within him something against them, either by word or deed, or both. (And nevertheless though a man be stirred and troubled in himself, and made unrestful, if so be it passeth not too much the bounds of reason, and that he keep his hands and his tongue, and be ready to forgive the trespass when forgiveness is asked, yet this man hath the virtue of patience, though it be but weak and nakedly. Forasmuch as he desires to have it, and laboureth busily in restraining his unruly passions to the end that he may have it, and also is sorry that he hath it not as he should.) But to a true lover of Jesus it is no great mastery for to suffer all this; for why? Love fighteth for him, and slayeth wondrous easily such stirrings of wrath and of melancholy; and maketh his soul so easy and so peaceable, so suffering and so goodly, through the spiritual sight of Jesus, with the feeling of His blessed love, that though he be despised and contemned of other men, or suffer wrong or harm, shame or villainy, he heedeth it not, he is not much stirred against them; he will not be angered nor stirred against them, for, if he were much stirred, he should forego the comfort which he feeleth within his soul, but that will he not. He can lightlier forget all the wrong that is done him than another man can forgive it, though forgiveness was asked him; and so he had rather forget it; for he thinketh it most easy to him. And love doth all this, for love openeth the eye of the soul to the sight of Jesus, and establisheth it with the pleasure and content of love that it feeleth by that sight, and comforteth it so mightily that it taketh no heed whatever men jangle or do against him; it resteth nothing upon him; the greatest harm that he can suffer is a forbearing of the spiritual sight of Jesus; and therefore it is better for him to suffer all harms than that alone. All this can the soul do well and easily without great disturbing of this spiritual sight, when the grievances fall outwardly and touch not the body, as do backbitings or scornings or spoiling of his goods. All these grieve him nought; but it goeth somewhat nearer when his flesh is touched, and he feeleth smart, then is it harder.

Nevertheless, though it be hard and impossible to the frail nature of man to suffer bodily penance gladly and patiently, without bitter stirrings of ire, anger and melancholy, and yet it is not impossible to love, that is, the Holy Ghost for to work this in a soul, when He toucheth it with the blessed gift of love. But He giveth a soul that is in that plight mightily the feelings of love, and wonderfully fasteneth it to Jesus, and separateth it very far from sensuality through His secret might, and comforteth it so sweetly by His blessed presence that the soul feeleth little pain or else none at all in the sensual part; and this is a special grace given to the holy Martyrs.

This grace had the Apostles, as holy Writ saith of them thus: Ibant Apostoli gaudentes, &c.—The Apostles went from the Council rejoicing, when they were beaten with scourges, and they were glad that they were accounted worthy to suffer any bodily pain for the love of Jesus. They were not stirred to anger, nor to bitterness, to be revenged on the Jews that beat them, as a worldly man would be when he suffered a little harm, were it never so little, from his neighbour. Nay, they were not stirred to any pride, nor highness of mind, nor to disdain or judge the Jews, as hypocrites and heretics are who will suffer much bodily pain, and are sometimes ready to suffer death with great gladness and with mighty will, as it were in the name of Jesus, for love of Him. Verily, that love and that gladness that they have in suffering of bodily mischief is not of the Holy Ghost, it cometh not from the fire that burneth on the High Altar of Heaven, but it is feigned by the enemy, inflamed of hell; for it is fully mingled with the height of pride, and of presumption of themselves, of despite and judging and disdaining of those that thus punish them. They imagine that all this is charity, and that they suffer all that for the love of God, but they are beguiled by the mid-day fiend.

A true lover of Jesus, when he suffereth harm from his neighbour, is so strengthened through grace of the Holy Ghost, and is made so humble, so patient, so peaceable, and that so really, that what harm or wrong soever he suffereth from his neighbour, he still preserveth his humility, he despiseth him not, he judgeth him not, but he prayeth for him in his heart, and hath pity and compassion on him much more tenderly than of another man that never did him harm; and verily loveth him better, and more fervently desireth the salvation of his soul, because he seeth that we shall have so much spiritual profit out of that evil deed of that man though it be against his will. But this love and this meekness is wrought only by the Holy Ghost above the nature of man in them whom He maketh true lovers of Jesus.

CHAPTER IX: HOW LOVE SLAYETH COVETOUSNESS, LECHERY AND GLUTTONY, AND THE FLESHLY DELIGHT AND SAVOUR IN ALL THE FIVE BODILY SENSES, SOFTLY AND EASILY, THROUGH A GRACIOUS BEHOLDING OF JESUS

COVETOUSNESS also is slain in a soul by the working of love, for it maketh the soul so covetous of spiritual good and so inflamed to heavenly riches that it setteth right nought by all earthly things. It hath no more joy in the having of a precious stone than a chalk-stone; no more love hath he in an hundred pounds than in a pound of lead. It setteth all things that must perish at one price; he heedeth no more the one than the other, as to his love; for he knows well that all these earthly things which worldly men set so great price by and love so dearly must pass away and turn to nothing, both the thing itself and the love of it. And therefore he worketh his thoughts betimes into that judgement and esteem of them which they must come to hereafter, and so accounteth them as nought. And when worldly lovers strive and fight and plead for earthly goods, who may first have them; the lover of Jesus striveth with no man, but keepeth himself in peace, and is well contented with that which he hath, and will strive for no more; for he thinketh that he needs no more of all the riches on earth than a scanty bodily sustenance for to sustain his bodily life withal, as long as it pleaseth God, and that he can easily have. And therefore would he have no more than he barely needeth for the time, that he may freely be discharged from the trouble of keeping and spending of it, and fully give his heart and his business about the seeking of Jesus for to find Him in cleanness of spirit; for that is all his covetousness; for why?—only the clean in heart shall see Him.

Also, the fleshly love of father and mother and other worldly friends hangeth not upon him. It is even cut from his heart with the sword of spiritual love, so that he hath no more affection to father or mother, or to any worldly friend than he hath to another man, except he see or feel in them more grace or more virtue than in other men, or except that his father or mother hath the selfsame grace that some other men have. But if they be not so, then loveth he other men better than them, and that is charity. And thus doth God's love slay covetousness of the world, and bringeth into the soul poverty of spirit. And that doth love, not only in them that have right nought of worldly goods, but also in some creatures that are in great worldly state and have earthly riches to spend. Love slayeth in some of them covetousness so far forth that they have no more liking nor savour in having of them than of a straw. No, though it should so happen that they should lose them through default of those that should look after them, yet set they nought thereby. For why?—the heart of God's lover is, through the gift of the Holy Ghost, taken so fully with the sight of the love of another thing, which is Jesus, and that is so precious and so worthy that it will receive no other love to rest in it that is contrary thereto.

And not only doth love this, but also it slayeth the liking of Lechery and all other bodily uncleanness, and bringeth into the soul true chastity, and turneth it into liking. For the soul feeleth so great delight in the sight of Jesus that it liketh for to be chaste, and it is no great difficulty to it to keep chastity, for therein is most ease and most rest.

And in the same manner the gift of love slayeth the lusts of Gluttony, and maketh the soul sober and temperate, and beareth it up so mightily that it cannot rest in the liking of meat and drink. But it taketh such meat and drink, whatever it be, as least hindereth or chargeth the bodily complexion, if it can easily come by it; nor for the love of itself, but for the love of God. On this wise the lover of God seeth well that he needeth to sustain his bodily life with meat and drink, as long as God will suffer them to continue together. Here, then, will be the discretion of the lover of Jesus, as far as I understand that hath feeling and working in love, that in what manner he may best keep his grace whole, and be least letted from working in it through taking of bodily sustenance, so shall he do. That kind of meat, which least letteth and least troubleth the heart, and may keep the body in strength, be it flesh, be it fish, be it bread and ale, that I suppose the soul chooseth for to have, if it can come thereby. For the whole business of the soul is to think on Jesus with reverent love, constantly, without letting of anything, if that it might. And therefore since it must needs be letted somewhat and hindered the less it is letted and hindered by meat or drink or any other thing the better it is. It had rather use the best meat and most costly if it less hinder the keeping of his heart, than to take only bread and water, if that hinder him more; for he hath no regard for to get great merit by the pain of fasting, and be put thereby from softness and quietness of heart, but all his business is for to keep his heart as stably as he can in the sight of Jesus and in the feeling of His love. And surely I am of the opinion that he may with less lust and liking use the best meat, that is good in its kind, than another man that worketh all by reason without the special gift of love can use the worst. Ever excepting such meat as is dressed with art and curiosity only for lust, for such manner of meat cannot at all accord with him. And also on the other side, if little meat, as only bread and beer, most helpeth and quieteth his heart, and keepeth it most in peace, that is most acceptable to him for to use; and, namely, if he feel his bodily strength sustained thereby, and have the gift of love withal.

And yet doth love more, for it slayeth sloth and fleshly idleness, and maketh the soul to be occupied in goodness, and, namely, inwardly in beholding of him, by virtue whereof the soul hath savour and spiritual delight in praying, in meditating, and in all manner of doing that belongeth to him to do according to the state he is in, without heaviness or painful bitterness, whether he be religious or secular.

Also, it slayeth the vain likings of the five bodily senses. As first of the sight of the eyes, so that the soul hath no liking in the sight of any worldly thing, but feeleth rather pain and disease in beholding of it, be it never so fair, never so precious, never so wonderful. And, therefore, as worldly lovers run out sometimes for to see new things, for to wonder at them, and so for to feed their hearts with the vain sight of them; right so a lover of Jesus is busy for to run away, and withdraw himself from the sight of such manner of things, that the inner sight be not letted; for he spiritually seeth another manner of thing, which is fairer and more wonderful, and that would he not forbear.

Right on the self-same wise is it of speaking and hearing. It is a pain to the soul of a lover of Jesus for to speak or hear anything that might let the freedom of his heart from thinking on Jesus, whatever song, or melody, or music outward it be, if it hinder the thought that it cannot freely and restfully pray, or think on him, it liketh him right nought. And the more delectable it is to other men, the more unsavoury it is to him. And also to hear any manner of speaking of other men, unless it be somewhat touching the working of his soul into the love of Jesus, it liketh him right nought, he is right soon weary of it. He had rather be in peace, and hear right nought, nay speak right nought, than for to hear the speaking and the teaching of the greatest Clerk on earth, with all the reasons that he can say to him by human wit, except he can speak feelingly and stirringly of the love of Jesus; for there lies his skill principally. And therefore would not he speak of anything else, nor hear, nor see anything, but what might help him, and further him into more knowledge, and to better feeling of Him.

Of worldly speech it is no doubt that he hath no savour in speaking, nor in hearing of it, nor in worldly tales, nor tidings, nor in any such vain jangling that belongeth not to Him. And the same is of smelling and tasting. The more the thoughts are distracted and broken from spiritual rest by the use either of smelling, or tasting, or of any of the senses, the more he avoideth it. The less that he feeleth of them, the better he is. And if he could live in the body without the feeling of any of them he would never feel them, for they trouble the heart oft-times, and put it from rest; but they cannot fully be eschewed. Nevertheless the love of Jesus is sometimes so mighty in a soul, that it overcometh and slayeth all that is contrary thereto for a time.

CHAPTER X: WHAT VIRTUES AND GRACES A SOUL RECEIVETH THROUGH OPENING OF THE INNER EYE INTO THE GRACIOUS BEHOLDING OF JESUS, AND HOW IT CANNOT BE GOTTEN ONLY BY MAN'S LABOUR, BUT THROUGH SPECIAL GRACE AND HIS OWN LABOUR ALSO

THUS worketh love in a soul, opening the ghostly eye into the beholding of Jesus by inspiration of special grace, and maketh it pure, subtle and able to the work of Contemplation. What this opening of the spiritual eye is the greatest scholar on earth cannot imagine by his wit nor show fully by his tongue; for it cannot be gotten by study, nor by man's industry alone, but principally by grace of the Holy Ghost, and with human industry. I am afraid to speak anything of it, for methinketh that I cannot, it passeth my attempt, and my lips are unclean. Nevertheless, because it seems to me that love asketh, yea, love biddeth that I should, therefore shall I say a little more of it as I hope love teacheth. This opening of the spiritual eye is that lightsome darkness and rich nought that I spake of before, and it may be called purity of spirit and spiritual rest, inward stillness and peace of conscience, highness of thought and loneliness of soul, a lively feeling of grace and retiredness of heart, the watchful sleep of the spouse and tasting of heavenly savour, burning in love and shining in light, the gate of Contemplation and reforming in feeling. All these expressions are found in holy writings of divers men, for every one of them speaketh according to his feeling in grace. And though all these be divers in show of words, yet are they all one in meaning and verity; for that soul which through visiting of grace hath one of them hath all. For why? a soul sighing to see the Face of Jesus when it is touched through special grace of the Holy Ghost, it is suddenly changed, and turned from the state that it was in into another manner of feeling. It is wonderfully separated and drawn first into itself, from the love and the liking of all earthly things, so much that it hath lost the savour of the bodily life, and of all things save only Jesus. And then is it clean from all the filth of sin, so far forth that the minding of itself, and all other inordinate affections to any creature is suddenly washed and wiped away, so that there remains no middle thing or impediment betwixt Jesus and the soul, but only the bodily life, and then it is in spiritual rest. For why? all painful doubts and fears, and all other temptations of spiritual enemies are driven out of the heart, that they trouble not, nor sink not into it for the time. It is in rest from the annoyance of worldly business, and painful hindrances of wicked stirrings; but it is full busy in the free spiritual working of love. And the more it laboureth so, the more rest it feeleth.

This restful labouring is full far from fleshly idleness and from blind security. It is full of spiritual working, but it is called rest, for that grace loseth the heavy yoke of fleshly love from the soul, and maketh it mighty and free through the gift of spiritual love for to work gladly, softly and delectably in all things to which grace stirreth it to work in. And therefore it is called an holy idleness and a rest most busy, and so it is in regard of stillness from the great crying of the beastly noise of fleshly desires and unclean thoughts. This stillness is made by the inspiration of the Holy Ghost through the beholding of Jesus. For why? His voice is so sweet and so mighty that it putteth to silence in a soul all the jangling of all other speakers; for it is a voice of power, softly founded in a pure soul, of the which the Prophet saith thus: Vox Domini in virtute.—The voice of our Lord Jesus is with power. This voice is a lively words and speedy, as the Apostle saith: Vivus est sermo Dei, &c.—The word of the Lord is lively and powerful, more piercing than any sword is. Through speaking of this word is fleshly love slain, and the soul kept in silence from all wicked stirrings. Of this silence it is said in the Apocalypse thus: Factum est silentium in coelo, &c.—Silence was made in heaven as it were half an hour. By Heaven is meant a pure soul lifted up through grace from earthly love to heavenly conversation, and so it is in silence. But forasmuch as that silence cannot last whole continually by reason of the corruption of the bodily nature; therefore it is compared to the time of half an hour, a very short time the soul thinketh it to be, though it be never so long; and therefore it is but half an hour.

And then hath it peace in conscience. For why? Grace putteth out the gnawing, pricking, striving and fighting of sins, and bringeth in peace and concord, and maketh Jesus and a soul both one in full agreement of will. There is no upbraiding of sins, nor sharp reproving of faults made at that time in a soul, for they have kissed and are made friends, and all is forgiven that was done amiss.

Thus feeleth the soul, then, with great humble security and great spiritual gladness, and conceiveth a full great certainty of salvation by this accordmaking; for it heareth a secret witnessing of the Holy Ghost to the conscience, that he is a chosen son to a heavenly heritage. Thus St Paul saith: Ipse Spiritus testimonium perhibet spiritui nostro, &c.—The Holy Spirit beareth witness to our spirit that we are God's sons.

This witnessing of conscience verily felt through grace is the very joy of the soul, as the Apostle saith: Gloria mea est testimonium, &c.—My joy is the witness of my conscience: and that is, when it witnesseth peace and accord, true love and friendship betwixt Jesus and a soul. And when it is in this peace, then is it in highness of thought.

When the soul is bound with the love of the world, then is it beneath all creatures; for everything goeth over it, and beareth it down by mastery, that it cannot see Jesus nor love Him. For even as the love of the world is vain and fleshly, right so the beholding and thinking and using of all creatures is fleshly; and that is a thraldom of the soul. But then through opening of the spiritual eye into Jesus the love is turned, and the soul is raised up according to its own nature above all bodily creatures. And then the beholding and thinking, and the using of them is spiritual, for the love is spiritual. The soul hath then great disdain to be obedient to the love of worldly things, for it is high set above them through grace. It setteth nought by all the world. For why? It will all pass away and perish. Unto this highness of heart, as long as the soul is kept therein, cometh no error nor deceit of the enemy; for Jesus is really in sight of the soul at that time, and all other things are beneath it. Of this the Prophet speaketh thus: Accedat homo ad cor altum et exaltabitur Deus.—Let a man come to a high heart, and God shall be exalted. That is, a man that through grace cometh to the highness of thought shall see that Jesus is only exalted above all creatures, and he in Him.

And then is the soul thus set aloft, estranged from the fellowship of worldly lovers, though his body be in the midst among them, full far is he parted from carnal affections of creatures. He careth not though he never see man, nor speak with him, nor have comfort from him, that he might for ever continue in that spiritual feeling. He feeleth so great familiarity of the blessed presence of our Lord Jesus, and so much savour of Him, that he can easily for love of Him forget the fleshly affection and the fleshly mind of all creatures. I say not that he shall not love nor think of other creatures, that he shall think on them in fitting time, and see them and love them spiritually and freely, not fleshly and painfully as he did before. Of this loneliness speaketh the Prophet thus: Ducam eam in solitudinem, &c.—I will lead her into solitude, and I will speak to her heart. That is, the grace of Jesus leadeth the soul from troublesome company of fleshly desires into loneliness of thought, and maketh it forget the liking of the world, and soundeth by sweetness of His inspiration words of love in the ears of the heart. A soul is thus lonely when it loveth Jesus, and attendeth fully to Him, and he hath lost the savour and the comfort of the world; and that it may better keep this loneliness, it fleeth the company of men as much as it can; and seeketh loneliness of body, which helpeth much to the loneliness of the soul, and to the free working of love, the less hindrance that it hath from without of vain janglings, or from within of vain thinking, the more free it is in spiritual beholding. And so it is in retiredness of heart.

A soul is all without, whilst it is overlaid and blinded with worldly love, it is as common as the highway, for every stirring which cometh from the flesh or from the fiend sinketh in or goeth through it. But then through grace it is drawn into the privy-chamber, into the sight of our Lord Jesus, and heareth His privy counsel, and is wonderfully comforted in the hearing. Of this speaketh the Prophet thus: Secretum meum mihi, secretum meum mihi.—My privity to me, my privity to me. That is, the lover of Jesus, through inspiration of grace, taken up from outward feeling of worldly love, and ravished into the privity of spiritual love, yieldeth thanks to Him, saying thus: My privity to me. That is, my Lord Jesus, Thy privity is showed to me, and privily hid from all lovers of the world; for it is called hidden Manna, which may easier be asked than told what it is. And that our Lord Jesus promiseth to His lover, saying thus: Dabo sibi Manna absconditum, &c.—I will give her the hidden Manna which no man knoweth but he that taketh it. This Manna is heavenly meat, and angels' food, as the Scripture saith; for angels are fully fed and filled with clear sight in burning love of our Lord Jesus, and that is Manna; for we may ask what it is, but cannot know what it is. But the lover of Jesus is not yet filled here, but is fed with a little taste of it, whilst he is bound in this bodily life.

This tasting of this Manna is a lively feeling of grace had through the opening of the spiritual eye. And this grace is not another grace from that which a chosen soul feeleth in the beginning of his conversion; but it is the self-same grace, only it is otherwise felt and showed to a soul. For why? Grace groweth with a soul, and the soul groweth with grace. And the clearer that a soul is parted from the love of the world, the more mighty is its grace, the more inward and more spiritual is the showing of the presence of our Lord Jesus come to be. So that the same grace which at first turneth him from sin, and maketh him beginning and profiting by gifts of virtue and exercise of good works, maketh him also perfect. And that grace is called a lively feeling of grace; for he that hath it feeleth it well, and knoweth well by experience that he is in grace. It is full lively to him; for it quickeneth the soul wonderfully, and maketh it so whole that it feeleth no painful disease of the body, though it be feeble and sickly. For why? Then is the body most mighty, most whole and most restful, and the soul also. Without this grace the soul cannot live but in pain; for it thinketh that it can keep it for ever, and nothing can put it away; but it is not so, for it passeth away full easily. Nevertheless though the sovereign feeling passeth away, and is withdrawn, the virtue of it stayeth still, and keepeth the soul in sobriety, and maketh it to desire the coming again thereof.

And this is the waking sleep of the Spouse, of the which the Scripture thus: Ego dormio, et cor meum vigilat.—I sleep, and my heart waketh. That is, I sleep spiritually when through grace the love of the world is slain in me, and wicked stirrings of fleshly desires are dead, insomuch that I scarce feel them. I am not held by them, my heart is made free. And then it waketh, for it is quick and ready to love Jesus, and see Him. The more I sleep from outward things, the more am I awake in knowing of Jesus and of inward things. I cannot be awake to Jesus, except I sleep to the world. And therefore the grace of the Holy Ghost, shutting the fleshly eye, causeth the soul to sleep from worldly vanities, and opening the spiritual eye, keepeth it awake to the sight of God's majesty covered under the cloud of His precious Humanity. As the Gospel saith of the Apostles, when they were with our Lord Jesus in His transfiguration, first they slept: Et evigilantes viderunt majestatem.—They waking beheld His glory. By sleep of the Apostles is understood the dying of worldly love through the inspiration of the Holy Ghost; by their awaking is understood their Contemplation of Jesus. Through this sleep the soul is brought into rest from the noise of fleshly lust, and through waking is raised up to the sight of Jesus and spiritual things. The more that the eyes are shut in this manner of sleep from the appetite of earthly things, the sharper is the inner sight in lovely beholding of heavenly beauty. This sleeping and this waking doth love work through the light of grace in the soul of the lover of our Lord Jesus.

CHAPTER XI: HOW SUCH SPECIAL GRACE FOR THE BEHOLDING OF OUR LORD JESUS IS WITHDRAWN SOMETIMES FROM A SOUL; AND HOW A SOUL IS TO BEHAVE HERSELF IN THE ABSENCE AND IN THE PRESENCE OF JESUS, AND HOW A SOUL SHALL ALWAY DESIRE (AS MUCH AS IS IN HER) THE GRACIOUS PRESENCE OF JESUS

SHOW me then a soul that through inspiration of grace hath this opening of the spiritual sight into the beholding of Jesus that is separated and drawn out from the love of the world, so far forth that it hath purity and privity of spirit, spiritual rest, inward silence and peace of conscience, highness of thought, loneliness and privity of heart, the waking sleep of the Spouse, that hath lost the liking and joys of the world, taken with delight of heavenly savour, ever thirsting and softly hasting after that blessed presence of Jesus; and I dare boldly pronounce that this soul burneth all in love, and shineth in spiritual light, worthy to come to the name and to the worship of the Spouse; for it is reformed in feeling, made able and ready to Contemplation. These are the tokens of inspiration in opening of the spiritual eye. For when the eye is opened, the soul is in full feeling of all the aforesaid virtues for that time.

Nevertheless it falleth out oftentimes that grace withdraweth in part by reason of the corruption of man's frailty, and suffereth then the soul to fall into itself in sensuality, as it was before; and then is the soul in pain and in sorrow, for it is blind and unsavoury and can do no good. It is weak and impotent, encumbered with the body and all the bodily senses. It seeketh and desireth after the grace of Jesus again, and it cannot find it; for the Scripture saith thus of our Lord: Postquam vultum suum absconderit, &c.—When our Lord hath hid His face, there is none that can behold Him. When He showeth His face, the soul cannot but see Him, for He is light; and when He hideth Himself, it cannot see Him, for the soul is dark.

His hiding is but a subtle trying of the soul. His showing is a wonderful merciful goodness in comfort of the soul. Wonder not though the feelings of grace be sometimes withdrawn from a lover of Jesus; for holy Writ saith the same of the Spouse, that it fareth thus with her: Quaesivi et non inveni illum, &c.— I sought Him, and I found Him not; I called, and He answered not. That is, when I fall down to my frailty and sin, then grace withdraweth; for my falling is the cause thereof, and not His flying, but then feel I pain of my wretchedness in His absence. And, therefore, I sought Him by great desire of heart, and He gave to me not so much as a feeble answer. And then I cried with all my soul: Revertere, dilecte mi—Turn again, Thou my beloved. And yet He seemed as if He heard me not. The painful feeling of myself, and the assailing of fleshly loves and fears in this time, and the wanting of my spiritual strength is a continual crying of my soul to Jesus. And nevertheless our Lord maketh strange, and cometh not, cry I never so fast; for He is sure enough of His lover, that he will not turn again to worldly loves quite; he can have no savour in them, and, therefore, stayeth He the longer.

But at the last when He pleaseth, He cometh again full of grace and faithfulness, and visiteth the soul that languisheth through desire, by sighings of love after His presence, and toucheth it, and anointeth it full gently with the oil of gladness, and maketh it suddenly whole from all pain. And then crieth the soul to Jesus in a spiritual voice with a glad heart thus: Oleum effusum Nomen tuum.—Thy Name is as oil poured out. Thy Name is Jesus, that is, health. Then as long as I feel my soul sore and sick by reason of sin, pained with the heavy burthen of my body, sorrowful and fearful for perils and wretchedness of this life, so long, Lord Jesus, Thy Name is oil shut up, not poured forth. But when I feel my soul suddenly touched with the light of Thy grace, healed and cured from all the filth of sin, and comforted in love and in light with spiritual strength and gladness unspeakable, then can I say with lusty, loving and spiritual might to Thee: Thy Name, O Jesu, is to me oil poured forth. For by the effect of Thy gracious visitation I feel well the true exposition of Thy Name, that Thou art Jesus, health, for only Thy gracious presence healeth me from sorrow and from sin.

Happy is that soul that is ever fed with feeling of love in His presence, or is borne up by desire to Him in His absence. A wise lover is he, and well taught, that soberly and reverently behaveth himself in His presence, and lovely beholdeth Him without dissolute lightness, and patiently and easily beareth His absence without venomous despair and over painful bitterness.

This changeability of the absence and presence of Jesus, which a soul feeleth, is neither the perfection of the soul nor is it contrary to the grace of perfection or of Contemplation, but only a state of less perfection; for the more letting that a soul hath of itself from the constant feeling of grace, the less is the grace; and yet, nevertheless, is the grace in itself grace of Contemplation. This changeability of absence and presence falleth as well in the state of perfection as in the state of beginning, but after another manner; for even as there is diversity of feeling in the presence of grace betwixt these two states, right so is there in the absence of grace. And, therefore, he that knoweth not the absence of grace is apt to be deceived. And he that maketh not much of the presence of grace is unthankful to the visiting thereof, whether he be in the state of beginners or of the perfect. Nevertheless, the more stableness that there is in grace unhurt and unbroken, the lovelier is the soul, and more like unto Him in whom is no changeableness, as the Apostle saith. And it is very meet that the

Spouse should be like her Bridegroom Jesus in manners and in virtues, fully according to Him in stableness of perfect love. But that falleth out seldom here in Spouses of this life; for he that perceiveth no changeableness in the feeling of his grace, but is all alike, whole, stable, unbroken and unhurt, as he thinketh, he is either very perfect or very blind. He is perfect if he be sequestered from all carnal affections and inclinations to creatures, and hath all hindrances of corruption and of sin betwixt Jesus and his soul broken away, and is fully united to Him with softness of love. But this is only from grace above man's nature. Or he is very blind if he imagineth himself to be in grace without spiritual feeling of God's inspiration, and setteth himself in a way of stableness, as if he were ever in feeling and in working of special grace, imagining all to be grace which he doth and feeleth, both inwardly and outwardly, thinking that whatsoever he doth or speaketh is grace, holding himself unchangeable in speciality of grace. If there be any such, as I hope there is none, he is full blind in feeling of grace.

But thou mayest object: That we ought to live only by Faith, and not covet spiritual feelings, nor regard them if they come; for the Apostle saith: The just shall live by faith.

Unto this I answer that bodily feelings, be they never so comfortable, are not to be desired nor regarded much if they come; but spiritual feelings, such as I have spoken of, if they come in that manner as I have said, should ever be desired. I mean the killing of all worldly love, the opening of the spiritual eye, purity of spirit, peace of conscience and all other spoken of before. We should ever covet to feel the lively inspiration of grace made by the spiritual presence of Jesus in our souls, if we could. And for to have Him in our sight with reverence, and ever feel the sweetness of His love by a wonderful familiarity of His presence. This should be our life and our feeling in grace after the measure of His gift in whom all grace is, to some more and to some less; for His presence is felt in divers manners as He pleaseth. And in this we should live and work that which belongeth to us to work, for without this we should not be able to live spiritually. For as the soul is the life of the body, right so is Jesus the life of the soul by His gracious presence.

And, nevertheless, this manner of feeling, though it be never so much, is but in faith in comparison of that which shall be of the selfsame Jesus in the bliss of Heaven. Lo, this feeling should we desire; for every reasonable soul ought to covet, with all its power, to approach to Jesus, and to be united to Him through feeling of His gracious invisible presence. How that presence is felt may better be known by experience than by any writing; for it is the life and the love, the might and the light, the joy and the rest of a chosen soul.

And therefore, he that hath once truly felt it cannot forbear it without pain, neither can he choose but desire it, it is so good in itself and so comfortable. What is more comfortable here for a soul than to be drawn out through grace from the noisomeness of worldly business and filth of desires, and from vain affection of all creatures, into rest and softness of spiritual love, secretly perceiving the gracious presence of Jesus, and feelingly fed with the savour of His invisible blessed Face? Verily, I think nothing can make the soul of a lover full of mirth but the gracious presence of Jesus, as He can show Himself to a pure soul; such an one is never heavy, never sorry but when he is with himself in sensuality. He is never full glad, nor merry, but when he is out of himself as being with Jesus in spirit.

And yet is that no full mirth, for there ever hangeth a heavy lump of bodily corruption on his soul, and beareth it down, and hindereth much the spiritual gladness, and this must ever be whilst it is here in this life. But whereas I have before spoken of the changeability of grace, how it cometh and goeth, that thou mistake me not; thou must understand that I mean not of common grace, that is had and felt in faith and in goodwill to God; without having and lusting of which, and continuing in it, none can be saved, for it is in the least chosen soul that liveth. But I mean of special grace felt by inspiration of the Holy Ghost in that manner as I have said before. Common grace, which is Charity, lasteth whole whatsoever a man doth, as long as his will and his intent is true to God, which will of his keepeth him from sinning deadly, and the deed that he wittingly doth is not forbidden under a mortal sin; for this grace is not lost but by mortal sins. And then is a sin mortal when his conscience witnesseth with deliberation that it is mortal sin, and yet nevertheless he doth it; or else his conscience is so blinded that he holdeth it no deadly sin, although he doth the deed wilfully, which is forbidden by God and holy Church as a deadly sin.

Special grace felt through the invisible presence of Jesus, which maketh a soul a perfect lover, lasteth not ever alike whole in the height of feeling, but changeably cometh and goeth, as I have said before. Thus our Lord saith: Spiritus ubi vult spirat, &c.—The spirit bloweth where it listeth, and thou hearest His voice, but thou knowest not whence He cometh, nor whither He goeth. He cometh secretly sometimes when thou art least aware of Him, but thou shalt know Him full well ere He go; for He wonderfully stirreth and mightily turneth thy heart into the beholding of His goodness, and then doth thy heart melt delectably as wax against the fire into softness of His love, and this is the voice that He soundeth. But then He goeth ere thou perceivest, for He withdraweth Himself somewhat, not wholly altogether, but from excess into moderation. The height of feeling passeth, but the substance and the effect of Grace dwelleth still. And that is as long as the soul of a lover keepeth himself pure, and falleth not wilfully into wretchedness or carelessness in sensuality, nor to outward vanity, as sometimes it doth (though it have no delight therein) out of frailty. This is the changeability of grace which I meant and spake of.

CHAPTER XII: A COMMENDATION OF PRAYER OFFERED UP TO JESUS BY A CONTEMPLATIVE SOUL, AND HOW STABLENESS IN PRAYER IS A SECURE WORK TO STAND IN; AND HOW EVERY FEELING OF GRACE IN A CHOSEN SOUL MAY BE CALLED JESUS. BUT THE MORE CLEAN THE SOUL IS, THE MORE WORTHY THE GRACE IS

THE soul of a man, whilst it is not touched with special grace, is blunt and gross for spiritual work, and can do nought therein. It skilleth not thereof by reason of its weakness. It is both old and dry, undevout and unsavoury in itself. But then cometh the light of grace, and through touching maketh it sharp and subtle, ready and able to spiritual work, and giveth it a great freedom and a perfect readiness in will to be pliable to all the stirrings of grace, ready to work after that grace stirreth the soul. For by opening of the spiritual eye it is wholly applied to grace, ready to pray. And how the soul then prayeth I shall tell thee.

The most special prayer that the soul useth and hath most comfort in, I suppose, is the Pater noster or else Psalms of the Psalter. The Pater noster for unlearned men; and Psalms and Hymns and other service of holy Church for the learned. The soul prayeth, therefore, not in that manner as it did before, after the common way of men by highness of voice, or by reasonable speaking out; but in full great stillness of voice and softness of heart. For why? His mind is not troubled nor hindered with outward things, but wholly gathered together into itself. And the soul is set, as it were, in the spiritual presence of Jesus, and, therefore, every word and every syllable is sounded savourly, sweetly and delectably, with full accord of mouth and of heart. For why? The soul is then turned all into the fire of love. And, therefore, every word that it secretly prayeth is like a spark rising out of a burning fire, which heateth all the powers of the soul, and turneth them into love, and enlighteneth them so comfortably that the soul listeth ever to pray and to do nothing else. The more it prayeth the better it may, and the mightier it is. For grace helpeth the soul well, and maketh all things light and easy, that it delighteth to chant and sing the praises of God with spiritual mirth in heavenly delight. This spiritual work is the food of the soul, and this prayer is of great virtue, for it wasteth and bringeth to nought all secret and open temptations of the enemy, and slayeth all the mind and all the liking of the world and of fleshly sins. It beareth up the body and the soul from painful feeling of the wretchedness of this life. It keepeth the soul in the feeling of grace and working of love, and nourisheth it ever alike hot, as sticks nourisheth the fire. It putteth away all irksomeness and heaviness of heart, and holdeth it in strength and spiritual gladness.

Of this prayer speaketh David thus: Dirigatur oratio mea sicut incensum &c.—Let my prayer be dressed as incense in Thy sight. For even as incense that is cast into the fire maketh a sweet smell by the smoke rising up to the air, right so a Psalm savourly and softly sung or said in a burning heart, giveth up a sweet smell to the face of our Lord Jesus, and to all the Court of Heaven. There dare no flesh-fly rest upon the pot's brink boiling on the fire. Even so can no fleshly delight rest upon a clean soul, that is all bilapped and warmed in the fire of love, boiling and blowing up Psalms and prayers to Jesus. This prayer is always heard of Jesus. It yieldeth grace to Jesus, and receiveth grace again. It maketh a soul familiar, and, as it were, hail-fellow with Jesus, and with all the Angels in Heaven, use it who so can. The work is good and gracious in itself. And though it be not altogether perfect Contemplation in itself, nor the working of love by itself, nevertheless it is in part Contemplation. For why? It cannot be exercised in this manner but by plenty of grace through opening of the spiritual eye. And, therefore, a soul that hath this freedom and this gracious feeling in praying with spiritual savour and heavenly delight hath the grace of Contemplation in the manner as it is.

This prayer is a rich offering filled all with fatness of devotion, received by Angels and presented to the face of Jesus. The prayer of other men, who are busy in active works, is made of two words; for they oftentimes form in their hearts one word through thinking of worldly business, and speak with their mouth another word of the Psalm sung or said. Yet, nevertheless, if his intent be true his prayer is good and acceptable, though it lack savour and sweetness. But this prayer of a Contemplative man is made but of one word; for as it is formed in the heart, right so doth it wholly sound in the mouth, as it were nothing but one and the same thing, both which formeth it and which soundeth it. And verily no more it is, for the soul, through grace, is made whole in itself so far parted from sensuality, that it is master of the body, and then is the body nothing else but as an instrument and a trumpet of the soul in the which the soul bloweth sweet notes of spiritual prayers to Jesus. This is the trumpet that David spake of thus: Buccinate in neomenia, &c.—Blow ye the trumpet in the new moon. That is, ye souls that are reformed in spiritual life through opening of the inner eye, blow ye devoutly the sounding of Psalms with the trumpet of your bodily tongue. And, therefore, since this prayer is pleasant to Jesus, and so profitable to the soul, it is good for him who is new converted to God (and desires to please Him, and coveteth to have some quaint feeling of grace) to covet this feeling, that he may through grace come to this liberty of spirit and offer his prayers and his Psalms to Jesus continually and stably and devoutly, with whole mind and burning affection towards Him, so that he may be ready for it through custom when grace will stir him up thereto. This is a secure feeling, and a true one. If thou canst attain unto it and keep it, thou shalt not need to run about here and there and ask questions of every spiritual man what thou shouldst do, how thou shouldst love God, and how thou shouldst serve God, and speak of spiritual matters, that pass thy understanding, as perhaps some do: Such kind of doings are not profitable unless in case of necessity. Keep thee to thy prayers, quietly at first with thy own great industry, that thou mayest afterwards come to this restful feeling of spiritual prayer, and that shall teach thee wisdom enough in verity without feigning or fancy; and hold thee on in such prayer if thou hast gotten it and leave it not; but if grace come otherwise, and removeth it from thee for a time, causing thee to work on another manner, then mayest thou leave it for a time, and after return again thereto. And he that hath this grace in prayer asketh not whereupon he should set the point of his thought in his prayer, whether upon the words that he speaketh, or else on God, or on the Name of Jesus, as some ask, for this feeling of grace will teach him well enough. For why? The soul is turned into the eye, and sharply beholdeth the face of Jesus, and is ascertained that it is Jesus that it feeleth and seeth. I do not mean Jesus as He is in Himself, in fulness of His blessed Godhead; but I mean Jesus, as He is pleased to show Himself to a clean soul, yet in the body according to the cleanness that it hath. For thou must know that every feeling of grace is Jesus, and may be called Jesus. And according as the grace is more or less, so feeleth the soul more or less of Jesus. Yea, the first feeling of special grace in a beginner, which is called grace of compunction and contrition for his sins, is verily Jesus. For why? He causeth that contrition in a soul by His presence. But Jesus is then very grossly and rudely felt, very far from this spiritual subtlety; for the soul can nor may do no better by reason of its uncleanness. Nevertheless, afterward, if the soul profit and increase in virtues and in cleanness, the same Jesus, and none other, is seen and felt by the same soul when it is touched with grace; but that is more spiritually, and nearer to His Divinity. And verily that is the chiefest thing that Jesus loveth in a soul, that it may be made spiritual and divine in sight and in love, like to Him in grace, as He is by nature; for that shall be the end of all lovers.

Then mayest thou be secure, that at what time thou feelest thy soul stirred by grace, specially in that manner as I have said before, by opening of thy spiritual eye that thou seest and feelest Jesus, hold Him fast whilst thou may, and keep thyself in grace, and let Him not easily go from thee. Look after none other Jesus but that same, by feeling of that self-same grace more divinely that it may increase in thee more and more. And be not afraid, though Jesus whom thou feelest be not Jesus as He is in His full Godhead, that thou therefore mayest be deceived if thou trust to that feeling. But trust thou well, if thou be a lover of Jesus, that thy feeling is true, and that Jesus is truly felt and seen of thee through His grace as thou canst see Him here. And therefore trust fully to thy feeling when it is gracious and spiritual, and keep it tenderly, and have great dainty, not of thyself, but of it, that thou mayest see and feel Jesus still better and better. For grace shall ever teach thee by itself, if thou wilt fall thereto, till thou come to the end.

But perchance thou beginnest to wonder why I say one time that grace worketh all this, and another time that love worketh, or God worketh?

Unto this I answer thus: That when I say that grace worketh, I mean both love, and Jesus, and God; for all is one, and nought but one; Jesus is love, Jesus is grace, Jesus is God. And because He worketh all in us by His grace for love, as He is God, therefore may I use which of these four words I list after my stirring in this writing.

CHAPTER XIII: HOW A SOUL THROUGH THE OPENING OF THE SPIRITUAL EYE RECEIVETH A GRACIOUS LOVE ENABLING TO UNDERSTAND THE HOLY SCRIPTURES, AND HOW JESUS, THAT IS HID IN THE HOLY SCRIPTURES, SHOWETH HIMSELF TO HIS LOVERS

WHEN a soul thus feeleth Jesus in prayer, he thinketh that he shall never feel otherwise. Nevertheless it happeneth that sometimes grace putteth vocal prayer to silence, and stirreth the soul to see and to feel Jesus in another manner. And that manner is first to see Jesus in the holy Scriptures; for Jesus, who is all truth, is hid and covered therein, folded in a soft Syndon, under fair words, that He cannot be known nor felt but of a clean heart. For why? Truth will not show itself to enemies, but to friends, that love and desire it with an humble heart. For Truth and Humility are full true sisters, fastened together in love and charity, and there is no distance of counsel betwixt them two. Humility presumeth upon Truth, and not at all on itself; and Truth esteemeth well of Humility, so they accord well together. Then forasmuch as the soul of a lover is made humble through inspiration of grace by opening of the spiritual eye, and seeth that it is nought of itself, but only hangeth on the mercy and the goodness of Jesus perpetually, being borne up by the favour and help of Him only, and truly desiring His presence, therefore seeth it Jesus; for it seeth the truth of holy Scriptures wonderfully showed and opened above study and industry and reason of man's natural wit. And that may well be called the feeling and the perceiving of Jesus. For Jesus is the fountain of Wisdom, and by pouring down of His Wisdom into a clean soul, by little and little, He maketh the soul wise enough for to understand all holy Scripture; not all at once in special beholding, but through that grace the soul receiveth a new ability and a gracious habit to understand it, particularly when it cometh to mind. This opening and this cleanness of understanding is made by the spiritual presence of Jesus: for right as the Gospel saith of the two Disciples going to Emmaus, burning in desire and speaking of our Lord Jesus, our Lord appeared to them presently as a pilgrim, and taught them the prophecies of Himself. And as the Gospel saith: Aperuit illis sensum, &c.—He opened their wits that they might understand the Scriptures. Right so the spiritual presence of Jesus openeth the wit of His lover, that it burneth in desire to Him and bringeth to His mind by ministration of Angels, the words and sentences of holy Writ unsought and unconsidered one after another and expoundeth them readily, be they never so hard nor so secret. The harder they be, and farther from man's understanding by reason, the more delectable is the true showing of them. When Jesus is the teacher, it is expounded and declared literally, morally, mystically, and heavenly, if the matter will bear it. By the literal (which is the easiest and plainest) corporal nature is comforted. By the moral, the soul is informed concerning vices and virtues, to be able wisely to distinguish the one from the other. By the mystical it is enlightened to see the works of Jesus in holy Church, readily to apply the words of holy Writ to Christ our head, and to holy Church, which is His mystical body. The fourth, which is heavenly, belongeth only to the working of love, and that is, when all truth in holy Writ is applied to love. And because this is most like to heavenly feeling, therefore I call it heavenly.

The lover of Jesus is His friend, not for that he deserveth it, but because Jesus of His merciful goodness maketh him His friend by true accord. And therefore to him He showeth His secrets, as to a true friend that pleaseth Him by love, not serveth Him through fear in slavery. Thus He saith Himself to His Apostles: Jam vos dixi amicos quia quaecumque audivi a Patre meo nota feci vobis.—Now have I called you friends, for I have made known unto you all that I have heard of the Father. To a clean soul whose palate is purified from filth of fleshly love, holy Writ is lively food and sustenance delectable, It savoureth wonderful sweetly when it is well chewed by spiritual understanding.

For why? The spirit of life is hid therein, that quickeneth all the powers of the soul, and filleth them full of sweetness of heavenly savour and spiritual delight. But verily he must have white teeth, and sharp, and well picked, that can bite of this spiritual bread; for fleshly lovers and heretics may not touch the inward flour of it. Their teeth are bloody, and full of filth, therefore must they be fasting from feeling of this bread. By teeth I understand the inward senses of the soul, which in fleshly lovers and heretics are bloody, full of sin and worldly vanities. They would, but they cannot come through curiosity to the truth in knowing of holy Writ; for their senses are corrupted by original and actual sin, and are not yet healed through grace. And therefore they do but gnaw upon the outward bark, speak they never so much thereof. The inner savour within they taste not of. They be not humble, they be not pure for to see it. They be not friends to Jesus, and therefore He showeth them not His counsel. The mystery of holy Writ is closed under a key, and sealed with a signet of Jesus' finger, which is the Holy Ghost, and therefore without His love and His leave may none come in. He alone hath the key of skill in His keeping, as holy Writ saith, and He Himself is the key: and He letteth in whom He will by inspiration of His grace, and breaketh not the seal.

And this doth Jesus to His lovers, but not to all alike, but to them that are specially inspired for to seek Truth in holy Writ, with great devotion in praying, and with much business in studying going before. These may come to the finding of it, when our Lord will be pleased to show it. See now, then, how grace openeth the spiritual eye, and Heareth the senses of the soul wonderfully above the frailty of corrupt nature. It giveth the soul a new ability whether it will read holy Writ, or hear it, or meditate in it, for to understand truly and savourly the truth of it in the manner aforesaid; and also for to turn readily all reasons and words that are literally spoken in spiritual understanding. And that is no great wonder, for the same Spirit that made the Scriptures, expoundeth it and declareth it to a clean soul for its comfort—namely, the Holy Ghost.

And this grace may be, and is, as well in laymen as in the learned, as to the substance and true feeling of the verity and spiritual savour of it in general, though they see not so many reasons in special; for that needeth not. And when the soul is thus enabled, and enlightened through grace, then he chooseth to be alone sometimes, out of the letting and meddling with all creatures, that he may freely exercise his instrument, which I call his reason of beholding of verity which is contained in holy Scriptures. And then will there fall into his mind words and reasons and senses enough to busy him, and that full orderly and full seriously. And what comfort and spiritual delight, what savour and sweetness a soul can then feel in that spiritual exercise through divers illuminations, inward perceivings, secret knowings and sudden touchings of the Holy Ghost, a soul can only know by experience, and not otherwise. And I hope that he shall not err, if so be his teeth, that is his inward senses, be kept white and clean from spiritual pride, and from curiosity of his natural wit. I believe David felt full great delight in this manner of working, when he said thus: Quam dulci faucibus meis eloquia Tua, &c.—How sweet are Thy words unto my taste! sweeter than honey to my mouth. That is, Lord Jesus, Thy holy words endited in holy Writ, brought to my mind by grace, are sweeter to my taste, that is the affections of my soul, than honey is to my mouth. Verily this is a fair work without painful travail for to see Jesus thus. This is one manner of sight of Jesus, as I said before; not as He is, but clothed under the likeness of works and of words, per speculum, in aenigmate.—In a glass, and by a likeness, as the Apostle saith. Jesus is endless might, wisdom and goodness, righteousness, truth, holiness and mercy. And what this Jesus is in Himself can no soul see nor hear; but by the effects of His working may be seen through the light of grace. As thus, His might is seen by making of all creatures of nothing; His wisdom in orderly disposing of them; His goodness in saving of them; His mercy in forgiveness of sins; His holiness in gifts of grace; His righteousness in severely punishing of sin; His gentleness in true rewarding of good works. And all this is expressed in holy Writ, and this a soul seeth there with all other attributes that pertain thereto. And be thou well assured, that such gracious knowings in holy Writ, or in other writings, which are made by the assistance of God's grace, are nought else but sweet letters sent and made betwixt a loving soul and Jesus the beloved. Or else, that I may speak trulier, betwixt Jesus the true lover and the souls beloved of Him. He hath full great tenderness of love to all his chosen children, that are here closed in clay of this bodily life. And therefore, though He be absent from them, high, hid above in the bosom of the Father, filled with the delights of the Blessed Godhead, yet notwithstanding He thinketh upon them, and visiteth them full oft through His gracious spiritual presence, and comforteth them by His letters of holy Writ, and driveth out of their hearts heaviness and wearisomeness, doubts and fears, and maketh them truly glad and merry in Him, believing in all His promises, and humbly continuing fulfilling His will.

St Paul saith thus: Quaecumque scripta sunt, &c.—Whatsoever things are written, are written for our instruction, that we might have hope through the comfort of the Scriptures. And this is another work of Contemplation, to see Jesus in the Scriptures after the opening of the spiritual eye. The cleaner the sight is in beholding, the more comforted is the affection in tasting. A full little savour felt in a clean soul of holy Writ in this manner abovesaid, should make the soul set little price by knowing of all the seven liberal arts, or of all the world, or all worldly wisdom; for the end of this knowing is the salvation of a man's soul in everlasting life; and the end of that other knowledge, as to himself, is but vanity and a fading delight, unless by grace it be turned to this end.

CHAPTER XIV: OF THE SECRET VOICE OF JESUS SOUNDING IN A SOUL, AND HOW IT MAY BE KNOWN. AND HOW ALL THE GRACIOUS ILLUMINATIONS MADE IN A SOUL BE CALLED THE SPEAKINGS OF JESUS

LO, these are fair new feelings in a clean soul; and if a soul were filled with such, it might be said, and that truly, that it were reformed somewhat in feeling, but not yet fully; for why? Yet Jesus showeth more, and leadeth the soul inward, and beginneth to speak more familiarly and more lovely to a soul, and maketh it more ready to follow the stirrings of grace. For the Prophet saith: Quocumque ibat spiritus, illuc gradiebantur et rotae sequentes eum.—Whithersoever the spirit went, thither went the wheels following him. By wheels are understood the true lovers of Jesus, for they are round in virtue, without angle of frowardness; and lightly whirling through readiness of will after the stirrings of grace; for according as grace stirreth and teacheth, so they follow and work, as the Prophet saith.

But first, they have a full secure experience, and a true knowing of the voice of grace, ere they do so; that they be not deceived by their own feigning, or by the mid-day fiend. Our Lord Jesus saith thus of His lovers: Oves meae vocem meam audiunt, &c.—My sheep hear My voice, and I know them, and they know Me. The privy voice of Jesus is full true, and it maketh a soul true; there is no feigning in it, nor on fancy, nor pride, nor hyprocrisy; but gentleness, humility, peace, love and charity. And it is full of life, love and grace. And therefore when it soundeth in a soul, it is of so great power sometimes, that the soul suddenly layeth aside all that was in hand, as praying, speaking, reading or thinking; in the manner abovesaid, and all manner of bodily work, and listeneth thereto fully, hearing and perceiving in rest and in love the sweet sound of this spiritual voice, as it were ravished from the mind of all earthly things, and then in this quiet, Jesus sometimes showeth Himself as an awful master, and sometimes as a reverend Father, and sometimes as a lovely Spouse. And it keepeth a soul in a wonderful reverence, and in a lovely beholding of Him, that the soul liketh well then, and never so well as then; for it feeleth so great security, and so great rest in Jesus, and so much savour of His goodness, that it would ever be so, and never do other work. It thinketh that it toucheth Jesus, and through virtue of that unspeakable touching, it is made whole and stable in itself, reverently beholding Jesus only, as if there were nothing but Jesus, one thing, and himself another, borne up only by the savour and the wonderful goodness of Him; that is that thing which he feeleth and seeth. And this feeling is ofttimes without special beholding of holy Writ, and with but few words formed in the mind; only there falls in among sweet words, according to the feeling either of loving, or worshipping, or admiring, or otherwise sounding, as the heart liketh. The soul is very much separated from love or liking of the world, through virtue of this gracious feeling, and also very much from minding of the world in that time. It taketh no heed thereof, for it hath no time thereto. But then sometimes anon, together with this, falleth into a soul divers illuminations through grace, which I call the speakings of Jesus, and the sight of spiritual things; for be thou assured, that all the business that Jesus maketh about a soul, is for to make it a true perfect spouse to Him in the height and the fulness of love, and that cannot be done suddenly. Therefore Jesus, who is love, and of all lovers the wisest, proveth by many ways, and by many wonderful means, ere this can come about. And therefore that it may come to the effect of true espousing, He hath such gracious speakings of a wooer to a chosen soul. He sheweth His privy jewels; many things He giveth, and more He promiseth; and showeth courteous dalliance. He often visiteth her with much grace and spiritual comfort, as I have said before; but how He doth this in particular, I cannot fully tell thee, for it needeth not. Nevertheless somewhat shall I say, according as grace enableth me.

The drawing of a soul fully to perfect love, is, first by the showing of spiritual things to a clean soul, when the spiritual eye is opened; not that a soul should rest therein, and make an end there, but should by that search Him and love Him who is highest of all, without any beholding of any other thing than He.

But thou wilt ask, what are these spiritual things, because I speak so oft of spiritual things?

To this I say that spiritual things may be said all the truth of holy Scripture. And therefore a soul that through light of grace can see the truth of Scripture, seeth spiritual things, as I have said before.

CHAPTER XV

SECTION I: HOW THROUGH GRACIOUS OPENING OF THE SPIRITUAL EYE A SOUL IS MADE WISE, HUMBLY AND TRULY TO SEE THE DIVERSITIES OF DEGREES IN HOLY CHURCH, AS MILITANT, AND FOR TO SEE THE NATURE OF ANGELS; AND FIRST OF THE REPROBATE

NEVERTHELESS, other spiritual things there be also, which through light of grace are showed to the soul, and are these: the nature of all reasonable souls, and the gracious workings of our Lord Jesus in them; the nature of angels, both good and bad, and their workings, and the knowledge of the Blessed Trinity, according as grace teacheth. Holy Writ saith of the Spouse thus in the Canticles: Surgam et circuibo civitatem, &c.—I will arise, and go about the city, and will seek Him whom my soul loveth. That is, I will rise into highness of thought, and go about the city. By this city is understood the University of all creatures, corporal and spiritual, ordered and ruled under God by laws of nature, of reason and of grace. I go about this city when I behold the natures and causes of bodily creatures, the gifts of grace, and the blisses of spiritual creatures. And in all these I seek Him whom my soul loveth. It is pleasant looking with the inner eye on Jesus in bodily creatures, to see His power, His wisdom and His goodness in ordering of their natures; but it is much more beautiful to look on Jesus in spiritual creatures: First in reasonable souls, both elect and reprobate, to see the merciful calling of them to election, how He turneth them from sin by the light of His grace, how He helpeth them, teacheth them, chasteneth them, comforteth them; He sanctifieth, cleanseth and feedeth them; how He maketh them burning in love and in light through plenty of His grace. And thus doth He, not to one soul only, but to all His chosen according to the measure of His grace.

Also concerning the reprobate, he seeth how justly he forsaketh them, and leaveth them in their sins, and doth them no wrong. How He rewardeth them in this world, suffering them to have the fulfilling of their own will, and after to punish them endlessly. Lo, this is a little beholding of holy Church, whilst it is militant in this life, by seeing how black and how foul it seemeth in souls that are reprobate; and how fair and how lovely it is in chosen souls.

And all this spiritual sight is nought else but the sight of Jesus, not in Himself but in His merciful secret works, and in His righteous judgements every day showed, remembered and renewed to reasonable souls. Moreover, to see with the spiritual eye the pains of the reprobate and the joy and bliss of chosen souls is full comfortable. For truth cannot be seen in a clean soul without great delight and wonderful content of blessed burning love.

Also the sight of the nature of Angels, first of the damned, then of the blessed; as it is a full pleasant contemplation concerning the devil in a clean soul. When grace bringeth the fiend into the sight of the soul, as a clumsy caitiff bound by the power of Jesus that he cannot hurt; then the soul beholdeth him not bodily, but spiritually, seeing his nature and his malice, and turneth him upside down and spoileth him and rendeth him all to nought, scorneth him and despiseth him, and setteth nought by his malice. Thus biddeth holy Writ, when it saith thus: Verte impium, et not erit.—Turn the wicked, that is, the fiend, upside down, and he shall be as nought. Much wonder hath the soul that the fiend hath so much malice and so little might. There is no creature so weak as he is; and therefore it is great cowardice that men fear him so much. He can do nothing without leave of our Lord Jesus, not so much as enter into a swine, as the Gospel saith , much less can he do then to annoy any man.

And therefore if our Lord Jesus give him leave to tempt us, it is full worthily and mercifully done, that he doth so; and therefore welcome be our Lord Jesus by Himself, and by all His messengers. The soul feareth no more the blustering of the fiend than the stirring of a mouse. Wondrous wroth is the fiend when we say nay to his temptations, but his mouth is stopped with his own malice. His hands are bound like a thieve's, worthy to be judged and hanged in hell. And then the soul accuseth him, and doth justly condemn him according to his deserts. Wonder not at this saying, for St Paul meant the same, when he saith thus: Fratres, nescitis, &c.—Brethren, know ye not that we shall judge the angels? namely, those that are wicked spirits through malice that were made good angels by nature. As who should say, yes; this judging is figured before the day of judgement in Contemplative souls, for they feel a little tasting in likeness of all that shall be done afterwards of our Lord Jesus openly in truth. Shamed and troubled is the fiend greatly in himself, when he is thus used by a clean soul. He would fain fly away, but he cannot, for the power of the Highest holdeth him still, and that grieveth him more than all the fire of hell. Then falleth the soul wonderfully humble under Jesus with hearty praises, for that He so mightily saveth a simple soul from all the malice of so cruel an enemy by His great mercy.

SECTION II: HOW BY THE SAME LIGHT OF GRACE THE NATURE OF THE BLESSED ANGELS IS SEEN. AND HOW JESUS IS GOD AND MAN ABOVE ALL CREATURES, ACCORDING TO THAT WHICH THE SOUL MAY SEE OF HIM HERE

AND then after this by the selfsame light may the soul spiritually see the beauty of the Angels, the worthiness of their nature, the subtlety of their substance, their confirming in grace, their fulness in endless bliss, the diversity of their orders; the distinctions of persons, how they all live in light of endless truth; and how they burn all in love of the Holy Ghost, according to the worthiness of their orders; how they see and love and praise Jesus in blessed rest without ceasing. There is no sight of a body, nor any figure in imagination, in this manner of working, but all spiritual, and of spiritual creatures.

Then beginneth the soul to have great acquaintance and great fellowship with the blessed spirits. They are full tender and full busy about such a soul to help it, they are masters to teach it. And often by their spiritual presence and touching of their light drive out fancies from the soul. They enlighten the soul graciously; they comfort the soul with sweet words suddenly sounded in a clean heart, and if any disease fall spiritually, they serve the soul and minister to it all that it needeth. Thus St Paul said of them: Know ye not that they are all ministering spirits, sent for them who shall be heirs of salvation? As if he had said thus: Know ye that all this spiritual working of words and of reasons, brought to the mind, and such fair likeness are made by the ministry of Angels, when the light of grace abundantly shineth in a clean soul. It cannot be told by tongue the feelings, the enlightenings, the graces and the comforts in special that clean souls perceive by the favourable fellowship of blessed Angels. The soul is so well pleased with beholding what they do that it would willingly attend to nothing else.

But then with the help of Angels the soul yet seeth more; for knowing in a clean soul riseth higher above all this, and that is to behold the blessed nature of Jesus. First of His glorious humanity, how it is worthily exalted above the nature of Angels, and afterwards of His blessed Divinity, for by knowing of creatures is known the Creator; and then beginneth the soul to perceive a little of the mysteries of the Blessed Trinity. And this it may do well enough, for the light of grace going before, she cannot err as long as she holdeth her in that light. Then is opened really to the eye of the soul the unity in substance, and distinction of persons in the Blessed Trinity, as it may be seen in this life, and much other truth of the Blessed Trinity pertinent to this matter; the which is openly declared and shown by writings of holy doctors of holy Church. And be you assured that one and the same verity concerning the Blessed Trinity that these holy doctors, inspired through grace, writ in their books for the strengthening of our truth, a clean soul may see in knowing through the same light of grace. I will not express too much of this matter here in particular, for it needeth not.

Wondrous great love feedeth the soul with heavenly delight in feeling of this truth, when it is wrought through special grace; for love and light go both together in a clean soul. There is no love that riseth out of knowing, and from special beholding that can sooner touch our Lord than this can. For why? This knowing of Jesus, God and Man, is alone in itself the worthiest and the highest, if it be specially shown by the light of grace. And therefore is the fire of flaming love hereof more burning than it is of any creature, corporal or incorporal. And all these gracious knowings of the university of all creatures felt in a soul in manner abovesaid, and of our Lord Jesus, the maker and keeper of all this fair university, I call fair words, and sweet speakings of our Lord Jesus to a soul, which He means to make His true Spouse. He showeth His mysteries, proffereth rich gifts out of His treasury, and arrayeth the soul with them full beautifully. She need not thenceforward be ashamed of the company of her fellows, to appear before the face of Jesus her Spouse. All this lovely dalliance of private conference betwixt Jesus and a soul may be called a hidden word; of the which Scripture saith thus: Porro ad me dictum est verbum absconditum, &c.—Moreover to me there was spoken a secret word, and the veins of His whispering mine ear hath perceived. The inspiration of Jesus is a hidden word, for it is privily hid from all lovers of the world, and shown to His lovers; through which a clean soul perceiveth readily the veins of His whispering, that is the special showings of His truth; for every gracious knowing of truth felt with inward savour and spiritual delight is a privy whispering of Jesus in the ear of a clean soul. He must have much cleanness and humility and all other virtues, and must be half deaf to the noise of worldly janglings, that will wisely perceive those sweet spiritual whisperings, that is the voice of Jesus. Of the which David saith thus: Vox Domini praeparantis cervos, &c.—The voice of the Lord prepareth harts, and shall discover thick woods. That is, the inspiration of Jesus maketh souls light as deer, that start from the ground over bushes and briars of all worldly vanities; and He showeth to them the thickets, that is, His mysteries, which cannot be perceived but by a sharp eye. These beholdings, solidly grounded in grace and humility, make a soul wise and burning in desire to the face of Jesus. These are the spiritual things that I spake of before, and they be called new gracious feelings; and I do but touch them a little for direction of a soul; for a soul that is pure, stirred up by grace to use this working, may see more of such spiritual matter in an hour than can be writ in a great book.

Thus finisheth this present book, which expoundeth many notable doctrines in Contemplation, which to me seemeth right expedient to those that set their felicity in busying themselves specially for their souls' health.

The following verses form the colophon to Wynkyn de Worde's edition of the "Scale," and are reprinted from the 1659 edition.

Infinite laud with thankings manifold,
I yield to God, me succouring with His grace;
This Book to finish, which as ye behold,
Scale of Perfection's called in every place:
Whereof th' Author Walter Hilton was,
And Wynkin de Word this hath set in print;
In William Caxton's house, so fell the case,
God rest his soul, in joy there may it stint.
This heavenly Book more precious than gold
Was lately directed with great humility,
For godly pleasure thereon to behold,
Unto the right noble Margaret as ye see,
The King's Mother of excellent bounty,
Harry the seventh, that Jesus him preserve,
This mighty Princess hath commanded me
T'imprint this Book, her grace for to deserve.

TREATISE WRITTEN TO A DEVOUT MAN

WALTER HILTON

AVAILABLE IN PAPERBACK.

CHRISTIAN DENOMINATIONS ROMAN CATHOLIC CHURCH

SCANNED AND EDITED BY HARRY PLANTINGA, 1995 THIS ETEXT IS IN THE PUBLIC DOMAIN.

PRINT EDITION PUBLISHED BY LONDON: ART AND BOOK COMPANY NEW YORK, CINCINNATI, CHICAGO: BENZINGER BROTHERS 1901

TREATISE WRITTEN TO A DEVOUT MAN

CHAPTER I

That he who intends to become a Spiritual Man must first use much Bodily Exercise in Penance, and in Destroying of sin

DEAR BROTHER IN CHRIST, —There be in the holy Church two kinds of life, by the which Christian souls do serve and please God, and procure their own salvation. The one is corporal, the other spiritual.

Corporal working appertaineth principally to the men and women of the world, who for the nature of their estate do lawfully use worldly goods, and intermeddle and deal with worldly businesses and affairs. This life also belongeth to all young beginners in spirituality who be but newly converted from sensual and worldly sins to the service of God; and this life is to dispose and enable such persons for spiritual working, by taming the body by corporal works and exercises, and thereby bringing it into obedience and subjection to the spirit, whereby it may become supple and ready, and not much contrarious to the spirit in her spiritual exercisings; for as St Paul saith, that woman was made for man, and not man for woman. Even so corporal working was ordained for spiritual, and not spiritual working for corporal. Corporal working is to go before, and spiritual working cometh after, as the same St Paul saith in these words: That is not first which is spiritual, but that which is sensible (or corporal), afterwards cometh that which is spiritual. And the reason why it should be so is this, that we are born in sin and in corruption of the flesh, by the which we are in souls so blinded and so overlaid that we neither have the spiritual sight or knowing of God by light of understanding, nor the spiritual tasting or feeling of Him by a clean desire of loving; and therefore we cannot suddenly start out of the dark night of this fleshly corruption into the spiritual light; for we are not as yet able to endure such spiritual light, by reason of the sickness of our souls, any more than we can with our bodily eyes, when they are sore, behold and look upon the light of the sun; and for that cause we must expect and work by degrees and process of time. First, by corporal works diligently, till we be discharged, or much lightened, or eased from this heavy burden of sin and sensuality, that hindereth us from spiritual working; and till our souls be somewhat cleansed from great outward sins, and enabled for spiritual workings.

By the corporal working that I speak of, thou must understand that I mean all manner of good works or deeds that thy soul doth by the senses or the members of thy body, either upon or towards thyself, as in fasting, watching, or in restraining thy fleshly or sensual desires, by penance-doing, or other acts of mortification. Or upon, or towards thy Christian brother, in performance of the works of mercy, spiritual or corporal. Or to, or towards God Himself, by suffering (for the love of Him and His justice) all manner of bodily pains and afflictions that shall occur for thee to undergo, either as immediately from His own hands, or by the means and from the hands of other creatures of His. All these kind of works done in faith and out of charity (without which they are of no worth) do please God. Therefore whoso desireth to become a spiritual man, it will be securest and profitable for him that he be first, for a long time, well exercised in these corporal workings, for these corporal deeds are practices and tokens of moral virtues, without which a soul is not able to work spiritually. Break down first pride within thee by bodily sufferings and bearings, and also by thinking in thy mind of something that will help to humble thee; and, moreover, by eschewing and avoiding all ostentations, boastings, or praising of thyself, either privately by thyself in thy mind, or by thy words or external deeds, or carriage towards, or with others; by this means casting away and mortifying within thee all vainglory and complacence in thyself for any talent, gift, or thing corporal or spiritual that God hath bestowed on thee. Also mortify and destroy within thee, so soon as thou art able, all envy and anger towards thy Christian brethren; whether they be rich or poor, good or bad, hate them not, nor disdain them, nor willingly offend them by words or by deeds. Likewise destroy and mortify in thee all coveting of worldly goods, and see that neither for the getting, or holding, nor saving of them, thou do not offend thy conscience, nor break verity with God, or thy Christian brother, for the love of any earthly thing; but what thou gettest, or hast, keep it without inordinate love or affection to it, and spend it as reasonable occasions shall require, for the honour of God, and the succour of thy Christian brother. Mortify also, and destroy as much as thou canst, all yielding to bodily sloth, and unnecessary bodily ease, and the sensual vices of gluttony and luxury, with the inordinations that rise out of them. And after that thou hast been well exercised and tried in all such kind of corporal works, thou mayest then by the grace of God, ordain thee and apply thee to spiritual working.

The grace and goodness of our Lord Jesus Christ, that He hath showed to thee, in withdrawing of thine heart from the love and liking of worldly vanity, and from the use of fleshly and sensual sins, and in turning of thy will entirely to His service, bringeth into mine heart much matter to love Him in His mercy; and also it greatly moveth and urgeth me to strengthen thee in thy good purpose, and in the work which thou hast begun between thee and God, so that it may be brought to a good end. And so far as may be in my power to help thee in it, my best endeavours in it I shall most willingly afford thee, first and principally for the service and honour of God, and next in requital of thy tender affection of love thou bearest to me, though I be a wretch, and unworthy of thy love or favour. I know well the desire of thy heart, as how that thou greatly covetest to serve our Lord both in soul and body, fully and wholly, without intermeddling or troubling thyself in worldly businesses, that so thou mayest, by the grace of God, attain to more knowledge, and spiritual feeling of God, and of spiritual things. Such desire of thine is (as I hope) good, and from God, for it is set upon Him in charity spiritually. Nevertheless, as in regard of external matters and workings in them, such desire of thine is to be moderated and ruled with discretion, according to the nature and quality of thy estate, which thou art to regard in thy spiritual intentions; for charity unruled, that is, not rightly ordered, turneth sometimes into a fault or vice. And therefore it is said of our Lord by a holy soul in the holy Scripture: He hath ordered charity in me; that is to say, our Lord giveth to me charity, hath set it in order and good rule within me, whereby it might not err in its exercise, nor be lost through my indiscreet doings. Even so the said desire and charity which our Lord hath wrought in thee, out of His goodness and mercy, must be so ruled and moderated, that in the exercises of it, it do regard the nature of thy estate and condition of life, and the manner of living, which in former time thou hast held, and the measure and quantity of virtues that now are in thee. Thou must not altogether follow thy said desire in giving over or neglecting those businesses and cares of the world that are necessary, and do belong to thee, either for thee upholding of thy own person in his degree, or in the ruling or ordering of other persons or things that pertain to thy charge, and give thee wholly to retiredness, spiritual devotions and holy meditations, as if thou wert a Friar or Monk, or another man that were not bound (as thou art) to the world by children or servants; for it is not for thee to do so, and if thou dost, then keepest thou not the order of charity. Also if thou wouldst altogether leave and forbear all spiritual exercises (especially now after the grace and calling that God hath given thee for them) and give thyself wholly to the businesses of the world, in fulfilling of the works of the active life, as fully as do other men, that never felt such devotions nor had such grace or calling as thou hast, thou dost then leave the order of charity; for thy state requireth of thee to attend to each of them in divers times. Thou shalt mingle the works of active life with the spiritual works of the contemplative life, and then thou dost well; for thou shalt sometimes be busy, with Martha, for to order and govern thine household, thy children, thy servants, thy neighbours and thy tenants. If they do well, comfort and help them therein; if they do amiss, then tell and teach them for their amendment, and chastise them as there shall be cause. Thou shalt also wisely look after and know thy things and thy worldly goods, as that they be well and duly used or preserved by thy servants, well ordered and reasonably spent, whereby thou mayest the more plenteously, out of thy temporal means, fulfil the deeds of mercy and charity towards thy Christian brethren. Also thou shalt sometimes, with Mary, leave or lay aside the businesses of the world, and shalt sit down at the feet of our Lord with humility, in prayers and holy thoughts, and in Contemplation of Him, according to the grace that He shall give thee for it, and so thou shalt go from that one to that other, profitably and fruitfully, and fulfil them both; and so doing thou observest well the order of charity.

CHAPTER II

To what kind of Men the Active Life pertaineth

BUT that thou mayest the less wonder at that that I have said, and that thou mayest better understand the reason thereof, therefore I shall declare the matter a little more fully to thee. Thou must understand that God is served by three kinds of life, as either by an active life, or by a contemplative, or by a third, that is mixed of them both, and therefore is commonly called a mixed life. The active life belongeth to worldly men and women that are gross and ignorant, as to the understanding or knowledge of spiritual exercises or ways, for they neither feel nor taste devotion by fervour of love as other men do, nor can they well conceive what it is or how it may be come by; and nevertheless, they have in them the fear of God and of the pains of Hell, and therefore they eschew and forbear sin, and have a desire for to please God, and to attain to Heaven, and a good will they bear to their Christian brethren. Unto these men it is needful and speedful to use the works of the active life as diligently as they can in the help of themselves and of their Christian brethren, for more they cannot do.

CHAPTER III

To whom the Contemplative Life appertaineth

THE Contemplative life appertaineth only to such men and women as for the love of God have forsaken all notorious sins, both of the flesh and of the world, and have given over all intermeddling with the affairs and businesses of the world, or with worldly goods, as also all care and charge over others, and all superiority or offices that concern the government of others (if ever they had any such) and make themselves poor and, as it were, naked from all the things of this life save for what their corporal nature doth merely need and of necessity require. Unto these men and women it appertaineth diligently and seriously to employ themselves in internal exercises for to get thereby (through the grace of our Lord) cleanness in heart and peace in conscience by destroying of sin and gaining of virtue, and so to come to Contemplation; since such cleanness (necessary for Contemplation) cannot be had without much exercise of body and continual travail or industry in spirit, by devout prayers, fervent desires and spiritual meditation.

CHAPTER IV

To whom appertained the Mixed Life

THE third kind of life that is called the mixed life belongeth to Prelates of holy Church and to pastors and curates who have charge and superiority over other men or women, for to teach and govern them, both as to their bodies and as to their souls, and principally to animate and guide them in the performance of the deeds of mercy both corporal and spiritual towards their Christian brethren. Unto these men of the mixed life it appertaineth sometimes to use the works of mercy in active life, in help and sustenance of themselves and of their subjects and of others also, and sometimes for to leave all manner of external businesses and to give themselves to contemplative exercises, as to prayer and meditations, reading of holy Scriptures or other good books or to some other spiritual exercises, according to what they shall feel themselves disposed. Also, this mixed life appertaineth to some temporal men, who are owners of much land and goods and have withal some dominion or mastership over other men, for to govern and sustain them, as a father hath over his children, and a master over his servants, and a lord over his tenants; the which men have received also of our Lord's gift, the grace of Devotion, and in some measure a taste and practice of spiritual exercise. Unto these men, I say, belongeth the foresaid mixed life, that is both active and contemplative; for if these men having (as they have) such external charge and cares lying on them, out of some obligation or necessity, would altogether leave or neglect such charge and businesses of the world pertaining to them, and give themselves wholly to the exercises of contemplative life, they would not do well in so doing, for they observe not the order of charity; for charity (as thou well knowest) consisteth in the love of God and of thy Christian brethren. And therefore he that hath charity in him, will not by occasion of his devotions, used immoderately towards God, omit that which he ought to do towards his Christian brother, but will serve both God and them for God, at divers times, as now the one and then the other; for he that for the loving of God in Contemplation leaveth the loving of his Christian brethren, and doth not perform towards them that which he ought, and is bound unto, he fulfilleth not the rule and obligation of charity. Likewise on the contrary side whoso hath so great a regard to the works of the active life and to the business of the world that for the love of his Christian brethren, and the serving of them, he leaveth or neglecteth all spiritual exercises, God having given him a call thereunto, he fulfilleth not charity, and so saith St Gregory. For though our Saviour Christ, for to stir up some to use the mixed life, took upon Himself the person of such manner of men, i.e., both of Prelates and of such other as are of the said mixed estate, and gave them example by His own working that they should upon occasion use the exercises of the mixed life, as He Himself did at those times that He spoke with men and meddled with them, showing and exercising His deeds of mercy towards them, taught the ignorant by His preaching, visited the sick and healed them of their diseases, fed the hungry and comforted the sorrowful; nevertheless, at other times He left the conversation of worldly men, and even of His own disciples, and went into the desert upon the hills, and continued there all night all alone in prayers, as the Gospel testifieth to us. And this mixed life did our Lord in Himself exercise, and show in the same manner, for an example to all other men that have taken on them the state or condition that requireth the exercises of the said mixed life, that is to say, that they should sometimes apply themselves to the external affairs and businesses belonging to their charge, and to the curing of such their Christian brethren as pertain to them to look to, instruct or provide for; and this to do according to reason and discretion and their need; and at another time to give themselves to devotion and to the exercises of a Contemplative life, being principally (as before I have said) reading and praying.

CHAPTER V

How holy Bishops held and used the said Mixed Life

THE said mixed life did holy Bishops hold and lead, who had charge over men's souls and had the ministration and disposal of temporal goods; for those holy men did not wholly forsake the administration looking to, and the disposal of worldly goods, and give themselves altogether, or unreasonably to Contemplation, notwithstanding the grace and gift they had for Contemplation; but very often left their own rest in Contemplation (which for their parts they had much rather have continued in still) for the love and service of their Christian brethren, and were contented to intermeddle with worldly businesses, for succouring and helping of those that were under their charge; and surely such doing of theirs was true charity. For justly and discreetly did they divide the time of their life into two parts, whereof the one they bestowed in the lower part of love and charity, that is to say, in the works of the active life (for they were bound thereto by taking on them their Prelacy): and another part of their time they spent in the higher part of love and charity, and that was in the contemplation of God, and of spiritual things by prayers and holy recollections; and so they had and held charity to God and their Christian brethren, both interiorly in affection of soul, and also exteriorly by doing and performing good corporal or external works. Other men that were only contemplatives, and were free from all cares and Prelacies, they also had charity towards God and their Christian brethren, but it was only interiorly in the affection of their soul, and not used outwardly in corporal deeds; and it may be it was so increased inwardly through their contemplations, that they needed not to intermeddle with external things for the bettering their charity, nor did it belong to their state of life to seek after such external workings, nor to intermeddle therewith, there being no necessity nor obligation for it on them; and so their internal charity sufficed for them. But those, whom before I mentioned, that were in Prelacy, and others also that were holy secular men, had perfect charity, both interiorly in their affection and did also exercise the same exteriorly in bodily working or deeds, and such doing is properly the mixed life which I have spoken of, consisting of the active and contemplative both together. And surely for such men that are in spiritual superiority, or have charge of the souls of others, as Prelates, Pastors and Curates have, or that are in temporal authority in the government of others, as worldly Lords and Masters are, I hold this mixed life best, and most expedient or necessary for them, so long as they remain in the said superiority and charge over others. But as for others that are free, and not obliged to any ministration or superiority, temporal or spiritual, I judge that the contemplative life alone by itself (if they have grace and calling to it) were, in truth, the best, the most expedient, most meritorious, most fair and most worthy for them to use, and not willingly to leave it for any outward working of the active life, unless it were in case of great need, as for the helping or comforting of some other men, either in their bodies or in their souls; and need requiring it, he to go about the doing of it, either when the party, or some other for him, requesteth, and craveth at his hands the doing of it; or that himself sees a mere necessity in the case, or else (being religious) when he is bidden by his superior to undertake or intermeddle with the work.

CHAPTER VI

That kind of Life was most fitting for him for whom this Treatise was made

BY that which I have said thou mayest partly understand the differences between one and another of the aforesaid three kinds of lives; and thou mayest by what I have said also judge which of them best fitteth thee, since that our Lord hath ordained and set thee in a state of superiority (of such nature as it is) and authority over others, and hath lent thee some store of worldly goods and lands, by the which thou mayest not only maintain and sustain thyself, but also all those other special persons that are under thy authority and government, and mightest withal govern them according to thy best knowledge and ability; and therewith also thou hast, through the goodness of our Lord, received from Him the grace for to know thyself, and a spiritual desire and taste of His love. I am of the mind that the life which I have termed to be mixed is best and most befitting thee; and thou accordingly to divide and dispose of thy time wisely and to the satisfaction of the foresaid rule of charity. For know thou well that if thou leave the necessary business or the active life belonging to thee, and be careless, and take no heed of thy worldly goods as how they be kept or spent, nor lookest after those that pertain to thy charge to see they do well, nor wilt afford thy help upon the necessity of thy Christian brother by reason of thy love and desire thou hast to apply thyself only to solitude and spiritual exercises, imagining that by so doing thou art excused and freed from thy foresaid obligations. If, I say, thou do so, thou dost not wisely nor profitably for thy soul; for what are thy works or exercises worth (be they spiritual or corporal) unless they be done according to justice and reason, to the honour of God and agreeable to His will? surely they are even nothing worth. Therefore if thou leave or neglect that thing which thou art bound unto by the law of charity, justice or other obligation, and wilt entirely give thee to another thing, voluntarily taken on thee, under pretense of better pleasing and serving of God, in a thing which thou art not bound unto, in so doing thou dost no discreet or acceptable service to Him. In so doing thou art careful to do honour and worship to His head and to His face, and to deck and adorn them fairly and curiously, but thou neglectest and leavest His body, with the feet, ragged and rent, and takest no care nor heed of them, nor dost thou anything honour Him; and it is but a shame and an indignity and no kind of honour for a man to be curiously dressed and decked about his head with pearls and precious stones, and therewith to have all his body naked and bare, as it were a beggar. Even so spiritually, it is no honour to God for one to crown His head and leave His body bare; for thou must understand that our Lord Jesus Christ, as a man, is the head of His spiritual body, which is the holy Church, the members or limbs of His body are all Christian men, some are arms, some are feet, and some are other members, according to the qualities, condition or estates they are of in the holy Church.

And now if thou be diligent with all thy skill and ability for to deck and adorn His head, that is, for to honour Him with the remembrance of His passion and of His other works done in His humanity, with devotion, love and thanks to Him for the same, and forgettest or neglectest His feet (which are thy children, thy servants, thy tenants and all thy Christian brethren) and lettest them to decay or perish for want of looking to, or to want clothing sufficient, or other necessaries, or otherwise not looked unto and provided for as they ought to be, then dost thou not please Him, nor doest Him any honour; thou seemest to kiss His mouth by devotion and spiritual prayer, but thou treadest upon His feet, and defilest them, inasmuch as thou wilt not tend to them (through thy negligence) that belong to thy charge and care. This is my opinion and advice to thee in this point; nevertheless if thou be of the mind that I say not aright in this matter, for that thou thinkest it were a fairer and more pleasing office to God for to do honour to His head, as to be all day devoutly thinking of His passion, and producing acts of inward affection upon it, than for to go home to other works that are more external, and make clean His feet, as for to employ thyself both in words and deeds about the helping or benefiting of thy Christian brethren, in so thinking thou thinkest amiss, and mistakest. For surely he will more thank thee and reward thee for the humble washing of His feet when they are very foul, and yield an ill savour to thee, than for all the curious painting and fair dressing or decking that thou canst make about His head, by the devoutest remembrance of His humanity; for it is fair enough, and needeth not much decking or dressing from thee; but for His feet, and other His limbs, that are sometimes ill-arrayed, and have need to be holpen by thee (namely, since thou art bound thereto), our Lord will render thee more thanks, if thou wilt humbly and charitably look unto them.

For the lower or meaner that the service which thou dost to thy Lord seemeth to be, in regard they are performed towards His members, and not immediately towards Himself, yet doing it for the love of Him, when reasonable occasions or need require it, and that with a cheerful and humble heart, thou much more pleasest Him than in service immediately done to Himself with omission of these offices of need or charity towards thy Christian brethren. And that thou mayest be the more willing to go about such an employment, thou shalt do well to think that it is sufficient, and best of all for thee to be employed in the very least degree, and lowest estate of His service, especially since it is His will that it be so. For thou must think, that since He hath put thee into that charge and estate of life, that it is the very best for thee, and that thou canst not do better than in performing what belongs thereto in the best manner and with all the willingness and gladness of mind that thou art able.

This I tell thee not as though that already thou dost it not, and better too; but to the end that thou shouldst do it with more alacrity and cheerfulness by occasion of this my writing; and shouldst not think it much sometimes to lessen or forbear thy spiritual exercise for to go and deal in worldly affairs pertaining to thee and thy estate, as to the looking and seeing too, that thy goods be well kept and spent according to reason, looking to the behaviour of thy servants and thy tenants, and doing other good deeds towards thy Christian brethren according to thy ability and their need, but shouldst perform both these works and exercises, that is to say, the internal and external, at divers and several times, and with as good a will the one as the other, so far as thou canst. As for example, if thou hast been at thy prayer and spiritual exercise, that finished thou shalt go and busy thyself in some corporal or external doing concerning thy Christian brethren, and therefore spend reasonable time with willingness and gladness of mind. And after that thou hast been busily employed for a time about thy servants, and other men with whom thou shalt have occasions, and hast profitably spent with them so much time as shall be truly needful, thou shalt then break from these external doings, and shalt return again to thy prayers and devotions, which thou shalt perform according to the grace that God shall give thee for it; and so doing, thou, by the grace of our Lord, shalt put away and avoid sloth, laziness, idleness and vain rest, which often creep upon us through the deceitfulness of our nature, under pretense or colour of contemplation or other spiritual recollections; whereby we come to omit the performance of good and meritorious external affairs and businesses pertaining to us and our charge by the appointment or providence of God. And thus thou shalt be always in some good exercise or other, internal or external, by turns, and in their proper times.

Therefore thou shalt do well to observe and do that spiritually, that is, in thy carriage in a spiritual life, which Jacob did in a matter that was only corporal or external. The holy Scripture telleth, how that Jacob, when he began to serve his master Laban, he coveted Rachel his master's daughter for her fairness to be his wife, and for the having of her he served seven years; but when he had thought for to have had her to his wife, he had first Leah, the other daughter, instead of Rachel, and afterwards he takes Rachel, and so he had both at the last. By Jacob in holy Scripture is understood an overcomer of sins; by those two wives are understood, as St Gregory saith, the two kinds of lives that are in the holy Church, which are the active life and the contemplative life. Leah is as much to say as labour and painful working, and betokeneth the active life. Rachel is as much as to say as a sight of the beginning, which is God, and betokeneth the contemplative life. Leah bore children, but she was sore-eyed. Rachel was fair and lovely, but she was barren. And now even as Jacob coveted Rachel for her fairness, and yet had her not when he would, but first took Lead and afterwards Rachel, even so, every man labouring, and heartily seeking (by compunction for his former great sins of the flesh and of the world) now to become a new servant to God in cleanness of good living, hath a great desire to have and come by Rachel, which is to have rest in spiritual sweetness, devotion and contemplation, for it is so fair, and so lovely a life, that in hope for to have it he determined with himself, by the grace of our Lord, for to serve Him with all his diligence and might; but oft-times when he thinketh to have Rachel, that is, rest in devotion, our Lord suffereth him to be well exercised and tried, either with the temptations of the world, or of the devil, or of his flesh, or else with some external businesses and doing, corporal or spiritual, in help or succour of his Christian brethren; and when he is thus well exercised, and in travails with Leah, and is well-nigh overcome, then our Lord giveth him Rachel, that is, grace and devotion, and rest in conscience, and then hath he both Rachel and Leah.

So shalt thou do, according to the example of Jacob, these two lives, active and contemplative, since God calleth and enableth thee for both, and use the one with the other of them. By the one life (which is the active) thou shalt bring forth the fruit of many good deeds in help of thy Christian brethren; and by the other shalt thou be made to become fair, clear-sighted and clean in the supreme brightness and beauty, which is God, the beginner and ender of all that is made, and then shalt thou be truly Jacob, and an out-goer and overcomer of all sins; and after that, by the grace of God, thy name shall be changed, as Jacob's name was, and turned into Israel, and Israel is as much as to say: a man seeing God. Therefore, if thou be first Jacob, and will discreetly use these two lives afterwards, in time thou shalt be Israel, that is, a true Contemplative, either in this life, if God will deliver thee, and make thee free from the charges and businesses which thou art bound to, or else after this life, fully and perfectly in the bliss of heaven when thou comest thither. A man shall desire a contemplative life, for it is fair and full of merit, therefore thou shalt ever have it in thy mind, and in thy desire; but thou shalt have in using active life, for it is both expedient and necessary. Therefore, if upon just occasions, either concerning thy children or thy servants or any other of thy Christian brethren, for their profit or their heart's ease, upon reasonable cause, asking it of thee, thou be put from thy rest in devotion, when thou hadst much rather stay still thereat, be not angry with them, nor heavy or sad within thyself, so far as thou art able to help it, nor afraid, as if God would be angry with thee, that thou leavest Him for any other business or doing, for He will not be angry but well pleased and delighted thou so do. And therefore in such a case readily leave off thy devotion of what kind soever it be, and go about the deed, being service to thy Christian brethren, and that as willing and readily, as if our Lord Himself had called and bidden thee to go about it. Do so, I say, and endure the difficulty thou findest in it for His love; and put away all grudging for it, so far as thou canst; as also all bitterness and offence taken against thy Christian brother for calling thee to the said employment.

CHAPTER VII

That a Man's Devotion sometimes will be the greater by reason of the outward Work which before out of Charity he had been in hand with

AND it may fall out sometimes that the greater trouble thou hast exteriorly had in doing of thy active works, the more inflamed desire shalt thou afterwards have to God and the more sight of God and spiritual things, through the grace of our Lord, in devotion when thou comest thereto; for it fareth thereby as if thou hadst a little coal of fire, and wouldst make a fire therewith, and make it burn; thou wouldst first lay to some sticks, and with them over-cover the coal so that there is as yet no show or seeming hope of fire by it; nevertheless when thou hast abiden awhile and afterwards blowest it a little, anon, suddenly there will arise out a great flame of fire, so that the sticks will be turned all into fire. Even so is it spiritually; thy will and thy desire that thou hast to God is as it were a little coal of fire in thy soul, for it giveth to thee somewhat of light and of spiritual heat; but it is very little that it giveth, for often it waxeth cold and turneth to a fleshly rest (or into a rest of flesh and sensuality) and sometimes into idleness and doing of no good; therefore it is expedient that thou put to sticks, that is, some works of the active life; and though it be so that those works do seem for a time to be a let to thy desire, so that it may not be so entire nor so fervent as thou wouldst it were, yet be not daunted nor troubled thereat, but abide and suffer awhile, and so blow at the fire; that is, first go and do thy works, and afterwards, go alone to thy prayers and devotions, and lift up thine heart to God, and pray Him that of His goodness He will accept thy works that thou doest and receive them to His honour and glory; hold them as nothing in thine own sight, nor to be of any worth save so far as God only out of His goodness shall vouchsafe to accept of them; humbly acknowledge thy wretchedness and frailty really attributing thy good deeds to Him; and so much as they have any goodness in them, and inasmuch as they are bad, or not done discreetly with all circumstances requisite for a good deed, ascribe them to thyself, and then for this humility shall all thy good deeds turn into a flame of fire as do sticks laid upon a coal; and thou thus doing, thy external good deeds shall not hinder thy devotion but rather increase it. And moreover, our Lord saith in holy Scripture thus: Fire shall always burn in My Alter, and the Priest rising up in the morning shall put wood thereunto, so that the fire may not be extinguished. This fire is love and desire to God in a soul, the which fire requireth that it be nourished and maintained by laying to sticks, so that it may not go out; and these sticks are of divers matters, as some of one kind of wood and some of another. A man that is learned and hath some understanding in the holy Scripture, if he have this fire of devotion in his heart, it is good for him to get him sticks of holy examples and devout prayers, and nourish the fire with them. Another man that is unlearned cannot so readily have at hand the sayings of holy Scripture, or of Doctors for the purpose, and therefore it is necessary for him to do many good external deeds to his Christian brethren, and thereby maintain and exercise towards them the love he beareth them for God.

And so it is good that each man in his degree, and according to what is most agreeable to the benefit and disposition of his soul, do get him sticks of one thing or another, as either by praying, considering, meditating or reading in some good and devout book, or in doing of some corporal or external work, thereby for to nourish in his soul the fire of love so that it may not become quenched; for the affection of love is dainty and tender, and will easily go out and vanish away unless it be well kept and continually nourished by good deeds or exercises, corporal or spiritual.

Now therefore, since our Lord hath put into thine heart a little sparkle of this blessed fire, that is Himself, (as holy Scripture saith, Our Lord is a consuming fire; for, as a material fire wasteth all bodily things that may be wasted, so a spiritual fire, that is God, wasteth all kind of sin, and therefore our Lord is likened to fire wasting) I pray thee to nourish this fire within thee. This fire is nothing else but Love and Charity. This hath He sent into the earth, as He saith in the Gospel: I came to send fire into the earth, and to what end, but that it might burn? that is, God hath put into man's soul a fire of love and a good desire, and a great good will for to please Him, and that He hath done to this end, that man should know it, keep it, and nourish it, and strengthen and increase it, and thereby be saved. The greater desire that thou hast to Him and for Him, the greater is the fire of love in thee, and the less that the desire is in thee, the less is the fire. The quantity or measure of thy desire within thee, how much it is, neither thyself doth know, nor doth any man know how great it is in him, much less the quantity of love that is in another man; God only knoweth it, or he to whom God shall reveal and make it known. And therefore dispute not with thyself as if thou wouldst know how great thy desire is; be busy and serious to desire as much as thou canst, but not to know the quantity or measure of thy desire.

CHAPTER VIII

What the Desire of God for Himself is and how that in Cleanness of Conscience is found true Comfort and Sweetness

SAINT AUGUSTINE saith that the life of every good Christian man is a continual desire to God, and such desire is of great power and virtue, for it is a great crying in the ears of God; the more fervently thou desirest, the higher thou criest, the better thou prayest, and the wiser are thy thoughts. And what is this desire? Surely nothing but a loathing of all this worldly bliss, a forsaking of all fleshly or sensual love in thine heart, and an extreme loving, with a most hungry longing and thirsting after God and the everlasting bliss of Heaven; this is that which may be called a desire of God for Himself.

If thou hast this desire, as I verily hope and believe that thou hast, I pray thee keep it well and nourish it diligently; and when thou shalt pray or meditate of God, make this desire of Him to be the beginning and final intention of such thy exercises, and of all other thy works and deeds, thereby to increase it. Seek and nourish only this, and seek not after any feeling in thy corporal senses, external or internal, nor any sensible sweetness or devotion, neither by the ear nor by the taste of thy palate, nor by any wonderful light or sight of thy eyes, nor seek the sight of Angels, no, though our Lord Himself would appear in His body to the sight of thy eyes, make no great matter of that; and therefore let all thy diligence be that thou mayest truly and really perceive and find in thy soul, and especially in thy will, a loathing and full forsaking of all manner of sin and of all manner of uncleanness, with a spiritual seeing or perceiving how foul, how ugly and how painful these things be; and that thou mayest have within thee a mighty desiring of virtues, and, namely, of humility and charity, and finally, of the bliss of Heaven. This that I shall now tell thee were (as I would think) a spiritual comfort, and a spiritual sweetness in a man's soul; and that is, to have cleanness in conscience from wickedness and from all worldly vanities, with a firm faith and humble hope and a full desire of God. Howsoever it be for having of other comforts and sweetnesses I esteem that sweetness to be true, sound and secure that is found in cleanness of conscience, with a strong will of forsaking and loathing of all sins, and with inward sight and fervent desire of spiritual things; all other comforts and sweetnesses caused by any manner of feelings, unless they lead or help to the said end, that is, to cleanness of conscience and spiritual desire of God, are not secure to rest on.

But now thou wilt perhaps ask, whether this desire be love to God?

As to that I answer and say: That this desire is not properly love, but a beginning and taste of love, for love properly is a perfect uniting and coupling together of the lover and the loved into one. Perfect love maketh God and the soul to be as if they both together were but one thing. But such perfect coupling and union may not be had in this life, but only in desire and longing thereto, as by the example that I shall now deliver thee. If a man love another man that is absent, he greatly desireth his presence. Even so spiritually, as long as we are in this life, our Lord is absent from us, so that here we may neither see Him nor feel Him as He is, and therefore are not able (for want of such sight and feeling) here to love Him in fulness and perfection and in reality as we might do if we had the sight of Him really, and as He is in His own being;

the which, because we have not, nor shall have in this life, therefore all that we can do here is to have a desire and a great longing and thirsting for to be present with Him and see Him in His bliss, and to be fully and perfectly united unto Him in love. This desire we may have in us (of His gift) in this life, by the which we shall be saved, for it is love unto Him, such as may here be had. St Paul saith thus: We know that while we are in this body we are pilgrims (or strangers) from God. That is, we abide in this earth, or banishment, absent from Heaven, for we here walk by faith, and not by sight (that is, we here live in faith, not in real sight of Him as He is); but we are bold, and have a good will rather to be absent from the body, and to be present to our Lord (that is, we, through cleanness of conscience and sure trust of salvation, dare desire parting from our body by bodily death, and thereupon to be present to our Lord); nevertheless, because as yet we may not, therefore we endeavour, whether present or absent, to please Him; that is, we strive against the sins of the world, and pleasures of the flesh, and sensuality, by desire to Him, seeking to burn and consume in the fire of such our desire all things that may let or hinder us from Him.

But thou wilt perhaps further ask me: Whether a man may continually have this desire in his heart? and thou perhaps thinkest that he cannot.

As to that I will answer according to my opinion in it, which is, that thou mayest have this desire in thine heart and intention virtually or habitually, always and continually; but thou canst not so have it as to working or exercising upon it, as thou mayest better understand by this example. If thou wert sick, thou wouldst have, as every man in such a case hath, continually a natural desire in thine heart of bodily health; and this whether thou be asleep or awake, but art thinking of some worldly things; thou hast then such a desire only in intention or habit, and not in using or acting upon it. But when thou thinkest on thy bodily sickness or on thy health, then hast thou thy said desire of health in using and acting. Even so it is spiritually in the desire of God. He who by the gift of God hath this desire, though he sleep, or else thinketh not on God, but on some other worldly things, yet hath he this desire in his heart and soul till he commit some deadly sin. But as soon as he thinketh on God or purity of life or the joys of Heaven, then his desire to God worketh actually, as long as he keepeth his thought and intention to please God, either in prayers, meditations, or any other good action, so that all his endeavour be to excite this desire, and discreetly use it sometimes in one deed, sometimes in another, according as he is disposed and hath grace thereto.

This desire is the root of all thy actions that are rewardable. For whatever good deed thou doest for God's sake, whether it be bodily or spiritual, as when thou prayest or meditatest, it is an exercising and using of this desire. And therefore when thou doest any good work, scruple not whether thou desirest God or no, for thy deed showeth thy desire. Some ignorantly conceive that they desire not God except they be ever calling upon Him either with their mouths or their hearts; and therefore they are continually saying, Lord save me, or some such-like words; which words indeed are good, because they stir up the heart to a desiring of God. Yet nevertheless, without any such words, a pure thought of God, or any spiritual thing, or of virtue, or the humanity of Christ, or joys of Heaven, or understanding of the holy Scriptures, with love, may be better than such words. And the more spiritual thy thought is, the more is thy desire. Be not, therefore, in doubt whether thou desirest God, when thou thinkest upon Him or doest any outward good work to thy neighbour, for thy deeds show it. Nevertheless, though all thy good actions, spiritual and corporal, are a demonstration of thy desire to God, yet is there a great difference between spiritual and corporal deeds, for deeds of a Contemplative life are not so outward as the other; and therefore when thou prayest unto, or meditatest upon God, thy desire to Him is more entire, more fervent, more spiritual than when thou doest external works of charity to thy neighbour.

Now, if thou ask me by what means thou shalt keep this desire, and nourish it, I shall tell a little in that point, not with the meaning that thou shalt or must use the self-same form that I tell thee for it; but that thou thereby have some kind of general example, whereof thou shalt make use upon thy need and according to thy manner —not my manner, unless mine seem more for thy purpose, for I neither may nor can tell thee fully what is best for thee to use; but I shall tell thee somewhat according to what I think.

CHAPTER IX

How thou shalt Dispose thee to Devotion

IN the night after thy sleep, if thou wilt rise to pray and serve our Lord, thou shalt feel thyself at the first to be fleshly, heavy, and, as it were, drowned in sensuality, and ofttimes impertinent thoughts of the world or other vanities pressing into thy mind. But then shalt thou dispose thee to pray, or to think some good thought, for to revive and quicken thine heart towards God, and do thou use all thy discreet industry, for the drawing up of thy thoughts from worldly vanities, and from vain imaginations that come into thy mind, that so thou mayest feel some devotion in such vocal prayers as thou shalt then use, if thou use any such; or else (if thou wilt) enter thou into some spiritual thoughts, whereby thou mayest not remain hindered and troubled with such vain thoughts of the world or of thy flesh. And now as for matter of good thoughts for thee, thou must know that there be divers matters of such thoughts or meditations, but which of them were best for thee to take and use I cannot tell thee.

But I trow that such matter and manner of thinking or meditating, wherein thou feelest greatest gust, facility and ease or pleasure, is best for thee to use so long as it continueth so grateful to thy spirit. Thou mayest (it thou wilt) sometimes think on thy sins heretofore committed, and of the frailties into which thou daily fallest, and ask mercy and forgiveness for them. Also after this thou mayest think on the frailties and sins and miseries, corporal and spiritual, of thy Christian brethren, with pity and compassion of them, and ask mercy and forgiveness for them as tenderly as for thyself, and as if thou hadst done them, and that is a good exercise for the time. For I tell thee for truth that thou mayest make of other men's sins a precious ointment for to heal thine own soul, when thou thinkest on them with compassion and sorrow for them; this ointment is precious and very medicinal, though the spicery or things whereof it is composed be not clean, or otherwise wholesome; for it is treacle or mithridate, made of poison for to do away and destroy poison; that is to say, thine own and other men's sins. If thou beat and bruise them well with sorrow of thine heart, pity and compassion, they turn into treacle or mithridate, that will cleanse and make whole thy soul from pride and envy, and bring into it love and charity to thy Christian brethren. Such thought is good for thee sometimes to take into thee.

CHAPTER X

How a Man is to Think on the Humanity of Christ

ALSO for thy exercise of devotion thou mayest think on the humanity of our Lord, as of His birth, of His Passion or of any other of His works, and feed thy thought with spiritual imagination thereof, for to move thine affection more to the love of Him. This thought (I mean of something of our Saviour's humanity) is good and expedient, namely, when it cometh freely of God's gift, with devotion and fervour of spirit, else a man will not likely find taste or devotion in it. And if he have it not with such facility and sending of God, I think it not expedient that a man should much force himself in it, as if he would get it by violence; for so doing he might hurt his head and body too, and yet be never the nearer. Therefore I think that it is good for a man to have in his mind and thought sometimes our Saviour's humanity, or some matter thereof; and if devotion come withal, and relish or gust found in it, then to hold it and follow it for a time, but leave off soon, and hang not long thereon. And if devotion come not by thinking of the Passion, strive not, nor press too much for to have and come by such devotion or feeling in it, but take what will easily come; and if it come not easily betake thee to some other matter, wherein thou thinkest or hopest to find more devotion or gust.

CHAPTER XI

How a Man shall think on Virtues and upon the Saints

ALSO other thoughts there be that are more spiritual, as to think on virtues, and to see by light of understanding the virtue of humility, what it is, and what great reasons be why a man should be humble; and also what is patience, cleanness in soul, justice, charity, sobriety and other such like virtues; and how worthy it is that a man should labour for the getting of them, and of the means by which they may be gotten, and by such thoughts to have a great desire and longing to the having of those virtues; and also for to have a spiritual sight of the three principal, or Theological Virtues, Faith, Hope and Charity. By the sight and desire of these virtues a soul should see and feel much grace of our Lord, without which grace a man's soul is half blind, and without spiritual sweetness or taste. Also, for to think on the saints, as the apostles, martyrs, confessors and holy virgins, beholding in his interior their holy living and the grace and virtues that our Lord gave them in their life, and by the remembrance and consideration hereof, to stir thy heart for to take example from them for leading a better and perfecter life.

CHAPTER XII

How a Man shall think of the Holiness of our Lord Jesus and of our Blessed Lady

ALSO the thinking and considering (above all other saints) of our Lady St Mary and her excellency in grace and virtues is a good matter for raising and exercise of devotion, by seeing with thy spiritual eye the abundance of grace that was in her holy soul when she was here living, which our Lord had given her, above what He gave to any of the other Saints; for she was replenished with all other virtues, without one spot of sin, showing and manifesting by her life perfect humility and fulness of charity, with the beauty and excellence of all other virtues, the which virtues altogether make her so holy, that there would no temptation, or motion of pride, envy, wrath or anger, sensual delight or of any other kind of sin or imperfection enter into her heart or defile her soul in any part of it. By the beholding of the beauty and excellency of this blessed soul, a man's heart should be moved and put into a great spiritual delight and comfort.

And much more and above that is the beholding of the soul of our Lord Jesus, the which soul of His was fully and wholly united to the divinity, excelling without any comparison our blessed Lady and all other creatures. For in the Passion of Jesus are two natures, that is, God and man, perfectly united together. By the virtue of this most blessed union, which cannot be expressed nor yet conceived by man's wit or understanding, the soul of Jesus hath received the perfection and fulness of all wisdom and goodness; as the Apostle saith: The fulness of the divinity doth dwell is Christ corporally; that is, the divinity of God was fully united to the humanity (or man's nature) in the soul of Jesus, and so, by the means of His soul dwelling in His body, the remembrance of the humanity of our Lord after this manner (that is, to regard the virtues and surpassing grace of the soul of Jesus) should be right comfortable to a man's soul.

CHAPTER XIII

Of seeing and beholding the Power (by some consideration or thinking), the Wisdom, the Goodness and the Mercy of God in His Creatures

ALSO the remembrance of the power, the wisdom and the goodness of our Lord in all His creatures; for as much as we living here on earth cannot see God fully and as He is in His essence, therefore we are to see and behold Him, love and fear Him upon the sight and consideration of His creatures and His works; and in them also are we to admire and wonder at His power and goodness. Also, for to think on the mercy of our Lord, that He hath showed to me and to thee, and to all sinful captives that sometimes were in bondage to the devil, through the greatness and multitude of our sins; how He patiently suffered us to live in our sin, and in our heinous contempts of Him, and work no revenge on us for the same, as He most justly might have done, and might most worthily have cast us down headlong into Hell, if His love had not hindered Him; but out of love He spared us, and sent His grace into our souls, taking us out of the state of heinous sins, and by His grace hath turned our will entirely unto Him, and made us thereby, for the having of Him, and for His love, to forsake all manner of sin. The remembrance of His mercy and goodness, in these and in other matters and points more and greater than I can now reckon up, may justly cause and bring into a soul a great truth and confidence in our Lord, and a full hope of salvation, and greatly inflameth the desire of love to aspire to the joys of Heaven.

CHAPTER XIV

How the Consideration and thinking on the Miseries and Perils of this Life is apt to breed in a soul the Desire of Heaven

ALSO to think upon the miseries, mischiefs and perils, corporal and spiritual, that happen in this life; and after that to think of the joys of Heaven, as how great happiness is there, and what wonderful joy and delight; for there is neither sin, nor sorrow, nor passion nor pain, hunger nor thirst, aches nor sickness, doubt nor fear, shame nor blame, nor want of power, nor strength, nor lack of light, nor coldness in love; but there is most excellent beauty, clearness, strength, health, everlasting delights, perfect wisdom, love, peace, honour, security, rest, joy and bliss in abundance without ever having any end. The consideration of these points ought to cause thee the more fervently to covet and desire those everlasting joys and rest of that same most blessed life. Many men are covetous of worldly goods, honours and earthly riches, and think both in dreaming and waking how and by what means they might come thereto; and then they forget all care of their souls' good, and all thoughts of the pains of Hell, or of the joys of Heaven. Surely these men are not wise; they are like to children that run after butterflies, and, because they look not to their feet, they sometimes easily fall down and break their legs. What is all the pomp, honours, riches and jollity of this world but a butterfly? Surely it is no more, yea, it is much less. Therefore, I pray thee, be covetous of the joys of Heaven, and thou shalt have honour and riches that shall last for ever. For at the latter day, when worldly covetous men bring no good in their hands (because all their honour and riches, which they only made account of, are turned into nothing but sorrow and pain) then the good men of the world, that have truly forsaken all vain honours and riches of this world, or else if they had them they made no account in their hearts of them, nor did set their love or delight in them, but have ever lived in the peace of God and in humility and in hope, and sometimes in sorrows or afflictions, and patiently expected the mercy of God; they (I say) shall then fully attain that which they here coveted, for they shall be crowned as kings, and shall ascend up with our Lord into the bliss of Heaven. Also there be many other good considerations or thoughts (more than I can speak of) that serve to stir and raise a man's mind and affection to loathe the vanities of this world and to desire the joys of Heaven.

These matters I have not mentioned unto thee as if I had withal fully showed the manner how they are exercised in a man's soul; but I have only touched them a little, to the end thou mightest, by so much the better, understand these things for such use as thou canst best make of them.

CHAPTER XV

How a Man shall do when he feeleth no taste nor comfort in his Mental Exercises

NEVERTHELESS I would think it were good for thee that when thou disposest thee to think on God, as I have before said, or in any other manner, and peradventure thou feelest no gust nor devotion in thy exercise, but only a naked mind and a weak will; by which thou wouldst fain think on God, but canst not; then I think it is good for thee that thou strive not too much with thyself, for so thou mayest fall into greater darkness, unless thou knowest how to work more subtlety, and more above in spirit, and with all quietness in the senses. But thou not knowing how to do so for want of experience or skill in it, I hold it more secure for thee in such a case for to say thy Pater noster and thine Ave Maria, or else thy Matins, or to read in thy Psalter, for that is evermore a sure standard that will not fail. Whoso may cleave thereto he shall not err; and if thou canst by thy prayer get devotion, look then that this devotion be only in affection, that is to say in a great desire toward God, with a spiritual delight. Hold on then such thy saying of those vocal prayers, and not easily break off; for oftentimes it happeneth that praying with the mouth getteth and keepeth devotion, and if in such a case thou cease from saying, thy devotion withal vanisheth away.

Nevertheless, if Devotion in prayer bring into thine heart a devout thought of the humanity of our Lord, or of any of the other matters before mentioned by me, and this thought should be hindered by thy saying of the vocal prayers, then will it be best for thee to cease from thy saying, and to feed thy mind and affection with the thought of the said good matter till it leave thee and be vanished away.

CHAPTER XVI

What a Man is to take heed of in his Prayers and Meditations

BUT of certain things it behoveth thee to beware in thy meditations; of some of them I shall tell thee. One is that when thou hast had a spiritual thought or imagination of the humanity of our Lord, or of other bodily things, and thy soul hath been comforted and fed therewith, and afterward it passeth away of itself; do not seek, as it were, by mastery or force to hold it still, for then it will turn thee into pain and bitterness. Also, if it pass not away, but dwell still in thy mind, without any travail or industry of thine, and thou, for the comfort thou findest in it, wilt not leave it, and thereupon it still continuing with thee, cometh to bereave or hinder thee of thy sleep at nights, or else in the day times hindereth thee from other good deeds, or else through the great fervour that it worketh in thy body, thy body or thine head by it falleth into a great feebleness, then must thou lessen or moderate, and sometimes forbear such exercise of thine, even when thou hast most devotion in it, or to it, and wouldst otherwise be most loth to forbear it, or part from it; and therefore thou must needs use discretion in the matter, for to avoid those mischiefs, or any of them, which now I have reckoned up to thee, or any other mischief or peril that may come to thee through indiscreet fervour or love to those thy exercises; and in particular, give it over when it is reasonable time to give it over, or when thy Christian brother may receive harm, or take just offence at thee by occasion of thy long stay at such thy devotions. If thou do otherwise in this matter than I have told thee, I think thou dost not well nor wisely in it.

A worldly man or woman that peradventure feels not devotion twice in a year, if he (through the grace of our Lord Jesus) feel great compunction for his sins, or think seriously or devoutly on the Passion of our Lord, or upon any other good matter, if he by occasion thereof, and his devotion therein, be put from his sleep and his rest, for one, or two, or three nights, until his head ache, it makes no great matter, nor will he be the worse for it; such devotion cometh but seldom upon such persons. But as for thee, or any other man or woman, that every day duly performest, or hath such devotions, and intendest to continue in pursuing of such daily exercises, it is expedient for thee to use and hold discretion in thy performance of those thy exercises, and not fully to yield and plunge thyself into devotion, so far as it will offer itself unto thee, but moderate thyself in it, and take it moderately, though it offer itself to thee in abundance.

Also I hold it good, that thou observe this discretion in thy exercise, which is, that thou tarry not too long at it, that thereby thou put thyself from taking thy meat or of thy sleep, when the time shall be for taking of them, or do give just cause of displeasure or damage to any other man, through occasion of overlong tarrying at such thy devotion. The wise man saith: That all things have their time.

Another thing which behoveth thee to beware of is that when thy mind hath been employed for a time in the imagination of the humanity of our Saviour, or any other good matter, and after this thou seekest with all the desire of thine heart, for to have a more spiritual knowing or feeling of the divinity; press not too much upon such desire, nor suffer the desire of thine heart to tarry too long therein, as if thou wert expecting and tarrying for some better or higher elevation of thy spirit, or for a feeling that had more worth or excelling in it than any thou hast hitherto had. Thou shalt not do so. It is enough for thee and for me for to have a desire and a longing to our Lord; and if He out of His grace and goodness will vouchsafe, over and above such desires of ours, freely, and of His own accord, to send us of His spiritual light, and open our spiritual eye, for to see or know more of Him than heretofore he did or could, by our own labour and industry, let us thank him for it; but if He do not (because we are not as yet humble enough, but were likely to grow proud by reason of such extraordinary favours, if He bestowed them on us, or are not disposed in other respects, and namely, by cleanness of conscience through well living, for to receive such grace and favour at His hands), then let us humbly acknowledge our own unworthiness, and hold ourselves satisfied with the desire we have of Him, and with other common good thoughts, that may easily be had and used by our imagination; as thinking of our sins, of Christ's Passion, or other such like things, or else with some vocal prayers of the Psalter or other vocal prayers, and thank Him with all our hearts, that He bestoweth upon us any portion of His grace or favour, though it be the least that any man hath. And if thou do otherwise, thou mayest easily be deceived (for thy presumption) by the spirit of error; for it is a great folly for a man of his own head or wilfulness to press or strain himself too much, to get into the sight or exercise of spiritual things further than he seeth well that he hath invitation and enablement for it. For the wise man saith that the searcher of the Majesty (of God) shall be oppressed by the glory of Him; for not having humility, cleanness and worthiness in soul, for such a sight he shall be cast down, and made to know himself better than he did through this confusion. And therefore the same wise man in another place saith thus: Do not seek for things that are higher, nor search into things that pass thy strength; that is to say, high things that are above thy natural reason and apprehension seek not after, and great matters that are above thy ability or strength do not search into. By these words the wise man doth not wholly forbid us to seek after and desire the knowing and having of spiritual and heavenly things, but he forbiddeth us to seek for them in a preposterous manner, which is too soon, and sooner than we are fit for them or that God calleth us to them, as when we are as yet sensual, and not cleansed from the vain love of the world; being in that degree, we are not to take upon us as if we could or would by our labour or industry, or by our own wit, enable ourselves to discern, see or know spiritual things, or procure in us great fervour of the love of God; so that albeit we see that we set at nought all worldly things, and it seem to us that we would for God's love forsake all the wealth, honour and joys of this world; yet for all this we are unfit and indisposed for to seek and behold spiritual things that are above us, until our souls through precedent exercises of the imagination, become to be more subtle, or as it were thin, or somewhat spiritual, and withal he become well mortified and settled in virtues by process of time and by increase in grace. For (as St Gregory saith) no man suddenly (or hastily) becometh supreme or perfect in grace, but beginneth with little, and proceedeth on by little and little, until that he come to be perfect, the which God grant that we all may one day be. Amen.

FINIS.

20387807R00138

Printed in Great Britain
by Amazon